W9-AAD-120

# *Uncle John's* BATHROOM READER®

# QUINTESSENTIAL COLLECTION OF "NOTABLE" QUOTABLES

FOR EVERY CONCEIVABLE OCCASION

By the
Bathroom Readers'
Institute

Bathroom Readers' Press
Ashland, Oregon

UNCLE JOHN'S
QUINTESSENTIAL COLLECTION
OF NOTABLE QUOTABLES
FOR EVERY CONCEIVABLE OCCASION®

For information, write:
The Bathroom Readers' Institute,
P.O. Box 1117, Ashland, OR 97520
*www.bathroomreader.com*
888-488-4642

Cover design by Michael Brunsfeld,
San Rafael, CA (*Brunsfeldo@comcast.net*)

*Uncle John's Quintessential Collection of Notable
Quotables for Every Conceivable Occasion*®
by the Bathroom Readers' Institute

ISBN-13: 978-1-59223-689-3
ISBN-10: 1-59223-689-8

Library of Congress Catalog Card Number:
2006938881

Printed in the United States of America

First Printing

1 2 3 4 5 6 7 8 9 10 09 08 07 06

# THANK YOU!

*The Bathroom Readers' Institute sincerely thanks the people whose advice and assistance made this book possible.*

| | |
|---|---|
| Gordon Javna | (Hello) Mary Lou Goforth |
| Jay Newman | Laurel Graziano |
| Amy Miller | Mana, Dylan & Chandra |
| Brian Boone | Maggie Javna |
| Julia Papps | (Mr.) Mustard Press |
| John Dollison | Publishers Group West |
| Thom Little | Rick Overton |
| Judy Plapinger | Malcolm & Jahnna |
| Angela Kern | Jennifer Thornton |
| Maggie McLaughlin | Jennifer P. & Melinda A. |
| Michael Brunsfeld | Steven Style Group |
| Claudia Bauer | Allen Orso |
| Jeff Altemus | Shobha Grace |
| Jennifer Massey | Susie Newman |
| Sydney Stanley | Eddie Deezen |
| JoAnn Padgett | Michelle Sedgwick |
| Scarab Media | Raincoast Books |
| Connie Vazquez | Chris Olsen |
| Kristine Hemp | Porter the Wonder Dog |
| Nancy Toeppler | Thomas Crapper |

...and everybody who has ever said anything.

"When you say that you agree to a thing in principle, you mean that you have not the slightest intention of carrying it out in practice." —**Otto von Bismarck**

# CONTENTS

# INTRODUCTION

*Greetings from the Bathroom Readers' Institute
in the peaceful hamlet of Ashland, Oregon.*

**W**elcome one and all to our second volume of quotations. Our tireless team of quotationeers has carefully sifted through tens of thousands of vocal and written utterances to bring you what we believe is the most unique collection of quotations ever assembled:

*Uncle John's Quintessential Collection of
Notable Quotables for Every Conceivable Occasion*

And we mean *all* occasions. You'll find simple wisdom (*"No one has ever drowned in sweat."* —Lou Holtz), the strangely profound (*"The funny thing about being humble is the moment you know you're being humble, you are no longer humble."* —T-Bone Burnett), the not-so-wise (*"Twenty-three is old. It's almost 25, which is like almost mid-20s."* —Jessica Simpson), the witty (*"If evolution really works, how come mothers only have two hands?"* —Milton Berle), the downright nasty (*"He never opens his mouth without subtracting from the sum of human knowledge."* —Thomas Reed), and the truly bizarre (*"To see the snowman is to dislike the snowman."* —Roger Ebert). But that's just the beginning.

We've gathered quotes by people named Jones, quotes about specific colors, quotes from people born on Christmas, and other unusual arrangements. But don't worry—we've got the basics covered, too: life and death, good and evil, God and beer. Plus quizzes, interesting facts, and the answer to one of the 20th century's most enduring quotation mysteries: What did Neil Armstrong *really* say when he stepped on the moon?

So sit back, relax, and enjoy the strange story of humanity as told by the humans themselves. And as always, Go with the Flow!

—**Uncle John, Porter the Wonder Dog, and the BRI staff**

# TOILET TALK

*We begin this book with important thoughts from the most important room in the house—the bathroom.*

"My kids always perceived the bathroom as a place where you wait it out until all the groceries are unloaded from the car."
—**Erma Bombeck**

"In awe I watched the waxing moon ride across the zenith of the heavens like an ambered chariot towards the ebon void of infinite space wherein the tethered belts of Jupiter and Mars hang forever festooned in their orbital majesty. And as I looked at all this I thought: I must put a roof on this lavatory."
—**Les Dawson**

"I don't use the toilet much to pee in. I almost always pee in the yard or the garden, because I like to pee on my estate."
—**Iggy Pop**

"You can almost judge how screwed up somebody is by the kind of toilet paper they use. Go in any rich house and it's some weird-colored embossed stuff."
—**Don Van Vliet**

"My wife and I were married in a toilet—it was a marriage of convenience!"
—**Tommy Cooper**

"There is only one immutable law in life—in a gentleman's toilet, incoming traffic has the right of way."
—**Hugh Leonard**

"We had this bidet in the bathroom full of cuddly toys, god knows why. It was quite terrifying sometimes when there was no toilet paper and you're sitting there with this real moral dilemma: Do I or do I not wipe my a** with a teddy bear?"
—**Rhys Ifans**

"You do live longer with bran, but you spend the last fifteen years on the toilet."
—**Alan King**

"I have this porcelain fetish. I've had it since I was a kid, because there were so many kids in my family, the only place I had any solace was in the bathroom."
—**Linda Fiorentino**

"Hollywood...it's like Picasso's bathroom." —**Candice Bergen**

# STAND-UP FOLKS

*They stand—we sit. They talk—we laugh.*

"You know when you put a stick in water and it looks bent? That's why I never take baths."
—**Steven Wright**

"With my wife I don't get no respect. I made a toast on her birthday to 'the best woman a man ever had.' The waiter joined me."
—**Rodney Dangerfield**

"I have never been jealous. Not even when my dad finished fifth grade a year before I did."
—**Jeff Foxworthy**

"I took my parents back to the airport today. They leave tomorrow."
—**Margaret Smith**

"There is one thing I would break up over, and that is if she caught me with another woman. I won't stand for that."
—**Steve Martin**

"I was a bank teller. That was a great job. I was bringing home $450,000 a week."
—**Joel Lindley**

"Before you judge a man, walk a mile in his shoes. After that, who cares? He's a mile away and you've got his shoes."
—**Billy Connolly**

"I've been on so many blind dates, I should get a free dog."
—**Wendy Liebman**

"My grandfather's a little forgetful, but he likes to give me advice. One day, he took me aside and left me there."
—**Ron Richards**

"Guys are lucky because they get to grow mustaches. I wish I could. It's like having a little pet for your face."
—**Anita Wise**

"I phoned my dad to tell him I had stopped smoking. He called me a quitter."
—**Steven Pearl**

"Of course, Washington is corrupt. You can't wave that amount of lobbyist money in front of Republicans and expect them to remain honest. It's like leaving food out at a campsite."
—**Rick Overton**

"I'm going to get a tattoo over my whole body, but taller." —Steven Wright

# SUPERSTITIONS

*We'd bet our lucky rabbit's foot that you—like most people—
have your own special good-luck rituals. These folks do.*

"Every time I fail to smoke a cigarette between innings, the opposition will score."
—**Earl Weaver, MLB manager**

"I have an irrational fear of antique furniture, and I won't get on a plane if the last word I hear ends in 'th' or 'd', because death ends in 'th', and dead ends in 'd'. Like, if you say to me, 'Have a nice trip, say hello to Fred,' I'll make you say something else."
—**Billy Bob Thornton**

"Basically all superstitions are a form of mind relaxation. They distract you from the day-to-day grind and make the day flow that much easier."
—**Wade Boggs, who ate chicken every single day of his 18 year Hall of Fame baseball career**

"I'm superstitious, and every night after I got a hit, I ate Chinese food and drank tequila. I had to stop hitting or die."
—**Tim Flannery, San Diego Padres 2nd baseman**

"For five years in the minor leagues, I wore the same underwear and still hit .250. So no, I don't believe in that stuff."
—**Dusty Baker, MLB manager**

"I have only one superstition. I make sure I touch all bases when I hit a home run."
—**Babe Ruth**

"I never change anything during tournaments. Maybe afterwards I will shave again. I also have two songs that I listen to every day before I leave the house. And we have six showers in the locker room, so each day I pick the same one. If it is occupied, I wait."
—**Goran Ivanisevic, tennis player**

"Everyone has his superstitions. One of mine has always been when I started to go anywhere, or to do anything, never to turn back or to stop until the thing intended was accomplished."
—**Ulysses S. Grant**

Napoleon, Herbert Hoover, and Franklin Delano Roosevelt all feared the number 13.

# OF MICE AND STEINBECK

*American novelist John Steinbeck (1902–68), author of* Of Mice and Men *and* The Grapes of Wrath, *is also one of a select group of writers who won both the Pulitzer Prize and the Nobel Prize for Literature.*

"A journey is like marriage. The certain way to be wrong is to think you control it."
—*Travels With Charley*

"It would be absurd if we did not understand both angels and devils, since we invented them."
—*East of Eden*

"Man, unlike any other thing organic or inorganic in the universe, grows beyond his work, walks up the stairs of his concepts, emerges ahead of his accomplishments."
—*The Grapes of Wrath*

"No man really knows about other human beings. The best he can do is to suppose that they are like himself."
—*The Winter of Our Discontent*

"Men do change, and change comes like a little wind that ruffles the curtains at dawn, and it comes like the stealthy perfume of wildflowers hidden in the grass."
—*Sweet Thursday*

"We spend our time searching for security and hate it when we get it."
—*America and Americans*

"If you're in trouble, or hurt or in need—go to the poor people. They're the only ones that'll help—the only ones."
—*The Grapes of Wrath*

"Man is the only kind of varmint who sets his own trap, baits it, then steps on it."
—*Sweet Thursday*

"I have never smuggled anything in my life. Why, then, do I feel an uneasy sense of guilt on approaching a customs barrier?"
—*Travels With Charley*

"How can we live without our lives? How will we know it's us without our past?"
—*The Grapes of Wrath*

"I am impelled, not to squeak like a grateful and apologetic mouse, but to roar like a lion out of pride in my profession."

"In utter loneliness a writer tries to explain the inexplicable." —John Steinbeck

# WORLDLY PROVERBS

*"Proverbs are always platitudes until you have personally experienced the truth of them." —Aldous Huxley*

A broken hand works, but not a broken heart.
**—Persia**

Treat the earth well. It was not given to you by your parents. It was loaned to you by your children.
**—Kenya**

The ship that will not obey the helm will have to obey the rocks.
**—England**

The rain that makes the Monday dreary also makes the Tuesday beautiful.
**—America**

A tree falls the way it leans.
**—Bulgaria**

Insults should be written in sand, compliments should be carved in stone.
**—Arab**

A wise man hears one word and understands two.
**—Yiddish**

How beautiful it is to do nothing, and then rest afterward.
**—Spain**

If you wish to die young, make your physician your heir.
**—Romania**

He who strains himself grows old quickly.
**—Greece**

A friend's eye is a good mirror.
**—Ireland**

He that falls by himself never cries.
**—Turkey**

Call on God, but row away from the rocks.
**—India**

A man should live if only to satisfy his curiosity.
**—Yiddish**

A book is like a garden carried in the pocket.
**—Arab**

**Who lies for you will also lie against you. —Bosnian proverb**

# THE CRITIC'S CRITIC

*BRI trivia: In the bathroom of our office, you won't find a Bathroom Reader. So what sits on our porcelain shelf? Two books of Roger Ebert's movie reviews. They make for great bathroom reading (especially when he doesn't like the film).*

"Vincent Gallo has put a curse on my colon and a hex on my prostate. He called me a 'fat pig' in the *New York Post* and told the *New York Observer* I have 'the physique of a slave-trader.' He is angry at me because I said his *The Brown Bunny* was the worst movie in the history of the Cannes Film Festival. It is true that I am fat, but one day I will be thin, and he will still be the director of *The Brown Bunny*."

"*Gone in 60 Seconds* is the kind of movie that ends up playing on the TV set over the bar in a better movie."

"Yes, I take notes during the movies. During a movie like *House of D*, I jot down words I think might be useful in the review. Peering now at my 3x5 cards, I read 'sappy,' 'inane,' 'cornball,' 'shameless,' and, my favorite, 'doofusoid.' I sigh. This film has not even inspired interesting adjectives, except for the one I made up myself."

"Mr. *Magoo* is a one-joke movie without the joke."

"*The Village* is so witless, in fact, that when we do discover the secret, we want to rewind the film so we don't know the secret anymore. And then keep on rewinding, and rewinding, until we're back at the beginning, and can get up from our seats and walk backward out of the theater and go down the up escalator and watch the money spring from the cash register into our pockets."

"I think the future of the Republic may depend on young audiences seeing more movies like *Whale Rider* and fewer movies like *Scooby-Doo 2*, but then that's just me."

"*Return to the Blue Lagoon* aspires to the soft-core porn achievements of the earlier film, but succeeds instead in creating a new genre, 'no-core porn.'"

"I hated this movie. Hated hated hated hated hated this movie. Hated it. Hated every simpering stupid vacant audience-insulting moment of it. Hated the sensibility that thought anyone would like it."
—*North*

"*Lake Placid* is the kind of movie that actors discuss in long, sad talks with their agents."

"I hope *Serendipity* never has a sequel, because Jon and Sara are destined to become the most boring married couple in history. For years to come, people at parties will be whispering, 'See that couple over there? The Tragers? Jon and Sara? Whatever you do, don't ask them how they met.'"

"I have often asked myself, 'What would it look like if the characters in a movie were animatronic puppets created by aliens with an imperfect mastery of human behavior?' Now I know."
—*Friends & Lovers*

"*Mad Dog Time* is the first movie I have seen that does not improve on the sight of a blank screen viewed for the same length of time."

"There is always the moment when the killer is unmasked and spews out his bitterness and hate and vindictive triumph over his would-be victims. How about just once, at the crucial moment, the killer gets squished under a ton of canned soup, and we never do find out who he was?"
—*Saw*

"This movie doesn't have a brain in its three pretty little heads."
—*Charlie's Angels*

"*Jack Frost* could have been co-directed by Orson Welles and Steven Spielberg and still be unwatchable, because of that damned snowman... Never have I disliked a movie character more...the most repulsive single creature in the history of special effects...To see the snowman is to dislike the snowman. It doesn't look like a snowman, anyway. It looks like a cheap snowman suit...It has a big, wide mouth that moves as if masticating Gummi Bears. And it's this kid's dad."

"If you, under any circumstances, see *Little Indian, Big City*, I will never let you read one of my reviews again."

# NAME THAT LINE

*Focus in and uncover that part of your brain that stores everything you learned in high-school English. Is it all coming back? See how you do on this quiz matching the title of a novel to its famous opening line.*

**1.** "It is a truth universally acknowledged, that a single man in possession of a good fortune, must be in want of a wife."

**2.** "It was a bright cold day in April, and the clocks were striking thirteen."

**3.** "If you really want to hear about it, the first thing you'll probably want to know is where I was born, and what my lousy childhood was like."

**4.** "Mother died today."

**5.** "All this happened, more or less."

**6.** "In my younger and more vulnerable years my father gave me some advice that I've been turning over in my mind ever since."

**7.** "You better not never tell nobody but God."

**8.** "In the late summer of that year we lived in a house in a village that looked across the river and the plain to the mountains."

**9.** "The cold passed reluctantly from the earth, and the retiring fogs revealed an army stretched out on the hills, resting."

**a.** Stephen Crane, *The Red Badge of Courage*

**b.** Alice Walker, *The Color Purple*

**c.** Albert Camus, *The Stranger*

**d.** J. D. Salinger, *The Catcher in the Rye*

**e.** George Orwell, *1984*

**f.** Ernest Hemingway, *A Farewell to Arms*

**g.** F. Scott Fitzgerald, *The Great Gatsby*

**h.** Jane Austen, *Pride and Prejudice*

**i.** Kurt Vonnegut, *Slaughterhouse-Five*

**Answers:**
1-h, 2-e, 3-d,
4-c, 5-i, 6-g,
7-b, 8-f, 9-a

# WINNING QUOTES

*Is winning really everything?*

"Winning may not be everything, but losing has little to recommend it."
—Dianne Feinstein

"If a tie is like kissing your sister, losing is like kissing your grandmother with her teeth out."
—George Brett

"You can't win unless you learn how to lose."
—Kareem Abdul-Jabbar

"I disagree with people who think you learn more from getting beat up than you do from winning."
—Tom Cruise

"Losers live in the past. Winners learn from the past and enjoy working in the present toward the future."
—Denis Waitley

"Win as if you were used to it, lose as if you enjoyed it for a change."
—Ralph Waldo Emerson

"A life of frustration is inevitable for any coach whose main enjoyment is winning."
—Chuck Noll

"The will to win is meaningless without the will to prepare."
—Joe Gibbs

"If you're not making mistakes, you're not going anywhere. The key is to make mistakes faster than the competition, so you have more chances to learn and win."
—John W. Holt, Jr

"Those that know how to win are much more numerous than those who know how to make proper use of their victories."
—Polybius

"You're not obligated to win. You're obligated to keep trying to do the best you can every day."
—Marian Wright Edelman

"I never did say that you can't be a nice guy and win. I said that if I was playing third base and my mother rounded third with the winning run, I'd trip her up."
—Leo Durocher

"If winning isn't everything, why do they keep score?"
—Vince Lombardi

From 1971 to '74, the UCLA Bruins won 88 straight basketball games.

"Show class, have pride, and display character. If you do, winning takes care of itself."

—Paul "Bear" Bryant

"The man who is swimming against the stream knows the strength of it." —Woodrow Wilson

# PICASSO

*Spanish artist Pablo Picasso (1881–1973) created 13,500 paintings, 100,000 prints, 34,000 book illustrations, and 300 sculptures. When did he have time to talk so much?*

"You mustn't always believe what I say. Questions tempt you to tell lies, particularly when there is no answer."

"Ah, good taste! What a dreadful thing! Taste is the enemy of creativity."

"As a child I could draw like Leonardo, as an adult I want to paint as a child."

"Youth has no age."

"Painting is a blind man's profession. He paints not what he sees, but what he feels, what he tells himself about what he has seen."

"I have a horror of people who speak about the beautiful."

"I hate that aesthetic game of the eye and the mind, played by these connoisseurs, these mandarins who 'appreciate' beauty. What is beauty, anyway? There's no such thing. I never 'appreciate,' any more than I 'like.' I love or I hate."

"We artists are indestructible; even in a prison, or in a concentration camp, I would be almighty in my own world of art, even if I had to paint my pictures with my wet tongue on the dusty floor of my cell."

"Now there is fame! Of all—hunger, misery, the incomprehension by the public—fame is by far the worst. It is the castigation of God by the artist. It is sad. It is true."

"Through art we express our conception of what nature is not."

"To finish a picture? What nonsense! To finish it means to be through with it, to kill it, to rid it of its soul, to give it its final blow."

"If there were only one truth, you couldn't paint a hundred canvases on the same theme."

"Every act of creation is first of all an act of destruction."

# THE NAKED TRUTH

*Time to let it all hang out.*

"I wish we were all naked all the time. I have always believed it's what's underneath that counts."
—**Celine Dion**

"When you've seen a nude infant doing a backward somersault, you know why clothing exists."
—**Stephen Fry**

"Golf is more fun than walking naked in a strange place, but not much."
—**Buddy Hackett**

"When I get a reaction from people like, 'Why do you do that?' it makes me want to do it again and again."
—**Will Ferrell, on appearing naked in many of his films**

"Eros will have naked bodies; Friendship naked personalities."
—**C. S. Lewis**

"Beware of the naked man who offers you his shirt."
—**Navjot Singh Sidhu**

"Nudity is the uniform of the other side."
—**Milan Kundera**

"I think on-stage nudity is disgusting, shameful and damaging to all things American. But if I were 22 with a great body, it would be artistic, tasteful, patriotic and a progressive religious experience."
—**Shelley Winters**

"I'd like to see a nude opera, because when they hit those high notes, I bet you can really see it in those genitals."
—**Jack Handy**

"There are those who so dislike the nude that they find something indecent in the naked truth."
—**Francis Herbert Bradley**

"Modesty is a vastly overrated virtue."
—**John Kenneth Galbraith**

"I come from a country where you don't wear clothes most of the year. I was born nude and I hope to be buried nude."
—**Elle MacPherson**

"Clothes make the man, but nakedness makes the human being."
—**Kevin Kearney**

**"The skin is an important interface between man and the environment." —OSHA pamphlet**

# LIFE AND DEATH

*Just like peaches and cream, you can't have one without the other.*

"The art of living well and the art of dying well are one."
—Epicurus

"If I think more about death than some other people, it is probably because I love life more than they do."
—Angelina Jolie

"Our days are numbered. One of the primary goals in our lives should be to prepare for our last day. The legacy we leave is not just in our possessions, but in the quality of our lives. The greatest waste in all of our earth, which cannot be recycled or reclaimed, is our waste of the time that God has given us each day."
—Billy Graham

"Life is better than death, I believe, if only because it is less boring, and because it has fresh peaches in it."
—Alice Walker

"The fear of death follows from the fear of life. A man who lives fully is prepared to die at any time."
—Mark Twain

"While I thought that I was learning how to live, I have been learning how to die."
—Leonardo Da Vinci

"We're all going to get old and die, and if we live long enough, we're going to forget things or lose our memories. That's just what happens. So why be in a hurry to forget something or undo something?"
—Viggo Mortensen

"Life is a fatal complaint, and an eminently contagious one."
—Oliver Wendell Holmes

"It is natural to die as to be born."
—Francis Bacon

"Ignore death up to the last moment; then, when it can't be ignored any longer, have yourself squirted full of morphine and shuffle off in a coma. Thoroughly sensible, humane, and scientific, eh?"
—Aldous Huxley

"Life is pleasant. Death is peaceful. It's the transition that's troublesome."
—Isaac Asimov

# WHAT CONSPIRACY?

*We personally don't believe in all of these crazy conspiracy theories.*
*That black helicopter hovering overhead is just…sightseeing?*
*For hours on end? Someone go get the tin foil.*

"In politics, nothing happens by accident. If it happened, you can bet it was planned that way."
—**Franklin D. Roosevelt**

"Give me control of a nation's money and I care not who makes the laws."
—**Mayer Amschel Rothschild**

"More things in politics happen by accident or exhaustion than happen by conspiracy."
—**Jeff Greenfield**

"The world is governed by people far different from those imagined by the public."
—**Benjamin Disraeli**

"The de facto censorship which leaves so many Americans functionally illiterate about the history of U.S. foreign affairs may be all the more effective because it is not official, heavy-handed or conspiratorial, but woven artlessly into the fabric of education and media. No conspiracy is needed."
—**William Blum**

"The ruling class has the schools and press under its thumb. This enables it to sway the emotions of the masses."
—**Albert Einstein**

"Anyone who knows how difficult it is to keep a secret among three men—particularly if they are married—knows how absurd is the idea of a worldwide secret conspiracy consciously controlling all mankind by its financial power, in real, clear analysis."
—**Oswald Mosley**

"I really wish there was some Big Brother conspiracy, but it's all about trying to make a dollar. If anyone doesn't think that this is about making money, then they're crazy."
—**Montel Williams**

"The real truth of the matter is, as you and I know, that a financial element in the large centers has owned the government of the U.S. since the days of Andrew Jackson."
—**Franklin D. Roosevelt**

"Those market researchers are playing games with you and me and with this entire country. Their so-called samples of opinion are no more accurate or reliable than my grandmother's big toe was when it came to predicting the weather."
—**Dan Rather**

"More history is made by secret handshakes than by battles, bills, and proclamations."
—**John Barth**

"The real rulers in Washington are invisible and exercise power from behind the scenes."
—**Justice Felix Frankfurter**

"The biggest conspiracy has always been the fact that there is no conspiracy. Nobody's out to get you. Nobody gives a sh*t whether you live or die. There, you feel better now?"
—**Dennis Miller**

## POTTER'S APHORISMS
*On the TV show M\*A\*S\*H, Col. Potter had some funny ways of expressing his dissatisfaction.*

Crock of beans!

Mule muffins!

Hot mustard!

Hot sausage!

Cow cookies!

Mule fritters!

Monkey muffins!

Buffalo bagels!

Beaver biscuits!

Pigeon pellets!

Pony pucks!

Sufferin' sheepdip!

Hell's bells!

Horse hockey!

Pig feathers!

Road apples!

Sufferin' saddlesoap!

Scuttlebug is as common as cooties in your skivvy!

What in the name of Sweet Fanny Adams?!

What in the name of Marco Blessed Polo!

What in the name of Great Caesar's Salad?!

# RATHERISMS

*We love former CBS newsman Dan Rather's colloquial analogies
as much as a three-legged dog loves chasing a one-legged cat!*

"This presidential race has been crackling like a hickory fire for at least the last hour."

"Texas: 32 electoral votes, another of the so-called big enchiladas or if not an enchilada at least a huge taco."

"This race is hotter than the Devil's anvil."

"You talk about a ding-dong, knock-down, get-up race."

"One's reminded of that old saying, 'Don't taunt the alligator until after you've crossed the creek.'"

"This situation in Ohio would give an aspirin a headache."

"If you ain't got the yolk, you can't emulsify the Hollandaise."

"No question now that John Kerry's rapidly reaching the point where he's got his back to the wall, his shirttails on fire, and the bill collector's at the door."

"In Southern states they beat him like a rented mule."

"She ran away with it like a hobo with a sweet potato pie."

"If you try to read the tea leaves before the cup is done you can get yourself burned."

"John Kerry's moon has just moved behind a cloud."

"The election is closer than Timmy and Lassie."

"I'd say [the Virginia Senate race] was as ugly as a hog lagoon after a bachelor party."

"It was as hot and squalid as a New York elevator in August."

"You would likelier see a hippopotamus run through this room than see George Bush appoint Ralph Nader to the Cabinet."

"What I say or do here won't matter much, nor should it."

**"Never eat spinach just before going on the air." —Dan Rather**

# JUSTICE AND THE LAW

*Where does the law end and justice begin? We don't know;
we just make* Bathroom Readers. *But these
people seem to think they have an idea.*

"Good people do not need laws to tell them how to act responsibly, while bad people will find a way around the laws."
—**Plato**

"In the Halls of Justice, the only justice is in the halls."
—**Lenny Bruce**

"The law, in its majestic equality, forbids the rich as well as the poor to sleep under bridges, to beg in the streets, and to steal bread."
—**Anatole France**

"The strictest law sometimes becomes the severest injustice."
—**Benjamin Franklin**

"The law must be stable, but it must not stand still."
—**Roscoe Pound**

"It is the spirit and not the form of law that keeps justice alive."
—**Earl Warren**

"Written laws are like spiders' webs: They only entangle and hold the poor and weak, while the rich and powerful will easily break through them."
—**Anacharsis**

"Justice without force is powerless; force without justice is tyrannical."
—**Blaise Pascal**

"Law and justice are not always the same. When they aren't, destroying the law may be the first step toward changing it."
—**Gloria Steinem**

"Oh, judge, your damn laws: the good people don't need them and the bad people don't follow them, so what good are they?"
—**Ammon Hennacy**

"Justice limps along...but it gets there all the same."
—**Gabriel García Márquez**

"At his best, man is the noblest
of all animals. Separated from law
and justice, he is the worst."

—Aristotle

# MOTHERHOOD

*It's the hardest job in the neighborhood.*

"Motherhood: All love begins and ends there."
—**Robert Browning**

"When you are a mother, you are never really alone in your thoughts. A mother always has to think twice, once for herself and once for her child."
—**Sophia Loren**

"Never marry a man who hates his mother, because he'll end up hating you."
—**Jill Bennett**

"A mother is not a person to lean on, but a person to make leaning unnecessary."
—**Dorothy Canfield Fisher**

"The future destiny of the child is always the work of the mother."
—**Napoleon Bonaparte**

"Before becoming a mother, I had a hundred theories on how to bring up children. Now I have seven children and only one theory: Love them, especially when they least deserve to be loved."
—**Kate Samperi**

"No matter how old a mother is, she watches her middle-aged children for signs of improvement."
—**Florida Scott-Maxwell**

"Mothers are fonder than fathers of their children because they are more certain they are their own."
—**Aristotle**

"A suburban mother's role is to deliver children obstetrically once, and by car forever after."
—**Peter De Vries**

"The phrase 'working mother' is redundant."
—**Jane Sellman**

"Blaming mother is just a negative way of clinging to her still."
—**Nancy Friday**

"The story of a mother's life: Trapped between a scream and a hug."
—**Cathy Guisewite**

"Anyone who doesn't miss the past never had a mother."
—**Gregory Nunn**

# BODY PARTS

*Some observations on body parts and the power they have.*

"If you ever need a helping hand, you'll find one at the end of your arm."
—**Yiddish Proverb**

"You start out happy that you have no hips or boobs. All of a sudden you get them, and it feels sloppy. Then just when you start liking them, they start drooping."
—**Cindy Crawford**

"I'm a 34 waist, 32 inseam, which is not a good look. You kind of want your legs to be longer than your waist circumference."
—**Jason Bateman**

"The only things I really love about myself physically are my ankles and my hair."
—**Valerie Bertinelli**

"Ankles are nearly always neat and good-looking, but knees are nearly always not."
—**Dwight D. Eisenhower**

"My mother told me I was dancing before I was born. She could feel my toes tapping wildly inside her for months."
—**Ginger Rogers**

"Yeah, some kids called me fish lips because I had these really full lips. Now I'm sure all those same girls are getting collagen injections, so I'm having the last laugh."
—**Denise Richards**

"You can go a long way with bad legs and a good head."
—**Gavin McDonald, Scottish Bicyclist**

"Although the whole mind seems to be united to the whole body, I recognize that if a foot or arm is cut off, nothing has thereby been taken away from the mind."
—**René Descartes**

"You can only hold your stomach in for so many years."
—**Burt Reynolds**

"If your body was a used car, you wouldn't buy it."
—**Jerry Seinfeld**

"Your body is not the real you, it's just the meat you live in. I like that: it means that the real me doesn't really have a humongous butt."
—**Jessica Zafra, author**

Hungarian food critic Egon Ronay took out a $400,000 insurance policy on his tastebuds.

# THE TRUMAN SHOW

*Truman Capote (1924–1984) said a lot in his novels* In Cold Blood *and* Breakfast at Tiffany's…*but he was also a prolific interviewer. Here are some choice bits gleaned from Capote's question-and-answer sessions.*

"A conversation is a dialogue, not a monologue. That's why there are so few good conversations: due to scarcity, two intelligent talkers seldom meet."

"Well, I'm about as tall as a shotgun, and just as noisy."

"I'm not a saint yet. I'm an alcoholic. I'm a drug addict. I'm homosexual. I'm a genius. Of course I could be all four of these dubious things and still be a saint. But I ain't."

"All being best-dressed ever takes is taste and money."

"I was so different from everyone, so much more sensitive and perceptive. I was having fifty perceptions a minute to everyone else's five. I always felt that nobody was going to understand me, going to understand what I felt about things. I guess that's why I started writing. At least on paper I could put down what I thought."

"The truth seems to be that no one likes to see himself described as he is. Well, even I can understand that—because I don't like it myself when I am the sitter and not the portraitist: the frailty of egos! —and the more accurate the strokes, the greater the resentment."

"I started writing when I was eight—out of the blue, uninspired by any example. I'd never known anyone who wrote; indeed, I knew few people who read."

"Style makes the middle class nervous."

"I love elegant women. They're like art and music. But I want them all to look as if they were living private lives. Not as if they were going on stage about to do the tarantella."

"I know a lot more about other people than I know about myself."

# HE SLUD INTO THIRD

*Sometimes the most entertaining things you'll find on sports broadcasts don't come from the field of play, but from the mouths of the broadcasters.*

"That's Hendrick's 19th home run. One more and he reaches double figures."
—Jerry Coleman

"The racecourse is as level as a billiard ball."
—John Francome

"He fakes a bluff."
—Ron Fairly

"He was a dead man walking —he didn't have a leg to stand on."
—Malcolm Boyden, after a soccer player was ejected

"Stern John had the easy task of rolling it into the net from six yards. He made it look easy, although it wasn't!"
—Chris Kamara

"Hawaii doesn't win many games in the United States."
—Lee Corso, football analyst

"Aw, how could he [Jorge Orta] lose the ball in the sun? He's from Mexico."
—Harry Caray

"Bruce Sutter has been around for a while, and he's pretty old. He's 35 years old. That will give you some idea of how old he is."
—Ron Fairly

"That is the most unheard-of thing I've ever heard of!"
—Harry Neale, after the Washington Capitals lost two consecutive hockey games in the final three seconds

"Next up is the Central African Republic...located in...central Africa.
—Bob Costas, during the 2000 Summer Olympics

"It's a partial sellout."
—Skip Caray

"In a sense, it's a one-man show—except there are two men involved, Hartson and Berkovic, and a third man, the goalkeeper."
—John Motson, BBC

"Fans, don't fail to miss tomorrow's game."
—Dizzy Dean

# UNCLE JOHN'S QUOTATIONARY

*Quotable people have a knack for coming up with new and clever definitions for everyday words. We've compiled our favorites into this quotationary.*

**ACTING:** standing up naked and turning around very slowly. (Rosalind Russell)

**ACTIVIST:** It's not the man who says the river is dirty—it's the man who cleans up the river. (Ross Perot)

**ADVERSITY:** an opportunity for heroism. (Marv Levy)

**ADVERTISING:** the science of arresting the human intelligence long enough to get money from it. (Stephen Leacock)

**ALCOHOLIC:** anyone you don't like who drinks more than you do. (Dylan Thomas)

**AMERICA:** a great social and economic experiment, noble in motive and far-reaching in purpose. (Herbert Hoover)

**ANATOMY:** something everyone has, but which looks better on a girl. (Bruce Raeburn)

**ANXIETY:** the dizziness of freedom. (Søren Kierkegaard)

**APPEARANCE:** but a glimpse of what is hidden. (Anaxagoras)

**APPEASEMENT:** the policy of feeding your friends to a crocodile, one at a time, in hopes that the crocodile will eat you last. (Franklin Delano Roosevelt)

**ART:** a house that tries to be haunted. (Emily Dickinson)

**ATHEISM:** the religion devoted to the worship of one's own smug sense of superiority. (Stephen Colbert)

**AUTOBIOGRAPHY:** an obituary in serial form with the last installment missing. (Quentin Crisp)

Poet Walt Whitman's day job: low-level Washington bureaucrat.

**AUTUMN:** a second spring when every leaf is a flower. (Albert Camus)

**BABY:** God's opinion that the world should go on. (Carl Sandburg)

**BAGEL:** an unsweetened doughnut with rigor mortis. (Beatrice and Ira Freeman)

**BANK:** a place that will lend you money if you can prove that you don't need it. (Bob Hope)

**BEAUTY:** an outward gift, which is seldom despised, except by those to whom it has been refused. (Ralph Waldo Emerson)

**BEER:** a high and mighty liquor. (Julius Caesar)

**BLOOD:** the ink of our life's story. (Jason Mechalek)

**BLUSHING:** the color of virtue. (Diogenes)

**BREAST IMPLANTS:** a close chemical relative of Silly Putty. (Barbara Ehrenreich)

**BURNOUT:** nature's way of telling you that you've been going through the motions, but your soul has departed; you're a zombie, a member of the walking dead, a sleepwalker. (Sam Keen)

**CAMERA:** an instrument that teaches people how to see without a camera. (Dorothea Lange)

**CAPITALISM:** the extraordinary belief that the nastiest of men, for the nastiest of reasons, will somehow work for the benefit of us all. (John Maynard Keynes)

**CAPITAL PUNISHMENT:** income tax. (Jeff Hayes)

**CELEBRITY:** the worst thing that can happen to an actor. (John Cusack)

**CENSORSHIP:** advertising paid for by the government. (Federico Fellini)

**CHANCE:** the pseudonym of God when he does not want to sign. (Anatole France)

**CHIC:** a convent for unloved women. (Anatole Broyard)

**CIVILIZATION:** a limitless multiplication of unnecessary necessities. (Mark Twain)

"People who throw kisses are hopelessly lazy." —Bob Hope

**COACHING:** eliminating mistakes before you get fired. (Lou Holtz)

**COMEDY:** the art of making people laugh without making them puke. (Steve Martin)

**COMMITTEE:** a cul-de-sac down which ideas are lured and then quietly strangled. (Sir Barnett Cocks)

**COMPROMISE:** the art of dividing a cake in such a way that everyone believes he has the biggest piece. (Ludwig Erhard)

**CONCENTRATION:** the ability to think about absolutely nothing when it is absolutely necessary. (Ray Knight)

**CONFIDENCE:** what you have before you understand the problem. (Woody Allen)

**CONSERVATION:** a state of harmony between men and land. (Aldo Leopold)

**COUNTRY MUSIC:** three chords and the truth. (Harlan Howard)

**CREATIVITY:** the sudden cessation of stupidity. (Edwin Land)

**CRITIC:** is someone who knows the way but can't drive the car. (Kenneth Tynan)

**CRIMINAL:** a person with predatory instincts without sufficient capital to form a corporation. (Howard Scott)

**CURIOSITY:** lying in wait for every secret. (Ralph Waldo Emerson)

**CYNICAL REALISM:** the intelligent man's best excuse for doing nothing in an intolerable situation. (Aldous Huxley)

*For more, see page 70.*

"Half our life is spent trying to find something to do with the time we have rushed through life trying to save."
—Will Rogers

Every 11 seconds, the U.S. population grows by one person.

"There are two kinds of
people in the world: those
who walk into a room and
say, 'There you are,' and
those who say, 'Here I am.'"
—**Abigail Van Buren**

# TWO KINDS OF PEOPLE

*Sure, dividing people into "types" is simplistic...but sometimes it works.*

"At every party there are two kinds of people—those who want to go home and those who don't. The trouble is, they are usually married to each other."
—**Ann Landers**

"There are two kinds of talent: man-made talent and God-given talent. With man-made talent, you have to work very hard. With God-given talent, you just touch it up once in a while."
—**Pearl Bailey**

"We need two kinds of friends: one to complain to, while to the others we boast."
—**Logan Pearsall Smith**

"There are two kinds of people in the world: those who love chocolate, and Communists."
—**Leslie Moak Murray**

"When it comes to the future, there are three kinds of people: those who let it happen, those who make it happen, and those who wonder what happened."
—**John M. Richardson**

"I'm scared! I don't know whether the world is full of smart men bluffing, or imbeciles who mean it."
—**Morrie Brickman**

"Don't matter how much money you got, there's only two kinds of people: saved people and lost people."
—**Bob Dylan**

"There are two types of forwards: scorers and bangers. Scorers score and bangers bang."
—**Ken Dryden, NHL forward**

"There are two kinds of truth; the truth that lights the way and the truth that warms the heart. The first of these is science, and the second is art."
—**Raymond Chandler**

"There are two kinds of adventurers: those who go truly hoping to find adventure, and those who go secretly hoping they won't."
—**William Least Heat Moon**

"I only like two kinds of men, domestic and imported."
—**Mae West**

# WHY WEIGHT?

*How do we stay in shape at the Bathroom Readers'
Institute? By pushing our luck, jumping to
conclusions, and ducking deadlines.*

"I've been on a diet for two weeks, and all I've lost is two weeks."
—**Totie Fields**

"There's a great new rice diet that always works—you use one chop stick."
—**Red Buttons**

"If nature had intended our skeletons to be visible, it would have put them on the outside of our bodies."
—**Elmer Rice**

"I'm tired of all this nonsense about beauty being only skin-deep. That's deep enough. What do you want, an adorable pancreas?"
—**Rita Mae Brown**

"Observe your dog: if he's fat, then you're not getting enough exercise."
—**Evan Esar**

"The best measure of a man's honesty isn't his income tax return. It's the zero adjustment on his bathroom scale."
—**Arthur C. Clarke**

"So far I've always kept my diet secret, but now I might as well tell everyone what it is. Lots of grapefruit throughout the day and plenty of virile young men."
—**Angie Dickinson**

"When we lose twenty pounds, we may be losing the pounds that contain our genius, our humanity, our love, and honesty."
—**Woody Allen**

"I feel about airplanes the way I feel about diets. It seems to me they are wonderful things for other people to go on."
—**Jean Kerr**

"The biggest seller is cookbooks and the second is diet books—how not to eat what you've just learned how to cook."
—**Andy Rooney**

"It's okay to be fat. So you're fat. Just be fat and shut up about it."
—**Roseanne Barr**

# THE ANIMAL KINGDOM

*Some thoughts on the animal kingdom from the strangest animal of them all—Homo sapiens.*

"Until one has loved an animal, a part of one's soul remains unawakened."
—**Anatole France**

"Penguins mate for life. Which doesn't surprise me that much, because they all look alike—it's not like they're gonna meet a better-looking penguin one day."
—**Ellen DeGeneres**

"Unlike humans, the boa constrictor, when he has had an adequate meal, goes to sleep, and does not wake until he needs another meal."
—**Bertrand Russell**

"I think animal testing is a bad idea; they get all nervous and give the wrong answers."
—**Joseph Blosephina**

"I don't like small birds. They hop around so merrily outside my window, looking so innocent. But I know that secretly, they're watching my every move and plotting to beat me over the head with a large steel pipe and take my shoes."
—**Jack Handey**

"A lion's work hours are only when he's hungry; once he's satisfied, the predator and prey live peacefully together.
—**Chuck Jones**

"I go about looking at horses and cattle. They eat grass, make love, work when they have to, bear their young. I am sick with envy of them."
—**Sherwood Anderson**

"My favorite animal is the mule. He has more horse sense than a horse. He knows when to stop eating—and he knows when to stop working."
—**Harry S. Truman**

"It's easy to forget the connection between a hamburger and the cow it came from. But I forced myself to acknowledge the fact that every time I ate a hamburger, a cow had ceased to breathe and moo and walk around."
—**Moby**

"When rats leave a sinking ship, where exactly do they think they're going?"
—**Douglas Gauck**

Myth-nomer: The lion, a.k.a. "King of the Jungle," lives mainly on the savannah grasslands.

# POOR RICHARD'S ALMANACK

*Yearly almanacs were popular in colonial America, featuring a calendar, weather forecasts, and astronomical information for the upcoming year. Using the pseudonym "Poor Richard," Benjamin Franklin published his own almanacs, adding aphorisms and bits of wisdom to the mix. Result: From 1732 to 1757, they were the bestselling annual books in the colonies.*

Visits should be short, like a winter's day. Lest you're too troublesome, hasten away.

Love well, whip well.

Hunger never saw bad bread.

A rich rogue is like a fat hog, who never does good 'til as dead as a log.

Beware of the young doctor & the old barber.

To lengthen thy life, lessen thy meals.

Great famine when wolves eat wolves.

Innocence is its own defense.

Take this remark from Richard poor and lame, Whate'er's begun in anger ends in shame.

Don't think to hunt two hares with one dog.

Who pleasure gives, shall joy receive.

Where there's marriage without love, there will be love without marriage.

He that cannot obey, cannot command.

An egg today is better than a hen tomorrow.

He that waits upon fortune is never sure of a dinner.

Great modesty often hides great merit.

You may delay, but time will not.

He that best understands the world, least likes it.

---

Benjamin Franklin spoke five languages fluently and could play violin, harp, and guitar.

Well done is better than well said.

Who has deceiv'd thee so oft as thy self?

If passion drives, let reason hold the reins.

Be slow in choosing a friend, and slower in changing.

Who is rich? He that rejoices in his portion.

Monkeys, warm with envious spite, their most obliging friends will bite.

'Tis easy to see, hard to foresee.

Those who in quarrels interpose, must often wipe a bloody nose.

Wars bring scars.

Neither trust, nor contend, nor lay wagers, nor lend; and you'll have peace to your live's end.

Tomorrow I'll reform, the fool does say; today itself's too late—the *wise* did yesterday.

When you speak to a man, look on his eyes; when he speaks to thee, look on his mouth.

He that spills the rum loses that only; he that drinks it often loses both that and himself.

Clean your finger before you point at my spots.

No wonder Tom grows fat; the unwi'ldy sinner makes his life but one continual dinner.

Promises may get thee friends, but nonperformance will turn them into enemies.

Let thy discontents be thy secrets; if the world knows them, it will despise thee and increase them.

None are deceived, but they that confide.

Genius without education is like silver in the mine.

Death takes no bribes.

Great spenders are bad lenders.

A slip of the foot you may soon recover, but a slip of the tongue you may never get over.

Diligence is the mother of good luck.

# THE COS

*Hey hey hey! It's the Bill Cosby page!*

"I am certainly not an authority on love because there are no authorities on love, just those who've had luck with it and those who haven't."

"Let us now set forth one of the fundamental truths about marriage: the wife is in charge."

"Like everyone else who makes the mistake of getting older, I begin each day with coffee and obituaries."

"My childhood should have taught me lessons for my own fatherhood, but it didn't because parenting can only be learned by people who have no children."

"Poets have said that the reason to have children is to give yourself immortality. Immortality? Now that I have five children, my only hope is that they are all out of the house before I die."

"Is the glass half full, or half empty? It depends on whether you're pouring or drinking."

"When you become senile, you won't know it."

"Humans are the only creatures on earth that allow their children to come back home."

"By the time a child is eight or nine, he has developed a passion for his own music that is even stronger than his passions for procrastination and weird clothes."

"Women don't want to hear what you think. Women want to hear what they think in a deeper voice."

"I was a physical education major with a child psychology minor, which means if you ask me a question about a child's behavior, I will advise you to tell the child to take a lap."

"It's more blessed to give than to receive. Especially kittens."

"You can turn painful situations around through laughter. If you can find humor in anything, even poverty, you can survive it."

# SCIENCE

*"Equipped with his five senses, man explores the universe
around him and calls the adventure Science."*
—Edwin Powell Hubble

"The greatest discoveries of
science have always been
those that forced us to rethink
our beliefs about the universe
and our place in it."
—Robert L. Park

"Science is the search for
truth. It's not a game in
which one tries to beat his
opponent. We need to have
the spirit of science in international affairs, to make the
conduct of international
affairs the effort to find the
right solution, the just
solution of international
problems, not the effort by
each nation to get the better
of other nations."
—Linus Pauling

"It requires a very unusual
mind to undertake the analysis
of the obvious."
—Alfred North Whitehead

"Whenever science makes a
discovery, the devil grabs it
while the angels are debating
the best way to use it."
—Alan Valentine

"The great tragedy of science:
the slaying of a beautiful
hypothesis by an ugly fact."
—Thomas H. Huxley

"Science is the great antidote
to the poison of enthusiasm
and superstition."
—Adam Smith

"Most institutions demand
unqualified faith; but the
institution of science makes
skepticism a virtue."
—Robert K. Merton

"I think science has enjoyed
an extraordinary success
because it has such a limited
and narrow realm in which to
focus its efforts. Namely, the
physical universe."
—Ken Jenkins

"True science teaches, above
all, to doubt and be ignorant."
—Miguel de Unamuno

"Science has made us gods
even before we are worthy of
being men."
—Jean Rostand

# PUN-ISHING QUOTES

*What did the one beaver say to the other beaver?*
*"This is the best dam page in the book!"*

"A bore is a person who opens his mouth and puts his feats in it."
—**Henry Ford**

"Art is just a pigment of your imagination."
—**Tony Follari**

"Old professors never die, they just lose their faculties."
—**Stephen Fry**

"I went to the doctor and he said I had acute appendicitis, and I said compared to who?"
—**Jay London**

"*The Passion of the Christ* opened up on Ash Wednesday, and had a Good Friday."
—**Billy Crystal**

"I almost didn't make it tonight. Had a flat tire— there was a fork in the road."
—**Bob Dylan**

"A jester unemployed is nobody's fool!"
—**Danny Kaye**

"I dream of a rural life—raising checks."
—**Dorothy Parker**

"A liberated woman is one who rises up and says to her menfolk, 'I will not be dictated to,' and proceeds to become a stenographer."
—**G. K. Chesterton**

"If you want to see a comic strip, you should see me in the shower."
—**Groucho Marx**

"I could not understand how it was that people could put a drug user on such a high pedestal."
—**Chet Baker**

"Putting your hands in the earth is very grounding."
—**John Glover**

"I'd call him a sadistic, hippophilic necrophile, but that would be beating a dead horse."
—**Woody Allen**

"An art thief is a man who takes pictures."
—**George Carlin**

"Down is up when the geese are flying."
—**Angela Kern**

"I love puns so much that my wife made a sign I hang over my desk: 'Caution! Incorrigible Punster. Please Don't Incorrige.'"
—**Bob Trowbridge**

"She was what we used to call a suicide blond—dyed by her own hand."
—**Saul Bellow**

"The hardest tumble a man can make is to fall over his own bluff."
—**Ambrose Bierce**

"The antiques my wife buys at auctions are keeping me baroque."
—**Peter De Vries**

Two vultures boarded an airplane, each carried two dead raccoons. The flight attendant looked at them and said, "I'm sorry, gentlemen, only one carrion allowed per passenger."

A motorcycle pulled alongside a speeding car on the highway. He was amazed to see that the woman behind the wheel was actually knitting. The cop yelled, "Pull over!" "Not quite!" the woman yelled back, "Scarf!"

"It was so quiet, you could hear a pun drop." —**Bugs Baer**

# THE WRATH OF AGNEW

*As vice president under Richard Nixon, Spiro T. Agnew (1918–96), served as a "mouthpiece" for the administration, saying the things that Nixon couldn't. His role was to throw verbal darts at the liberal establishment—intellectuals, hippies, and the press—anyone who disagreed with the administration. His remarks were antagonistic, outrageous, controversial…and very quotable.*

"I have often been accused of putting my foot in my mouth, but I will never put my hand in your pockets."

"A spirit of national masochism prevails, encouraged by an effete corps of impudent snobs who characterize themselves as intellectuals."

"Some newspapers are fit only to line the bottom of birdcages."

"An intellectual is a man who doesn't know how to park a bike."

"Ultraliberalism today translates into a whimpering isolationism in foreign policy, a mulish obstructionism in domestic policy, and a pusillanimous pussyfooting on the critical issue of law and order."

"In the United States today, we have more than our share of nattering nabobs of negativism."

"Yippies, hippies, yahoos, Black Panthers, lions and tigers alike—I would swap the whole damn zoo for the kind of young Americans I saw in Vietnam."

"The lessons of the past are ignored and obliterated in a contemporary antagonism known as the generation gap."

"If you've seen one city slum, you've seen them all."

"They have formed their own 4-H club: the hopeless, hysterical hypochondriacs of history."

"Perhaps the place to start looking for a credibility gap is not in the offices of the Government in Washington but in the studios of the networks in New York."

"Three things have been difficult to tame: the oceans, fools, and women. We may soon be able to tame the oceans; fools and women will take a little longer."

"Now we are in a fix. Peace has been declared." —Napoleon Bonaparte

# HERE'S WHAT I THINK...

*A few wise comments from a wide array of speakers.*

"There's a bit of magic in everything, and some loss to even things out."
—Lou Reed

"Your vision will become clear only when you look into your heart. Who looks outside, dreams. Who looks inside, awakens."
—Carl Jung

"The greatest danger for most of us is not that our aim is too high and we miss it, but that it is too low and we reach it."
—Michelangelo

"The doctor sees all the weakness of mankind; the lawyer all the wickedness, the theologian all the stupidity."
—Arthur Schopenhauer

"Education is when you read the fine print; experience is what you get when you don't."
—Pete Seeger

"The weak are more likely to make the strong weak than the strong are likely to make the weak strong."
—Marlene Dietrich

"He who cannot obey himself will be commanded. That is the nature of living creatures."
—Friedrich Nietzsche

"Most people aren't appreciated enough, and the bravest things we do in our lives are usually known only to ourselves. No one throws ticker tape on the man who chose to be faithful to his wife, or the lawyer who didn't take the drug money."
—Peggy Noonan

"To think is easy. To act is difficult. To act as one thinks is the most difficult."
—Goethe

"Wisdom is knowing what to do next, skill is knowing how to do it, and virtue is doing it."
—David Starr Jordan

"Think what a better world it would be if we all, the whole world, had cookies and milk about three o'clock every afternoon and then lay down on our blankets for a nap."
—Barbara Jordan

"I don't really think, I just walk." —Paris Hilton

# TRUE VS. FALSE

*What is truth? What is false? What is the difference?*

"All truths are easy to understand once they are discovered; the point is to discover them."
—Galileo Galilei

"It takes two to speak truth—one to speak, and another to hear."
—Henry David Thoreau

"Every violation of truth is not only a sort of suicide in the liar, but is a stab at the health of human society."
—Ralph Waldo Emerson

"The truth, of course, is that a billion falsehoods told a billion times by a billion people are still false."
—Travis Walton

"Truth can be a dangerous thing. It is quite patient and relentless."
—R. Scott Richards

"One comes to believe whatever one repeats to oneself sufficiently often, whether the statement be true or false. It comes to be dominating thought in one's mind."
—Robert Collier

"Lying became part of my life. I lied if I needed to lie to get something or get out of something."
—James Frey,
*A Million Little Pieces*

"I made a mistake. I left the impression that the truth does not matter, and I am deeply sorry about that, because that is not what I believe."
—Oprah Winfrey,
apologizing for endorsing James Frey's memoir
*A Million Little Pieces*

"In an age of universal deceit, telling the truth is a revolutionary act."
—George Orwell

"Say not, 'I have found the truth,' but rather, 'I have found a truth.'"
—Khalil Gibran

"The truth is what is, not what should be. What should be is a dirty lie."
—Lenny Bruce

"Truth is such a rare thing, it is delightful to tell it."
—Emily Dickinson

"A fact will fit every other fact in the universe, and that is how you can tell whether it is or is not a fact. A lie will not fit anything except another lie."
—Robert G. Ingersoll

"A lie told often enough becomes the truth."
—Vladimir Lenin

"The third time you say a thing, it sounds like a lie."
—Harrison Ford

"Truth, like light, blinds. Falsehood, on the contrary, is a beautiful twilight that enhances every object."
—Albert Camus

"Truth isn't always beauty, but the hunger for it is."
—Nadine Gordimer

"What the imagination seizes as beauty must be truth."
—John Keats

"Chase after the truth like all hell and you'll free yourself, even though you never touch its coattails."
—Clarence Darrow

"The way I feel about music is that there is no right and wrong. Only true and false."
—Fiona Apple

"But are not the dreams of poets and the tales of travelers notoriously false?"
—H. P. Lovecraft

"The surest way to remain poor is to be an honest man."
—Napoleon Bonaparte

"It is easier to perceive error than to find truth, for the former lies on the surface and is easily seen, while the latter lies in the depth, where few are willing to search for it."
—Goethe

"Do not be misled by what you see around you, or be influenced by what you see. You live in a world which is a playground of illusion, full of false paths, false values and false ideals. But you are not part of that world."
—Sai Baba

"You shall know the truth, and the truth shall make you mad as hell."
—Aldous Huxley

"I believe that in the end the truth will conquer."
—John Wycliffe

"They say that in the end truth will triumph, but it's a lie."
—Anton Chekhov

# THAT'S MY NAME

*What does your name say about you? Maybe someday you can become famous enough to tell your story in a quotation book, like these people.*

"My name is more important than myself."

—**Pierre Cardin**

"I've made up so many stories about my where my name comes from, I can't remember."

—**Joaquin Phoenix**

"Cara is not my real name, and I'm not going to tell you what it is. Only because I do live in New York and enough people already know who my parents are."

—**Irene Cara, born Irene Escalera**

"My full name is Damieon Dante Hall. But I go by Dante because I don't like the name Damieon because of the movie *The Omen*."

—**Dante Hall**

"I wasn't lucky enough to be born with a body that responded well to acid-washed jeans and Lycra, so I had to rely on my last name to get past bodyguards."

—**Moon Unit Zappa**

"It has not been an easy name, yet it has brought me many a laugh."

—**Sister Parish**

"The C stands for Christopher. The Screen Actors Guild makes you do it if there's another union member with the same name. I wasn't going to change my name, so I just included the middle one. It was a decision I had to make on *Casualties of War*, my first film in 1989. I got a phone call and had to fly out to Thailand where Brian De Palma was shooting, so it was a sudden decision, and I'm stuck with it. But I'm glad I didn't go for a stupid and exotic-sounding name just to grab attention, or you could be talking to a man named Tallulah or something."

—**John C. Reilly**

"I've always thought that a name says a lot about a person. So naturally, being named Howard, I always wanted to crawl into a hole."

—**Howard Stern**

# CLOSE ENCOUNTERS

*Does alien life exist? These people sure think so.*

"It was the darnedest thing I've ever seen. It was big, it was very bright, it changed colors, and it was about the size of the moon. We watched it for ten minutes, but none of us could figure out what it was. One thing's for sure, I'll never make fun of people who say they've seen unidentified objects in the sky. If I become president, I'll make every piece of information this country has about UFO sightings available to the public and the scientists."

**—Jimmy Carter, 1976, who was elected, but never released the UFO info**

"I certainly believe in aliens in space. They may not look like us, but I have very strong feelings that they have advanced beyond our mental capabilities....I think some highly secret government UFO investigations are going on that we don't know about—and probably never will unless the Air Force discloses them."

**—Barry Goldwater**

"At no time when the astronauts were in space were they alone: there was a constant surveillance by UFOs."

**—Scott Carpenter, who photographed a UFO while in orbit in 1962. NASA has not released the photo.**

"Since, in the long run, every planetary society will be endangered by impacts from space, every surviving civilization is obliged to become spacefaring—not because of exploratory or romantic zeal, but for the most practical reason imaginable: staying alive."

**—Carl Sagan**

"My own present opinion, based on two years of careful study, is that UFOs are probably extraterrestrial devices engaged in something that might very tentatively be termed 'surveillance.'"

—Dr. James E. McDonald, 1968, speaking to Congress

"It followed us during half of our orbit. We observed it on the light side, and when we entered the shadow side, it disappeared completely. It was an engineered structure, made from some type of metal, approximately 40 meters long with inner hulls. The object was narrow here and wider here, and inside there were openings. Some places had projections like small wings. The object stayed very close to us. We photographed it, and our photos showed it to be 23 to 28 meters away."

—Cosmonaut Victor Afanasyev, who saw a UFO on his way to the *Solyut 6* space station in 1979. His photos have never been made public.

"The unidentified craft appeared to take efficient controlled evasive action."

—FBI Memo, describing chase of a UFO over the North Sea, 1947

"I think that we all know that we're not alone in the universe. I can't imagine that we are the only intelligent biological life form out there. I'm a little less sure in my 50s than I was in my late 20s whether we're actually ever going to find out."

—Steven Spielberg

"People ask if there is life out there, but why is it that the only people who get abducted are morons? Why would intelligent life with advanced technology come out to Earth and pick out a drunk idiot that nobody believes in the first place?"

—Michael Stoneman

# BILL O'REILLY

*He speaks his mind and doesn't apologize for it.*

"You gotta look people in the eye and tell them they're irresponsible and lazy. Because in this country, you can succeed if you get educated and work hard. Period. Period."

"Winston Churchill said that democracy was the worst possible form of government, except for all the others. Maybe we can say the same about capitalism. For all of its faults, it gives most hardworking people a chance to improve themselves economically, even as the deck is stacked in favor of the privileged few. Here are the choices most of us face in such a system: Get bitter or get busy."

"In a country of 300 million, I'd say 15% of us are evil."

"I don't get invited to parties. Nobody wants me. When I do go, everyone is exceedingly polite to me."

"Conservative people tend to see the world in black and white terms, good and evil. Liberals see grays."

"Public misbehavior by the famous is a powerful teaching tool."

"My advice to homosexuals, whether they're in the Boy Scouts, or in the Army or in high school: Shut up, don't tell anybody what you do. Your life will be a lot easier."

"We cannot intervene in the Muslim world ever again. What we can do is bomb the living daylights out of them."

"The children of America have seen with their own eyes that liars can win and cheaters can prosper. They know that our nation will accept venal behavior and, in some cases, reward it with tremendous wealth and power. So why wouldn't they lie, cheat, and steal?"

"What's wrong for you is not wrong for your neighbor if he doesn't think his actions are wrong."

"Lots of people want to hurt me. That's the price you pay for being a big mouth."

# HUH?

*"Most of the pages in this quotation book all generally tend to have a lot of quotations on them." —Uncle John*

"I think we won that game against Liverpool because we scored and they didn't."
—José Mourinho

"Those who enter the country illegally violate the law."
—George W. Bush

"I've always thought that under populated countries in Africa are vastly underpopulated."
—Lawrence Summers, chief economist of the World Bank

"It's only puffy when it's swollen."
—Charlie Hough, MLB pitcher, describing a broken finger

"Wherever I have gone in this country, I have found Americans."
—Alf Landon, 1936 presidential candidate

"We are trying to change the 1974 Constitution, whenever that was passed."
—Donald Kennard, Louisiana state representative

"I think you can't repeat the first time of something."
—Natalie Imbruglia, her first Grammy nomination

"There is no housing shortage in Lincoln today, just a rumour put out there by people who have nowhere to live."
—G. L. Murfin, Lincoln (U.K.) mayor

"We'd like to avoid problems, because when we have problems, we can have troubles."
—Wesley Bolin

"There is certainly more in the future now than back in 1964."
—Roger Daltrey

"It's almost impossible for referees these days—they need eyes in the back of their heads, which they haven't got."
—Graham Taylor, soccer player

"The reality of it is is that we are in reality."
—Scott Johnson, soccer coach

# BOB DYLAN

*The reluctant spokesman of a generation sure has lots to say.*

"If I wasn't Bob Dylan, I'd probably think that 'Bob Dylan' has a lot of answers, too."

"I never wanted to be a prophet or savior, but I could easily see myself becoming Elvis."

"A man is a success if he gets up in the morning and gets to bed at night, and in between he does what he wants to do."

"I define nothing. Not beauty, not patriotism. I take each thing as it is, without prior rules about what it should be."

"There is nothing so stable as change."

"People seldom do what they believe in. They do what is convenient, then repent."

"All the truth in the world adds up to one big lie."

"It was like a flying saucer landed. That's what the '60s were like. Everybody heard about it, but only a few really saw it."

"There doesn't seem to be any tomorrow. Every time I wake up, no matter in what position, it's always been today."

"I've never written a political song. Songs can't save the world. I've gone through all that."

"I accept chaos; I'm not sure whether it accepts me."

"This land is your land and this land is my land, sure, but the world is run by those that never listen to music anyway."

"Experience teaches us that silence terrifies people the most."

"Even the President of the United States sometimes must have to stand naked."

"Some people—you're born, you know, the wrong names, wrong parents. I mean, that happens. You call yourself what you want to call yourself. This is the land of the free."
    —*on why he changed his name from Robert Zimmerman*

"All I can do is be me,
whoever that is."

—Bob Dylan

"Real beauty knocks you a little bit off kilter." —David Byrne

# GUYS NAMED DICK

*The trickiest page in the book.*

"The basic tool for the manipulation of reality is the manipulation of words. If you can control the meaning of words, you can control the people who must use the words."
—**Philip K. Dick**

"I cannot tell you what it means when children recognize me. This is about the third generation for me. And when kids that small recognize me, it really pleases me."
—**Dick Van Dyke**

"Saying 'no' politely is a necessity if one wants to lead any kind of stable life."
—**Richard Chamberlain**

"Principle is OK up to a certain point, but principle doesn't do any good if you lose."
—**Dick Cheney**

"I'm not so mean. I wouldn't ever go out to hurt anybody deliberately—unless it was, you know, important, like a league game or something."
—**Dick Butkus**

"I never believed in Santa Claus because I knew no white dude would come into my neighborhood after dark."
—**Dick Gregory**

"Pretty much every TV show that had anything to do with comedy made its version of an Andy Dick joke. I don't need any help making myself look like a fool. I do it all on my own, thank you very much."
—**Andy Dick**

"Finishing second in the Olympics gets you silver. Finishing second in politics gets you oblivion."
—**Richard M. Nixon**

"My advice to an aspiring sportswriter is to accept criticism and guidance from someone whose sensibilities you trust, and then work your butt off."
—**Dick Schaap**

"Reality must take precedence over public relations, for nature cannot be fooled."
—**Richard P. Feynman, physicist**

# ANGELINA JOLIE

*She's an outspoken movie star, a humanitarian, and very weird.*

"Some people say you are going the wrong way, when it's simply a way of your own."

"I wish I could find people who just would fight me and break through to me and hold me down and scream their life into my face."

"If being sane is being normal, I'd rather be completely mental."

"When other little girls wanted to be ballet dancers, I kind of wanted to be a vampire."

"I think scars are sexy because it means you made a mistake that led to a mess."

"If I make a fool of myself, who cares? I'm not frightened by anyone's perception of me."

"I've never liked being touched. Ever. People used to say I held my breath when they were hugging me. I still do."

"I always play women I would date."

"If you ask people what they've always wanted to do, most people haven't done it. That breaks my heart."

"If you have enough people telling you you're wonderful, then you start believing you're fabulous. Then someone tells you you stink and you believe that, too."

"I love to put on lotion. Sometimes I'll watch TV and go into a lotion trance for an hour. I try to find brands that don't taste bad in case anyone wants to taste me."

"People have really odd opinions. They tell me I'm skinny, as if that's supposed to make me happy."

"I like everything. Boyish girls, girlish boys, the heavy and the skinny. Which is a problem when I'm walking down the street."

"I want to say my opinions and I hope they're taken in the right way. I don't want to stop being free. And I won't."

# CRAZY TALK

*Patient: Doc, my wife thinks I'm crazy because I like chicken wings.*
*Psychiatrist: Doesn't sound so bad—I like chicken wings, too.*
*Patient: Great! Come over and see my collection! I've got thousands of them!*

"There was never a genius without a tincture of madness."
—**Aristotle**

"A question that sometimes drives me hazy: am I or are the others crazy?"
—**Albert Einstein**

"What sane person could live in this world and *not* be crazy?"
—**Ursula K. Le Guin**

"For me, insanity is super sanity. The normal is psychotic. Normal means lack of imagination, lack of creativity."
—**Jean DeBuffet, French artist**

"A neurotic is a man who builds a castle in the air. A psychotic is the man who lives in it. A psychiatrist is the man who collects the rent."
—**Jerome Lawrence**

"There is no salvation in becoming adapted to a world which is crazy."
—**Henry Miller**

"It's hard to fight an enemy who has outposts in your head."
—**Sally Kempton**

"Some people never go crazy. What truly horrible lives they must lead."
—**Charles Bukowski**

"Insanity is often the logic of an accurate mind overtaxed."
—**Oliver Wendell Holmes**

"All of the people in my building are insane. The lady across the hall tried to rob a department store…with a pricing gun. She said, 'Give me your money, or I'm marking down everything in the store.'"
—**Steven Wright**

"Where does the violet tint end and the orange tint begins? Distinctly we see the difference of the colors, but where, exactly, does the one first blending enter into the other? So with sanity and insanity."
—**Herman Melville**

---

"There is no rejection in life quite like a canceled shrink appointment." —Bill Scheft

# APRIL 19th

*What do these people have in common? Not much, except that they were all born on the 19th of April.*

"Tough girls come from New York. Sweet girls are from Georgia. But us Kentucky girls, we have fire and ice in our blood. We can ride a horse, be a debutante, throw a left hook, and drink with the boys, all the while making sweet tea, darlin'."
  —**Ashley Judd (b. 1968)**

"Anytime you have somebody doing positive stuff and just doing their time and minding their own business, people will sit up there and lie."
  —**Suge Knight (b. 1965)**

"Dad taught me everything I know. Unfortunately, he didn't teach me everything he knows."
  —**Al Unser, Jr. (b. 1962)**

"When I am in the Parliament chamber, I often sit for the entire debate. It's only courteous to listen to what everyone has to say, although I often find myself desperate to say something but too scared to stand up in case I regret it."
  —**Margo MacDonald (b. 1943)**

"I certainly did feel inferior. Because of class. Because of strength. Because of height. I guess if I'd been able to hit somebody in the nose, I wouldn't have been a comic."
  —**Dudley Moore (b. 1935)**

"Our Nation is at risk. The educational foundations of our society are being eroded by a rising tide of mediocrity that threatens our very future as a Nation and as a people. If an unfriendly foreign power had attempted to impose on America the mediocre educational performance that exists today, we might well have viewed it as an act of war."
  —**Glenn T. Seaborg, Nobel Laureate in Chemistry (b. 1912)**

"To make history you cannot be horrified by it."
  —**Ricardo Bacchelli, Italian writer/poet (b. 1891)**

"A 41-inch bust and a lot of perseverance will get you more than a cup of coffee... a lot more."
  —**Jayne Mansfield (b. 1932)**

# MALE CHAUVINIST PIGS

*Open mouth—insert hoof.*

"It *was* a man's world. Then Eve arrived."
—**Richard Armour**

"I am not a chauvinist. I believe in women's rights for every woman but my own."
—**Harold Washington**

"In my opinion, it's OK for a man to commit adultery if his wife is ugly."
—**Howard Stern**

"Educating a beautiful woman is like pouring honey into a fine Swiss watch: everything stops."
—**Kurt Vonnegut**

"When a woman becomes a scholar there is usually something wrong with her sexual organs."
—**Friedrich Nietzsche**

"Women should have labels on their foreheads saying, 'Government Health Warning: women can seriously damage your brains, genitals, bank account, confidence, razor blades, and good standing among your friends.'"
—**Jeffrey Bernard**

"If I had a choice of having a woman in my arms or shooting a bad guy on a horse, I'd take the horse. It's a lot more fun."
—**Kevin Costner**

"Direct thought is not an attribute of femininity. In this, women are now centuries behind man."
—**Thomas Edison**

"Women should be obscene and not heard."
—**Groucho Marx**

"A woman's place is in the wrong."
—**James Thurber**

"Ask a woman's advice, and whatever she advises, do the reverse and you are sure to be wise."
—**Thomas More**

"All men hear is blah, blah, blah, SEX, blah, blah, blah, FOOD, blah, blah, blah, BEER."
—**Denis Leary**

"Men are pigs. Too bad we own everything."
—**Tim Allen**

"Men are superior to women.
For one thing, men can urinate
from a speeding car."

—**Will Durst**

"Women are an alien race set down among us." —John Updike

# WHY ASK WHY?

*Sometimes answers are irrelevant—it's the question that counts. Take a moment to ponder these cosmic queries.*

"In elementary school, in case of fire you have to line up quietly in a single file line from smallest to tallest. What is the logic? Do tall people burn slower?"
—**Warren Hutcherson**

"Sometimes when I'm talking, my words can't keep up with my thoughts. Why do we think faster than we speak? Probably so we can think twice."
—**Calvin,**
*Calvin and Hobbes*

"If stupidity got us into this mess, then why can't it get us out?"
—**Will Rogers**

"Why is it that our memory is good enough to retain the least triviality that happens to us, and yet not good enough to recollect how often we have told it to the same person?"
—**Francois de La Rochefoucauld**

"Why do they call it 'rush hour,' when nothing moves?"
—**Robin Williams**

"If Dracula can't see his reflection in a mirror, how come his hair is always so neatly combed?"
—**Steven Wright**

"If it's the Psychic Network, why do they need a phone number?"
—**Robin Williams**

"Why isn't there a special name for the tops of your feet?"
—**Lily Tomlin**

"If evolution really works, how come mothers only have two hands?"
—**Milton Berle**

"If man evolved from monkeys and apes, why do we still have monkeys and apes?"
—**Art Bell**

"Some people see things that are and ask, 'Why?' Some people dream of things that never were and ask, 'Why not?' Some people have to go to work and don't have time for all that crap."
—**George Carlin**

Popeye the Sailor is 5'6".

# MEN ARE...

*What women have to say about men.*

"A man's got to do what a man's got to do. A woman must do what he can't."
—Rhonda Hansome

"Women speak because they wish to speak, whereas a man speaks only when driven to speech by something outside himself, like, for instance, he can't find any clean socks."
—Jean Kerr

"I refuse to consign the whole male sex to the nursery. I insist on believing that some men are my equals."
—Brigid Brophy

"The male chromosome is an incomplete female chromosome. In other words the male is a walking abortion; aborted at the gene stage. To be male is to be deficient, emotionally limited; maleness is a deficiency disease and males are emotional cripples."
—Valerie Solanos

"The one nice thing about sports is that they prove men do have emotions and are not afraid to show them."
—Jane O'Reilly

"A lot of guys think the larger a woman's breasts are, the less intelligent she is. I don't think it works like that. I think it's the opposite. I think the larger a woman's breasts are, the less intelligent the men become."
—Anita Wise

"I like men to behave like men—strong and childish."
—Françoise Sagan

"The world men inhabit is rather bleak. It is a world full of doubt and confusion, where vulnerability must be hidden, not shared; where competition, not co-operation, is the order of the day; where men sacrifice the possibility of knowing their own children and sharing in their upbringing, for the sake of a job they may have chosen by chance, which may not suit them and which in many cases dominates their lives to the exclusion of much else."
—Anna Ford

"Man is not the enemy here, but the fellow victim."
—Betty Friedan

# BUSHISMS

*Some of the funniest gaffes ever uttered by President George W. Bush.*

"You teach a child to read, and he or her will be able to pass a literacy test."

"I glance at the headlines just to kind of get a flavor for what's moving. I rarely read the stories, and get briefed by people who probably read the news themselves."

"It was not always a given that the United States and America would have a close relationship."

"I can't imagine someone like Osama bin Laden understanding the joy of Hanukkah."

"We cannot let terrorists hold this nation hostile or hold our allies hostile."

"There will be a momentum, momentum will be gathered. Houses will begat jobs, jobs will begat houses."

"I don't know why you're talking about Sweden. They're the neutral one. They don't have an army."
—**mistaking Sweden for Switzerland**

"Africa is a nation that suffers from incredible disease."

"See, free nations are peaceful nations. Free nations don't attack each other. Free nations don't develop weapons of mass destruction."
—**at the time, the U.S. had 9,960 nuclear warheads**

"I like my buddies from West Texas. I liked them when I was young, I liked them then I was middle-age, I liked them before I was president, and I like them during president, and I like them after president."

"If this were a dictatorship, it'd be a heck of a lot easier, just so long as I'm the dictator."

"The relations with, uhh, Europe are important relations, and they've, uhh, because, we do share values. And they're universal values, they're not American values or, you know, European values, they're universal values. And those values, uhh, being universal, ought to be applied everywhere."

"I don't understand how poor people think." —George W. Bush

"You took an oath to defend our flag and our freedom, and you kept that oath underseas and under fire."
 —in a speech to veterans

"We look forward to hearing your vision."

"When I take action, I'm not going to fire a $2 million missile at a $10 empty tent and hit a camel in the butt. It's going to be decisive."

"When I was coming up, it was a dangerous world and you knew exactly who they were. It was us versus them and it was clear who them was. Today we are not so sure who the they are, but we know they're there."

"One of the things I've used on the Google is to pull up maps. It's very interesting to see—I've forgot the name of the program—but you get the satellite, and you can—like, I kinda like to look at the ranch. It reminds me of where I wanna be sometimes."

"Wow! Brazil is big!"
 —after being shown a map of Brazil by Brazilian president Luiz Inacio Lula da Silva

"All in all, it's been a fabulous year for Laura and me."
 —*December 20, 2001*

"You never know what your history is going to be like until long after you're gone."

Q: Mr. Bush, can you name the biggest mistake you've made as president?
A: Uhh…I wish you'd have given me this written question ahead of time so I could plan for it. I'm sure something will pop into my head here in the midst of this press conference, with all the pressure of trying to come up with answer, but it hadn't yet. I don't want to sound like I have made no mistakes. I'm confident I have. I just haven't—you just put me under the spot here, and maybe I'm not as quick on my feet as I should be in coming up with one.

# A *BIT* OVER THE TOP

*This is by far the finest, most fascinating, most incredible
page of quotations in any quotation book in the
history of publishing, period!*

"I can't think of a comparable level of cultural excitement about something since Neil Armstrong landed on the Moon in the 1960s."
—**Gil Schwartz, CBS publicist, on the *Survivor* finale**

"It's probably the most famous phrase said by a human being in history."
—**Michael Buffer, on why he trademarked his catchphrase, "Let's get ready to rumble!"**

"Please forgive me, but sometimes I get very emotional when I talk about my son. My heart fills with so much joy when I realize that this young man is going to be able to help so many people. He will transcend this game and bring to the world a humanitarianism which has never been known before. The world will be a better place to live in by virtue of his existence and his presence. I acknowledge only a small part in that, in that I know that I was personally selected by God himself to nurture this young man and bring him to the point where he can make his contribution to humanity. This is my treasure. Please accept it...and use it wisely. Thank you."
—**Earl Woods, father of Tiger Woods**

"I am such a strong admirer and supporter of George W. Bush that if he suggested eliminating the income tax or doubling it, I would vote yes on first blush."
—**Jerry Falwell**

"I have 100 billion dollars... You realize I could spend 3 million dollars a day, every day, for the next 100 years? And that's if I don't make another dime. Tell you what—I'll buy your right arm for a million dollars. I give you a million bucks, and I get to sever your arm right here."
—**Bill Gates**

# THAT STUPID SO-AND-SO…

*Apparently, being smarter than everyone else around you isn't enough—you have to be able to express how unbelievably stupid your inferiors are.*

"…has a brain of feathers, and a heart of lead."
—**Alexander Pope**

"…is a mental midget with the IQ of a fence post."
—**Tom Waits**

"…can compress the most words into the smallest idea of any man I know."
—**Abraham Lincoln**

"…lacks the power of conversation, but not the power of speech."
—**George Bernard Shaw**

"…is sharp as a sack full of wet mice."
—**Foghorn Leghorn**

"…is a next-day delivery in a nanosecond world."
—**Van Jacobson**

"…is one of the least benightedly unintelligent organic life forms it has been my profound lack of pleasure not to be able to avoid meeting."
—**Douglas Adams**

"…never opens his mouth without subtracting from the sum of human knowledge."
—**Thomas Brackett Reed**

"…doesn't know much, but leads the league in nostril hair."
—**Josh Billings**

"…is an end-of-season sale at the cerebral department."
—**Gareth Blackstock**

"…is differently clued."
—**Dave Clark**

"…has the mathematical abilities of a Clydesdale."
—**David Letterman**

"…has the attention span of a lightning bolt."
—**Robert Redford**

"…knows so little, and knows it so fluently."
—**Ellen Glasgow**

"…is brilliant to the top of his boots."
—**David Lloyd George**

How stupid? "…his golf bag does not contain a full set of irons." —Robin Williams

# LARRY DAVID

*Co-creator of* Seinfeld *and star of* Curb Your Enthusiasm, *comedian Larry David gives the impression that he's a prickly, cynical, horrible man…which he is. But he's also pretty clever.*

"When I was living in New York and didn't have a penny to my name, I would walk around the streets and occasionally I would see an alcove or something. And I'd think, 'That'll be a good spot for me when I'm homeless.'"

"Women love a self-confident bald man. Anybody with a full head of hair can be confident, but a bald man—there's your diamond in the rough."

"My new house was nearly destroyed by a fire the day before we moved in. I was actually kind of hoping it would burn down. I mean, we hadn't moved anything in yet. Some TV news guy could have interviewed me the next day going through the rubble and I would just be shrugging my shoulders saying, 'Actually, we had no memories here. I'm just trying to find this phone number I think I might have dropped somewhere.'"

"Trying on pants is one of the most humiliating things a man can suffer that doesn't involve a woman."

"Sometimes I like to pretend that I'm deaf, and try to imagine what it's like not to be able to hear the birds. It's not that bad."

"If you tell the truth about how you're feeling, it becomes funny."

"If someone says to you, 'Why don't you go f*ck yourself,' you simply respond, '*Touché*,' and you're out of there. It's a great way to make someone think they said something clever even if you don't mean it."

"I've led this empty life for over 40 years, and now I can pass that heritage on and ensure that the misery will continue for at least one more generation."
    —**on the birth of his child**

# UNCLE JOHN'S QUOTATIONARY

*Here's Part 2 of our quotation dictionary.*
*(Part 1 begins on page 33.)*

**DEATH:** the black backing on the mirror that allows us to see anything at all. (Saul Bellow)

**DEMOCRACY:** the recurrent suspicion that more than half of the people are right more than half of the time. (E. B. White)

**DEPRESSION:** melancholy minus its charms. (Susan Sontag)

**DESPAIR:** the price one pays for setting oneself an impossible aim. (Graham Greene)

**DETERRENCE:** the art of producing, in the mind of the enemy, the fear to attack. (Dr. Strangelove, *Dr. Strangelove*)

**DIET:** a system of starving yourself to death so you can live a little longer. (Totie Fields)

**DIPLOMAT:** a man who always remembers a woman's birthday but never remembers her age. (Robert Frost)

**DOG:** a yes-animal, very popular with people who can't afford to keep a yes-man. (Robertson Davies)

**DRAMA CRITIC:** a person who surprises a writer by informing him what he meant. (Wilson Mizner)

**DREAMS:** answers to questions we haven't yet figured out how to ask. (Dana Scully, *The X-Files*)

**EDUCATION:** a progressive discovery of our own ignorance. (Will Durant)

**ELEGANCE:** forgetting what one is wearing. (Yves Saint Laurent)

**ENTREPRENEUR:** what you're called when you don't have a job. (Ted Turner)

**EULOGY:** praise of a person who has either the advantages of wealth and power, or the consideration to be dead. (Ambrose Bierce)

**EUPHEMISMS:** unpleasant truths wearing diplomatic cologne. (Quentin Crisp)

**EVIL:** good or truth misplaced. (Mahatma Gandhi)

**EVOLUTION:** a tinkerer. (Francois Jacob)

**EXCELLENCE:** the gradual result of always striving to do better. (Pat Riley)

**EXERCISE:** the yuppie version of bulimia. (Barbara Ehrenreich)

**EXPERIENCE:** what you get while looking for something else. (Federico Fellini)

**EXPERT:** a person who has made all the mistakes that can be made in a very narrow field. (Niels Bohr)

*For more, see page 103.*

## COMBINE AND CONQUER

"There are only five notes in the musical scale, but their variations are so many that they cannot all be heard. There are only five basic colors, but their variations are so many that they cannot all be seen. There are only five basic flavors, but their variations are so many that they cannot all be tasted. There are only two kinds of charge in battle, the unorthodox surprise attack and the orthodox direct attack, but variations of the unorthodox and the orthodox are endless. The unorthodox and the orthodox give rise to each other, like a beginningless circle—who could exhaust them?"

—**Sun Tzu,** *The Art of War*

# MIXED METAPHORS

*If you want to get to the top of the mountain with your speech, then you better rev up that handbasket and put the pedal to the pail.*

"If you don't have a leg to stand on, you can't put your foot down."
—**Dave Weinbaum**

"That was a Trojan horse, and it had more holes than a piece of Swiss cheese."
—**Gray Davis**

"Please don't ask me to do that which I've just said I'm not going to do, because you're burning up time. The meter is running through the sand, and I am now filibustering."
—**George H. W. Bush**

"Mr. Speaker, I smell a rat forming in the air and darkening the sky, but I'll nip him in the bud."
—**Sir Boyle Roche, Dublin politician**

"My appetite is so good that I can eat the tablecloth right off the chair."
—**Joseph Moakley**

"Bond's knees, the Achilles heel of all skiers, were beginning to ache."
—**Ian Fleming**

"I think with a lifetime appointment to the Supreme Court, you can't play, you know, hide the salami, or whatever it's called."
—**Howard Dean**

"There comes a time in the affairs of man when he must take the bull by the tail and face the situation."
—**W. C. Fields**

"It's time to plant some seeds. What that means is, hit them in the mouth. Ya know, show 'em what time it is."
—**Levon Kirkland**

"I can see the carrot at the end of the tunnel."
—**Stuart Pearce**

"I think they'll have to throw the kitchen sink at them now. Maybe not the whole sink, with all the plumbing—maybe just the taps."
—**David Pleat**

"Some days, the sun even shines on a dog's butt."
—**Wade Redden, NHL player, on a come-from-behind win**

"People who speak in metaphors should shampoo my crotch." —Jack Nicholson

# BARBARA EHRENREICH

*This bestselling author and columnist has been writing about feminism and social change since 1969. And she's still going strong today.*

"Of all the nasty outcomes predicted for women's liberation…none was more alarming than the suggestion that women would eventually become just like men."

"*Time*'s list of the 20 most important 'leaders and revolutionaries' of the 20th century contains only three women, or 15% of the total. Naturally, my first response was to demand a recount."

"Thanks to 30 years of feminist striving, the category 'woman' has expanded to include anchorpersons, soccer moms, astronauts, firefighters, and even Senator or Secretary of State. But 'female' still tends to connote the oozing, bleeding, swelling, hot-flashing, swamp-creature side of the species, its tiny brain marinating in the primal hormonal broth."

"This is a nation founded in revolution, birthed by rebels and dissidents. They had a lot to say on many subjects—and none of it was 'shut up.'"

"Patriotism should bring us together, but not so close that we begin to look like sheep."

"We need a little less talk about the work ethic, and a little more ethics in relation to work."

"There is the fear, common to all English-only speakers, that the chief purpose of foreign languages is to make fun of us. Otherwise, you know, why not just come out and say it?"

"We seem to believe that leadership is expressed, in no small part, by a willingness to cause the deaths of others."

"America is addicted to wars of distraction."

"Perhaps every revolution is doomed to be betrayed, sooner or later, by its progeny."

"Like the dodo snuggling into its nest, we have found our evolutionary niche, which turns out to be the couch in the den."

# OVERPAID?

*Here are quotes from a few people who make more money in a few months than many of us will make in our entire lives.*

"How can a guy climb trees, say, 'Me Tarzan, You Jane,' and make a million?"

—Johnny Weissmuller

"Whenever I think of the high salaries we are paid as film actors, I think it is for the travel, the time away, and any trouble you get into through being well known. It's not for the acting, that's for sure."

—Bill Murray

"I just want the money and the fame and the adoration, and I don't want any of the other stuff."

—Matthew Broderick

"I don't want to become this actor who's going to be doing this occasional good work in the theater and then ever-diminishing bad television. I thought I'd rather do bad movies than bad television, because you get more money for it."

—Brian Cox

"This film cost $31 million. With that kind of money, I could have invaded some country."

—Clint Eastwood

# LOVE...AND MARRIAGE

*Some thoughts from people who know
the true meaning of "wedded bliss."*

"If I get married again, I want a guy there with a drum to do rimshots during the vows."
—**Sam Kinison**

"Husbands are awkward things to deal with; even keeping them in hot water will not make them tender."
—**Mary Buckley**

"My wife is a sex object—every time I ask for sex, she objects."
—**Les Dawson**

"The world has suffered more from the ravages of ill-advised marriages than from virginity."
—**Ambrose Bierce**

"I walked down the aisle as Conan the Barbarian and walked back up again as Arnold the Meek."
—**Arnold Schwarzenegger**

"The best way to get husbands to do something is to suggest that perhaps they are too old to do it."
—**Shirley MacLaine**

"Marriage is a lottery, but you can't tear up your ticket if you lose."
—**F. M. Knowles**

"Marriage is an adventure, like going to war."
—**G. K. Chesterton**

"Nearly all marriages, even happy ones, are mistakes: in the sense that almost certainly both partners might be found more suitable mates. But the real soul-mate is the one you are actually married to."
—**J. R. R. Tolkien, in a 1941 letter to his son**

"Love is blind, but marriage restores its sight."
—**Georg C. Lichtenberg**

"My husband and I have never considered divorce... murder sometimes, but never divorce."
—**Joyce Brothers**

"I first learned the concepts of non-violence in my marriage."
—**Mahatma Gandhi**

# TO SLEEP...

*Some thoughts to ponder while you're trying to nod off tonight.*

"There are 12 hours in the day, and above 50 in the night."
—Marie de Rabutin-Chantal

"The best bridge between despair and hope is a good night's sleep."
—E. Joseph Cossman

"Sleep is the interest we have to pay on the capital which is called in at death; and the higher the rate of interest and the more regularly it is paid, the further the date of redemption is postponed."
—Arthur Schopenhauer

"Sleep is the golden chain that ties health and our bodies together."
—Thomas Dekker

"It is a common experience that a problem difficult at night is resolved in the morning after the committee of sleep has worked on it."
—John Steinbeck

"Sleep opens within us an inn for phantoms. In the morning we must sweep out the shadows."
—Gaston Bachelard

"The bed is a bundle of paradoxes: we go to it with reluctance, yet we quit it with regret; we make up our minds every night to leave it early, but we make up our bodies every morning to keep it late."
—Charles Caleb Colton

"The worst thing in the world is to try to sleep and not to."
—F. Scott Fitzgerald

"Sleeplessness is a desert without vegetation or inhabitants."
—Jessamyn West

"How do people go to sleep? I'm afraid I've lost the knack. I might try busting myself smartly over the temple with the nightlight. I might repeat to myself, slowly and soothingly, a list of quotations beautiful from minds profound, if I can remember any of the damn things."
—Dorothy Parker

"You know you're in love when you can't fall asleep because reality is finally better than your dreams."
—Dr. Seuss

# PERCHANCE TO DREAM

*Welcome to that other world where we spend
so much time, yet know so little about.*

"All men whilst they are awake are in one common world; but each of them, when he is asleep, is in a world of his own."
—**Plutarch**

All dreams spin out from the same web.
—**Hopi proverb**

"Dreams are free therapy. Consult your inner Freud."
—**Grey Livingston**

"Dreams are illustrations… from the book your soul is writing about you."
—**Marsha Norman**

"Dreams are today's answers to tomorrow's questions."
—**Edgar Cayce**

"All the things one has forgotten scream for help in dreams."
—**Elias Canetti**

"Dreams say what they mean, but they don't say it in daytime language."
—**Gail Godwin**

"A dream which is not interpreted is like a letter not read."
—**The Talmud**

"I am accustomed to sleep and in my dreams to imagine the same things that lunatics imagine when awake."
—**Rene Descartes**

"The butcher's the poet's equal there."
—**E. M. Cioran**

"Dreams are excursions into the limbo of things, a deliverance from the human prison."
—**Henri-Frédéric Amiel**

"Dreaming is an act of pure imagination, attesting in all men a creative power, which if it were available in waking, would make every man a Dante or Shakespeare."
—**H. F. Hedge**

"To sleep, perchance to dream. Ay, there's the rub."
—**William Shakespeare,
Hamlet**

If you're average, you'll spend 2,100 days of your life dreaming. Have fun!

# DISSING QUOTES

*This page is dedicated to Alice Roosevelt Longworth, who famously said, "If you haven't got anything nice to say about anybody, come sit next to me."*

"Someone tried the monkeys-on-typewriters bit trying for the plays of Shakespeare, but all they got was the collected works of Francis Bacon."
—**Bill Hirst**

"She was good at being inarticulately abstracted for the same reason that midgets are good at being short."
—**Clive James, on Marilyn Monroe**

"Groucho Marx? He's a male chauvinistic piglet."
—**Betty Friedan**

"I've been working so hard, I'm about to have a Mariah Carey."
—**Usher, referring to Carey's rumored breakdown**

"Is he just doing a bad Elvis pout, or was he born that way?"
—**Freddie Mercury, on Billy Idol**

"The stupid person's idea of a clever person."
—**Elizabeth Bowen, on author Aldous Huxley**

"Yoko Ono's voice sounds like an eagle being goosed."
—**Ralph Novak**

"He's nothing more than a well-meaning baboon."
—**General George McClellan, on Abraham Lincoln**

"He's like a monkey with arthritis, trying to go on stage and look young. I have great respect for the Stones but they would have been better if they had thrown Keith out 15 years ago."
—**Elton John, on Keith Richards**

"His writing is limited to songs for dead blondes."
—**Keith Richards, on Elton John**

"Dan Quayle is more stupid than Ronald Reagan put together."
—**Matt Groening**

"She's about as modest as Mussolini."
—**David Crosby, on Joni Mitchell**

"A hack writer who would have been considered fourth-rate in Europe, who tried out a few of the old proven 'sure-fire' literary skeletons with sufficient local color to intrigue the superficial and the lazy."
—**William Faulkner, on Mark Twain**

"I've got three words for him: Am. A. Teur."
—**Charlie Sheen, on Colin Farrell**

"He was dull in company, dull in his closet, dull everywhere. He was dull in a new way and that made people think him great."
—**Samuel Johnson, on fellow poet Thomas Gray**

"Erick Dampier is soft. Quote it, underline it, tape it, send it to him. Don't ask me about that guy ever again."
—**Shaquille O'Neal**

"If that boy billionaire thinks he can shut me up, he should stick his head in a can of paint."
—**Myron Cope, Pittsburgh Steelers announcer, on Washington Redskins owner Daniel Snyder**

"He has the vocal modulation of a railway-station announcer, the expressive power of a fencepost, and the charisma of a week-old head of lettuce."
—**critic Fintan O'Toole, on Quentin Tarantino**

"Shannon [Sharpe] looks like a horse. I'll tell you, that's an ugly dude. You can't tell me he doesn't look like Mr. Ed."
—**Ray Buchanan, Atlanta Falcons, three days before Super Bowl XXXIII**

"Ray said that? Well, I think he's ugly, but did I ever call him that? No. Tell Ray to put the eyeliner, the lipstick, and the high heels away. I'm not saying he's a cross-dresser; that's just what I heard."
—**Shannon Sharpe, Denver Broncos, 20 minutes later**

# CLASSIC MOVIE LINES

*They sure don't make films like these any more.*

**Capt. Renault:** What on earth brought you to Casablanca?
**Rick:** My health. I came to Casablanca for the waters.
**Capt. Renault:** The waters? What waters? We're in the desert.
**Rick:** I was misinformed.
—*Casablanca*

"I've wrestled with reality for 35 years, Doctor, and I'm happy to state I finally won out over it."
—Elwood Dowd (James Stewart), *Harvey*

"I love him because he's the kind of guy who gets drunk on a glass of buttermilk, and I love the way he blushes right up over his ears. I love him because he doesn't know how to kiss, the jerk!"
—Sugarpuss O'Shea (Barbara Stanwyck), *Ball of Fire*

"Men like my father cannot die. They are with me still. real in memory as they were in flesh, loving and beloved forever."
—Huw Morgan (Roddy McDowall), *How Green Was My Valley*

"Insanity runs in my family. It practically gallops."
—Mortimer (Cary Grant), *Arsenic and Old Lace*

**Charlie Allnut:** A man takes a drop too much once in a while; it's only human nature.
**Rose Sayer:** Nature, Mr. Allnut, is what we are put into this world to rise above.
—*The African Queen*

"Why don't you get out of that wet coat and into a dry martini?"
—Albert (Robert Benchley), *The Major and the Minor*

"You see, boys forget what their country means by just reading 'The Land of the Free' in history books. Then they get to be men; they forget even more. Liberty's too precious a thing to be buried in books, Miss Saunders. Men should hold it up in front of them every single day of their lives and say: 'I'm free to think and to speak. My ancestors couldn't, I can, and my children will.' Boys ought to grow up remembering that."
—Jefferson Smith (James Stewart), *Mr. Smith Goes to Washington*

In the 1951 film *The Tall Target*, Dick Powell played a reporter who tries...

# FREDERICK DOUGLASS

*Frederick Douglass (1818–95) escaped slavery at the age of 20
and went on to become a fiery abolotionist, author, and
one of the most popular speakers in American history.*

"No man can put a chain about the ankle of his fellow man without at last finding the other end fastened about his own neck."

"I expose slavery in this country, because to expose it is to kill it. Slavery is one of those monsters of darkness to whom the light of truth is death."

"Where justice is denied, where poverty is enforced, where ignorance prevails, and where any one class is made to feel that society is an organized conspiracy to oppress, rob and degrade them, neither persons nor property will be safe."

"I prayed for 20 years, but received no answer until I prayed with my legs."

"I prefer to be true to myself, even at the hazard of incurring the ridicule of others, rather than to be false, and to incur my own abhorrence."

"Find out just what any people will quietly submit to, and you have the exact measure of the injustice and wrong which will be imposed on them."

"It is easier to build strong children than to repair broken men."

"A man's character takes its hue from the form and color of things about him."

"People might not get all they work for in this world, but they must certainly work for all they get."

"To suppress free speech is a double wrong. It violates the rights of the hearer as well as those of the speaker."

"If there is no struggle, there is no progress. Those who profess to favor freedom, and deprecate agitation, are men who want crops without plowing up the ground; they want rain without thunder and lightning."

# THE BOOB TUBE

*Television is like the weather: We complain about it all the time,*
*but the worse it gets, the more we seem to pay attention.*

"They say that ninety percent of TV is junk. But ninety percent of everything is junk."
—**Gene Roddenberry**

"The worst thing about television is that everybody you see on television is doing something better than what you're doing. You never see anybody on TV just sliding off the front of the sofa, with potato chip crumbs all over their shirt."
—**Jerry Seinfeld**

"I think television has betrayed the meaning of democratic speech, adding visual chaos to the confusion of voices. What role does silence have in all this noise?"
—**Federico Fellini**

"Just because your voice reaches halfway around the world doesn't mean you are wiser than when it reached only to the end of the bar."
—**Edward R. Murrow**

"All television is educational television. The question is: what is it teaching?"
—**Nicholas Johnson**

"Don't you wish there were a knob on the TV to turn up the intelligence? There's one marked 'Brightness,' but it doesn't work."
—**Gallagher**

"The one function TV news performs very well is that when there is no news we give it to you with the same emphasis as if there were."
—**David Brinkley**

"Your cable television is experiencing difficulties. Please do not panic. Resist the temptation to read or talk to loved ones. Do not attempt sexual relations, as years of TV radiation have left your genitals withered and useless."
—**Homer Simpson**

"If you came and you found a strange man teaching your kids to punch each other, or trying to sell them all kinds of products, you'd kick him right out of the house, but here you are; you come in and the TV is on, and you don't think twice about it."
—**Jerome Singer**

Dave Thomas, the founder of Wendy's, appeared in a record 652 TV commercials.

"I hate television. I hate it as much as peanuts. But I can't stop eating peanuts."

—Orson Welles

# COMPARING PLACES

*Sometimes the best way to describe a place is to compare it to another.*

"When it's three o'clock in New York, it's still 1938 in London."
—**Bette Midler**

"In America, only the successful writer is important, in France all writers are important, in England no writer is important, and in Australia you have to explain what a writer is."
—**Geoffrey Cottrell**

"There have been many definitions of hell, but for the English the best definition is the place where the Germans are the police, the Swedish are the comedians, the Italians are the defense force, Frenchmen dig the roads, the Belgians are the pop singers, the Spanish run the railways, the Turks cook the food, the Irish are the waiters, the Greeks run the government, and the common language is Dutch."
—**David Frost and Antony Jay**

"Everywhere outside New York City is Bridgeport, Connecticut."
—**Fred Allen**

"Europeans, like some Americans, drive on the right side of the road, except in England, where they drive on both sides of the road; Italy, where they drive on the sidewalk; and France, where if necessary they will follow you right into the hotel lobby."
—**Dave Barry**

"In Washington, the first thing people tell you is what their job is. In Los Angeles you learn their star sign. In Houston you're told how rich they are. And in New York they tell you what their rent is."
—**Simon Hoggart**

"Cities have sexes: London is a man, Paris a woman, and New York a well-adjusted transsexual."
—**Angela Carter**

"Germans are flummoxed by humor, the Swiss have no concept of fun, the Spanish think there is nothing at all ridiculous about eating dinner at midnight, and the Italians should never, ever have been let in on the invention of the motor car."
—**Bill Bryson**

# PHILOSOPHERS

*Not everyone who majors in philosophy
ends up working at Burger King.*

"Beauty is no quality in things themselves. It exists merely in the mind which contemplates them."
—**David Hume**

"Knowledge which is acquired under compulsion obtains no hold on the mind."
—**Plato**

"Few men think, yet all will have opinions."
—**George Berkeley**

"We are not human beings having a spiritual experience. We are spiritual beings having a human experience."
—**Pierre Teilhard de Chardin**

"Desire to know why, and how —curiosity, which is a lust of the mind, and a perseverance of delight in the continued-generation of knowledge— exceedeth the short vehemence of any carnal pleasure."
—**Thomas Hobbes**

"Anyone who has begun to think, places some portion of the world in jeopardy."
—**John Dewey**

"Three-fourths of philosophy and literature is the talk of people trying to convince themselves that they really like the cage they were tricked into entering."
—**Gary Snyder**

"Dreams will get you nowhere; a good kick in the pants will take you a long way."
—**Baltasar Gracián**

"Time is the father of truth, its mother is our mind."
—**Giordano Bruno**

"All philosophy lies in two words, sustain and abstain."
—**Epictetus**

"Neither should a ship rely on one small anchor, nor should life rest on a single hope."
—**Epictetus**

"Necessity is an interpretation, not a fact."
—**Friedrich Nietzsche**

"True excellence is rarely found, even more rarely is it cherished."
—**Goethe**

"Religion is a man using a divining rod. Philosophy is a man using a pick and shovel." —Anonymous

# ONE GIANT MISQUOTE FOR MANKIND

*Here's the story behind one of the most famous quotations of all time.*

## MAN ON THE MOON

Neil Armstrong knew the world would be listening to the first human words spoken on another world, so he thought long and hard about what he would say before he placed his foot on the surface of the Moon. After much deliberation, the *Apollo 11* astronaut decided on these words: "That's one small step for a man, one giant leap for mankind."

On July 20, 1969, with an audience of half a billion people, Armstrong hopped off the ladder of *Apollo 11*, took a step on the moon, and attempted his quotation, which was beamed back to Earth, 250,000 miles away. But what exactly did he say? Here is what the world heard: "That's one small step for man, one giant leap for mankind."

Big difference. Without the word "a" before "man," the quote made little sense. He essentially said: "One small step for mankind, one giant leap for mankind."

## TO "A" OR NOT TO "A"

"Damn, I blew the first words on the Moon, didn't I?" Armstrong lamented to NASA officials when he got home…except he wasn't entirely sure he *had* botched his famous line. Inside his helmet, he could hear the same static-drenched audio feed that was beamed back to Earth and couldn't remember if he said the "a"—or if it had been drowned out by static.

For nearly 40 years, Armstrong deflected criticism of his goof, citing the distinct possibility that he had said the "a." Few believed him, but no one could argue that the sentiment wasn't there; everyone knew what he was trying to say. "Certainly the 'a' was intended," he explained, "because that's the only way the statement makes any sense." Official quotation books acknowledged the "a" by placing it in brackets, but it still bothered

---

Absentee ballot? Astronaut John Blaha became the first American to vote from space, in 1997.

Armstrong. He wanted to know the truth—the most famous words of the 20th century were still in question.

## MODERN SCIENCE TO THE RESCUE

One man who also wanted to know the truth was an Australian computer expert named Peter Shann Ford. In 2006 Ford obtained the NASA recording of Armstrong's feed and ran it through a sophisticated sound-editing software system. After careful review, Ford picked up a nearly undetectable acoustic vibration after the word "for." He slowed it down, scrutinized the vibration, and concluded that it was a vocal utterance lasting only 35 milliseconds. It was, undoubtedly, Armstrong's missing "a." It seems that the astronaut—who had been awake for 24 hours when he said the famous words, and was nervous and excited to be the first person on the Moon (who wouldn't be?)—had hurried through his speech so quickly that the "a" got lost in the static.

Ford presented his results to NASA. "I find the technology interesting and useful," a relieved Armstrong told reporters. "And I find his conclusion persuasive."

### [Audible] Quotes from the Moon Landings

"The surface is fine and powdery. I can kick it up loosely with my toe. It does adhere in fine layers, like powdered charcoal, to the sole and sides of my boots. I only go in a small fraction of an inch, maybe an eighth of an inch, but I can see the footprints of my boots and the treads in the fine, sandy particles. There seems to be no difficulty in moving around, as we suspected."

—**Neil Armstrong**

"Magnificent desolation."

—**Buzz Aldrin**

"Whoopee! Man, that may have been a small one for Neil, but it's a long one for me!"

—**Charles "Pete" Conrad, *Apollo 12* commander, third man on the moon, and the shortest Apollo astronaut**

# FARTS

*This page is dedicated to our beloved canine companion,
Porter the Wonder Dog, who needs neither to speak
nor growl to let us know he's in the room.*

"Men have too many disgusting habits, like scratching themselves all the time. And it's really weird how they think that passing gas is the funniest thing in the world."
—Jennifer Lopez

"He couldn't ad-lib a fart at a bean-eating contest."
—**Johnny Carson, who used this line to describe many of his comedic competitors**

"I went to my doctor and asked for something for persistent wind. He gave me a kite."
—Les Dawson

"I did not win the Nobel Fart Prize."
—**Bart Simpson, written on the chalkboard during the opening credits**

"If I fail, the film industry writes me off as another statistic. If I succeed, they pay me a million bucks to fly out to Hollywood and fart."
—George A. Romero

"I don't wanna talk to you no more, you empty-headed animal food trough wiper! I fart in your general direction! Your mother was a hamster and your father smelt of elderberries!"
—**French soldier (John Cleese),** *Monty Python and the Holy Grail*

"During job interviews, when they ask: 'What is your worst quality?' I always say: 'Flatulence.' That way I get my own office."
—**Dan Thompson**

"I have bubbles in my tummy. It's just air. It's not stink. Promise."
—Jessica Simpson

"Love is the fart of every heart: It pains a man when 'tis kept close, and others doth offend, when 'tis let loose."
—**Sir John Suckling**

"A dog is not intelligent. Never trust an animal that's surprised by its own farts."
—Frank Skinner

**John Cleese reached the height of 6'4 ¾" when he was 13 years old.**

# CHARLIE CHAPLIN

*The most enduring performer from the
silent film era was anything but silent.*

"No matter how desperate
the predicament is, I am
always very much in earnest
about clutching my cane,
straightening my derby hat,
and fixing my tie, even
though I have just landed
on my head."

"It takes courage to make a
fool of yourself."

"A day without laughter is a
day wasted."

"The saddest thing I can
imagine is to get used to
luxury."

"I remain just one thing,
and one thing only, and that
is a clown. It places me on a
far higher plane than any
politician."

"I do not have much patience
with a thing of beauty that
must be explained to be
understood. If it does need
additional interpretation by
someone other than the creator, then I question whether
it has fulfilled its purpose."

"To truly laugh, you must be
able to take your pain, and
play with it."

"I hate the theatre. I also hate
the sight of blood, but it's in
my veins."

"Failure is unimportant. It
takes courage to make a fool
of yourself."

"Actors search for rejection.
If they don't get it, they reject
themselves."

"Acting is ninety-nine percent
sweat and one percent talent.
But that talent had better be
good."

"I went into show business for
the money, and the art grew
out of it. If people are disillu-
sioned by that remark, I can't
help it. It's the truth."

"Life is a tragedy when seen
in close-up, but a comedy in
long-shot."

"Laughter is the tonic, the
relief, the surcease for pain."

# FOOD FOR THOUGHT

*Some words to sink your teeth into.*

"Health food may be good for the conscience, but Oreos taste a hell of a lot better."
—Robert Redford

"Only the pure in heart can make a good soup."
—Ludwig van Beethoven

"Everything you see I owe to spaghetti."
—Sophia Loren

"The only kind of seafood I trust is the fish stick, a totally featureless fish that doesn't have eyeballs or fins."
—Dave Barry

"I would like to find a stew that will give me heartburn immediately, instead of at three o'clock in the morning."
—John Barrymore

"As a child my family's menu consisted of two choices: take it or leave it."
—Buddy Hackett

"Inhabitants of undeveloped nations and victims of natural disasters are the only people who have ever been happy to see soybeans."
—Fran Lebowitz

"A bagel is a doughnut with the sin removed."
—George Rosenbaum

"Life is too short to stuff a mushroom."
—Shirley Conran

"Bad cooks—and the utter lack of reason in the kitchen—have delayed human development longest and impaired it most."
—Friedrich Nietzsche

"No man is lonely while eating spaghetti."
—Robert Morley

"Mustard's no good without roast beef."
—Chico Marx

"Eating takes a special talent. Some people are much better at it than others. In that way it's like sex, and as with sex, it's more fun with someone who really likes it."
—Alan King

"It requires a certain kind of mind to see beauty in a hamburger bun."
—Ray Kroc, founder of McDonald's

Charles Lindbergh's only food on his trans-Atlantic flight: four sandwiches.

# FUNNY PRESIDENTS

*It would be impossible to handle the incredible
stress of the Executive Office without a sense of humor.*

"Before I refuse to take your questions, I have an opening statement."
—**Ronald Reagan**

"When we got into office, the thing that surprised me most was to find that things were just as bad as we'd been saying they were."
—**John F. Kennedy**

"Some folks look at me and see a certain swagger, which in Texas is called 'walking.'"
—**George W. Bush**

"If I were two-faced, would I be wearing this one?"
—**Abraham Lincoln**

"When things haven't gone well, call in a secretary or a staff man and chew him out. You will sleep better and they will appreciate the attention."
—**Lyndon Johnson**

"Things are more like they are now than they have ever been."
—**Gerald Ford**

"If President Reagan could be an actor and become president, maybe I could become an actor. I've got a good pension. I can work for cheap."
—**Bill Clinton**

"Fluency in the English language is something I'm not accused of."
—**George H. W. Bush**

"Richard Nixon was just offered $2 million by Schick to do a television commercial …for Gillette."
—**Gerald Ford**

"When they call the roll in the Senate, the senators do not know whether to answer 'Present' or 'Not guilty.'"
—**Theodore Roosevelt**

"McCarthyism is now McCarthywasm."
—**Dwight D. Eisenhower**

"I have often wanted to drown my troubles, but I can't get my wife to go swimming."
—**Jimmy Carter**

---

"Never insult seven men when all you're packin' is a six-gun." —**Zane Grey**

# A ROOSTER
# IN THE HEN HOUSE

**The story goes** that President Calvin Coolidge and his wife, Grace, were visiting a government farm. Led on separate tours, Mrs. Coolidge asked as she walked past the hen house, "Does the rooster…you know, service the hens more than once a day?"

"Dozens of times," answered the farmer.

"Please tell that to my husband," said the First Lady.

A little while later, the president passed the same hen house and was told of his wife's request.

"Hmm," he asked, "Same hen every time?"

"Oh no, Mr. President, a different one each time."

The president responded, "Please tell that to my wife."

# SELF-HELP

*Everyone can use a little advice sometimes. Here are a few tidbits of New Age wisdom from some of the most popular self-help gurus.*

"You can't change what you don't acknowledge."
—**Dr. Phil**

"Even when you think you have your life all mapped out, things happen that shape your destiny in ways you might never have imagined."
—**Deepak Chopra**

"Lots of people want to ride with you in the limo, but what you want is someone who will take the bus with you when the Limo breaks down."
—**Oprah Winfrey**

"If you don't have confidence in yourself, get off your rear end and do anything that will make you feel better about yourself."
—**Wayne Dyer**

"Formulate and stamp indelibly on your mind a mental picture of yourself as succeeding. Hold this picture tenaciously. Never permit it to fade. Your mind will seek to develop the picture."
—**Norman Vincent Peale**

"If you don't have daily objectives, you qualify as a dreamer."
—**Zig Ziglar**

"Life is our greatest possession and love its greatest affirmation."
—**Leo Buscaglia**

"All my life I used to wonder what I would become when I grew up. Then, about seven years ago, I realized that I was never going to grow up—that growing is an ever ongoing process."
—**M. Scott Peck**

"Be aware that even if you meant your words as honey, other people can turn what you said into poison."
—**Don Miguel Ruiz**

"If you hear anything that I say, then I invite you to take it and use it as your own. If you resonate with it...make it your own. And if you don't, then throw it away. Don't try to wear a shoe that pinches."
—**Gary Zukav**

# TIME FOR TEE

*Golf is a strange game. And golfers are strange people.*
*But to be fair, golf probably made them that way.*

"They call it golf because all of the other four-letter words were taken."
—**Raymond Floyd**

"The Oscar I was awarded for *The Untouchables* is a wonderful thing, but I can honestly say that I'd rather have won the U.S. Open."
—**Sean Connery**

"Golf is an open exhibition of overweening ambition, courage deflated by stupidity, skill scoured by a whiff of arrogance."
—**Alistair Cooke**

"The reason the pro tells you to keep your head down is so you can't see him laughing."
—**Phyllis Diller**

"Swing hard in case you hit it."
—**Dan Marino**

"Man blames fate for other accidents but feels personally responsible for a hole in one."
—**Martha Beckman**

"I have a tip that can take five strokes off anyone's golf game: it's called an eraser."
—**Arnold Palmer**

"Golf appeals to the idiot in us and the child. Just how childlike golf players become is proven by their frequent inability to count past five."
—**John Updike**

"Talking to a golf ball won't do you any good. Unless you do it while your opponent is teeing off."
—**Bruce Lansky**

"Golf is twenty percent mechanics and technique. The other eighty percent is philosophy, humor, tragedy, romance, melodrama, companionship, camaraderie, cussedness, and conversation."
—**Grantland Rice**

"Hockey is a sport for white men. Basketball is a sport for black men. Golf is a sport for white men dressed like black pimps."
—**Tiger Woods**

# A RAINBOW OF QUOTES

*"Sit in reverie and watch the changing color of the waves that break upon the idle seashore of the mind."* —Henry Wadsworth Longfellow

## WHITE

"The first of all single colors is white."
—Leonardo Da Vinci

"White is not a mere absence of colour; it is a shining and affirmative thing, as fierce as red, as definite as black...God paints in many colours; but He never paints so gorgeously, I had almost said so gaudily, as when He paints in white.
—G. K. Chesterton

"The white music I like is white."
—Kanye West

## ORANGE

"Orange is the happiest color."
—Frank Sinatra

"Orange is red brought nearer to humanity by yellow."
—Wassily Kandinsky

## YELLOW

"It is the color closest to light. In its utmost purity it always implies the nature of brightness and has a cheerful, serene, gently stimulating character. Hence, experience teaches us that yellow makes a thoroughly warm and comforting impression."
—Goethe

"The road to the City of Emeralds is paved with yellow brick."
—L. Frank Baum

"There are painters who transform the sun into a yellow spot, but there are others who, thanks to their art and intelligence, transform a yellow spot into the sun."
—Pablo Picasso

"Yellow wakes me up in the morning. Yellow gets me on the bike every day. Yellow has taught me the true meaning of sacrifice. Yellow makes me suffer. Yellow is the reason I'm here."
—Lance Armstrong

## PINK

"A profusion of pink roses being ragged in the rain speaks to me of all gentleness and its enduring."
—William Carlos Williams

"Mauve is just pink trying to be purple."
—James Whistler

"I was shown Tutankhamun's tomb in the 1920s. I saw all this wonderful pink on the walls and the artifacts. I was so impressed that I vowed to wear it for the rest of my life."
—Barbara Cartland

"An optimist is a person who sees a green light everywhere, while a pessimist...

"It was always my nickname when I was a little girl. My friends named me that because I was the only girl in my clique."
—Pink

"We were on the dark side of the Earth when we started to see outside the window this soft pink glow, which is a lot of little angry ions out there going very fast. We were hitting them *very* fast."
—Robert Crippen, Space Shuttle astronaut

## GREEN

"Green, I love you green. Green wind. Green branches."
—Federico Garcia Lorca

"Green is my favorite color, except for flesh."
—Tom Robbins

"Green is my favorite because it's the color of my wife's eyes, grass, trees, life, and money."
—Casper Van Dien

## GRAY

"Gray skies are just clouds passing over."
—Frank Gifford

"Gray is the color of all theory."
—Goethe

"The moon is essentially gray, no color. It looks like plaster of Paris, like dirty beach sand with lots of footprints in it."
—James Lovell, *Apollo 13* commander

## BLUE

"If the sight of the blue skies fills you with joy, rejoice, for your soul is alive."
—Eleanora Duse

"Blue color is everlastingly appointed by the Deity to be a source of delight."
—John Ruskin

"I never get tired of the blue sky."
—Vincent van Gogh

## RED

"I can't stand to see red in my profit-or-loss column. I'm Taurus the Bull, so I react to red. If I see red, I sell my stocks quickly."
—Barbra Streisand

"Beauty, to me, is about being comfortable in your own skin. That, or a kick-ass red lipstick!"
—Gwyneth Paltrow

"Out of the ash I rise with my red hair/ And eat men like air."
—Sylvia Plath

## PURPLE

"Purple is black blooming."
—Christopher Smart

"I think it pisses God off if you walk by the color purple in a field somewhere and don't notice it."
—Alice Walker

"I won't eat any cereal that doesn't turn the milk purple."
—Calvin, *Calvin and Hobbes*

# THE DOUBLE STANDARD

*No one's ever said the world is fair…at least, no woman has.*

"A man has to be Joe McCarthy to be called ruthless. All a woman has to do is put you on hold."
—**Marlo Thomas**

"We have a double standard, which is to say, a man can show how much he cares by being violent—see, he's jealous, he cares—a woman shows how much she cares by how much she's willing to be hurt; by how much she will take; how much she will endure."
—**Andrea Dworkin**

"It gets me so angry. A man can sleep around, no questions asked. But if a woman makes 19 or 20 mistakes, she's a tramp."
—**Joan Rivers**

"When a man speaks his mind, it is accepted as charming, interesting, sexy, but when a woman speaks hers, she is unattractive, pushy—some might even say a bitch."
—**Lauren Bacall**

"Men are taught to apologize for their weaknesses, women for their strengths."
—**Lois Wyse**

"Because I am a woman, I must make unusual efforts to succeed. If I fail, no one will say, 'She doesn't have what it takes.' They will say, 'Women don't have what it takes.'"
—**Clare Boothe Luce**

"When women are the advisers, the lords of creation don't take the advice till they have persuaded themselves that it is just what they intended to do; then they act upon it, and if it succeeds, they give the weaker vessel half the credit of it; if it fails, they generously give her the whole."
—**Louisa May Alcott,** *Little Women*

"Why is it that men can be bastards and women must wear pearls and smile?"
—**Lynn Hecht Schafren**

"The failure of women to produce genius of the first rank has been used to block the way of all women of talent in a manner that would be amusingly absurd were it not so monstrously unjust and socially harmful."
—**Anna Garlin Spencer, 1912**

# IMAGINE

*More than 25 years after his death, John Lennon's voice is as clear as ever.*

"I believe in everything until it's disproved. So I believe in fairies, myths, dragons. It all exists, even if it's in your mind. Who's to say that dreams and nightmares aren't as real as the here and now?"

"My role in society, or any artist's role, is to express what we all feel. Not as a preacher, not as a leader, but as a reflection of us all."

"Part of me suspects that I'm a loser, and the other part of me thinks I'm God Almighty."

"Music is everybody's possession. It's only publishers who think that people own it."

"The only one who controls me is me, and that's just barely possible."

"When real music comes to me—the music that surpasseth understanding—that has nothing to do with me, because I'm just the channel. The joy for me is to transcribe it like a medium. Those moments are what I live for."

"I'm not going to change the way I look or the way I feel to conform to anything. I've always been a freak. So I have to live with that, you know. I'm one of those people."

"I don't believe in yesterday. I am only interested in what I am doing now."

"I've always thought there was this underlying thing in Paul's 'Get Back.' When we were in the studio recording it, every time he sang the line 'Get back to where you once belonged,' he'd look at Yoko."

"We're all Christ and we're all Hitler. We want Christ to win. What would he have done if he had advertisements, TV, records, films, and newspapers? The miracle today is communication. So let's use it."

"Walking away is much harder than carrying on. I've done both."

"I really thought that love would save us all."

Canadian journalist Sandy Gardiner coined the phrase "Beatlemania."

# DID WE REALLY LAND ON THE MOON?

*No matter how much hard evidence there is to refute them, some comspiracy theories just won't go away.*

"I received a call from a Margaret Hardin of Portland, Oregon. She said that she had met a hooker in Reno in 1970 who admitted to her that two NASA engineers told her the Moon trips were a hoax."
—**Bill Kaysing, author of** *We Never Went to the Moon: America's Thirty Billion Dollar Swindle*

"Bill Kaysing is wacky. His position makes me feel angry. We spent a lot of time getting ready to go to the Moon. We spent a lot of money, we took great risks, and it's something everybody in the country ought to be proud of."
—**Jim Lovell,** *Apollo 13* **commander**

"An old carpenter asked me if I really believed it happened. I said sure, I saw it on television. He disagreed; he said that he didn't believe it for a minute, that 'them television fellers' could make things look real that weren't. Back then, I

thought he was a crank. During my eight years in Washington, I saw some things on TV that made me wonder if he wasn't ahead of his time."
—**Bill Clinton**

"The event was so removed, however, so unreal, that no objective correlative existed to prove it had not been an event staged in a television studio—the greatest con of the century."
—**Norman Mailer**

"If the late unlamented Evil Empire was still around, I might have suspected some of being communist sympathizers attempting to discredit the one achievement for which the U.S.A. may be remembered a thousand years from now. Remembering how quickly Watergate unraveled, how could any sane person imagine that a conspiracy involving *hundreds of thousands of people over more than a decade* would not have done

Real Conspiracy Theory: The fake Moon landing footage was produced by Stanley Kubrick.

the same? Ben Franklin put it well: 'A secret known to three people can be kept—as long as two of them are dead.'"
—**Arthur C. Clarke**

"And here's the Smithsonian Institute's Air and Space Museum, where you can see the original rocks from the soundstage where they faked the Moon landing. It's a part of Hollywood history."
—**Stephen Colbert,**
***The Colbert Report***

"Who are these Looneytoons that do not believe in science, history, personal endeavor, heroic feats, and rock-solid facts? Forgive me, but I find these folks an utter waste of time, the 'didn't happen crowd.' I wish they'd just all go back to their beer, and shuffleboard, and wondering if the Earth is really not, after all, going around the Sun."
—**Bobby Charles, NASA oversight committee, 1999**

"NASA is going to spend a few thousand dollars trying to prove to some people that the United States did indeed land men on the Moon. They've been so rattled, they hired someone to write a book refuting the conspiracy theorists."
—**Peter Jennings, 2002**

"The body of physical evidence that humans did walk on the Moon is simply overwhelming."
—**Dr. Robert Park, physicist**

"In my research at NASA I uncovered, deep in the archives, one mislabelled reel from the *Apollo 11* mission to the Moon. What is on the reel and on the label are completely different…It contains an hour of unedited, colour television footage that is dated by NASA's own atomic clock three days into the flight. Identified on camera are Neil Armstrong, Edwin 'Buzz' Aldrin, and Michael Collins. They are doing multiple takes of a single shot of the mission, from which only about ten seconds was ever broadcast…Really! It means they did not walk on the Moon!"
—**Bart Sibrel**

"You are a coward and a liar and a thief!"
—**Bart Sibrel, to Buzz Aldrin in 2002. Aldrin responded by punching Sibrel in the face.**

"I can remember walking on the Moon."
—**Alan Bean,**
***Apollo 12* astronaut**

# REAL GENIUS

*What is genius? Here are some quotes from people who know a thing or two about it.*

"What is genius, but the power of expressing a new individuality?"
—**Elizabeth Barrett Browning**

"Genius sees the answer before the question."
—**J. Robert Oppenheimer**

"Men give me credit for some genius. All the genius I have lies in this; when I have a subject in hand, I study it profoundly. Day and night it is before me. My mind becomes pervaded with it. Then the effort that I have made is what people are pleased to call the fruit of genius. It is the fruit of labor and thought."
—**Alexander Hamilton**

"Neither a lofty degree of intelligence nor imagination nor both together to the making of genius. Love, love, love is the soul of genius."
—**Wolfgang Amadeus Mozart**

"Intellectuals solve problems; geniuses prevent them."
—**Albert Einstein**

"Simplicity is the most difficult thing to secure in this world; it is the last limit of experience and the last effort of genius."
—**George Sand**

"Intelligence is like four-wheel drive. It only allows you to get stuck in more remote places."
—**Garrison Keillor**

"You don't have to be a genius to recognize one. If you did, Einstein would never have gotten invited to the White House."
—**Tom Robbins**

"The distance between insanity and genius is measured only by success."
—**Bruce Feirstein**

"The fact that some geniuses were laughed at does not imply that all who are laughed at are geniuses. They laughed at Columbus, they laughed at Fulton, they laughed at the Wright brothers. But they also laughed at Bozo the Clown."
—**Carl Sagan**

# MAMA ALWAYS SAID…

*It is the job of the elders to pass down the wisdom of the ages to the younger generation, even if that wisdom is suspect.*

"'Be like a duck,' my mother used to tell me. 'Remain calm on the surface and paddle like hell underneath.'"
—**Michael Caine**

"My father told me that if you saw a man in a Rolls Royce you could be sure he was not a gentleman unless he was the chauffeur."
—**Earl of Arran**

"My father used to say, 'You would worry less about what people think if you knew how little they did.'"
—**Dr. Phil McGraw**

"My mom always said, 'Don't say *if* I make it, say *when* I make it!'"
—**Mariah Carey**

"Like my boy tells me: 'If it looks like a rat and smells like a rat, by golly, it is a rat.'"
—**Terrell Owens**

"My mother used to tell me that 'man gives the award, God gives the reward.' I don't need another plaque."
—**Denzel Washington**

"My dad always used to tell me that if someone challenges you to an after-school fight, tell them you won't wait—you can kick their ass right now."
—**Cameron Diaz**

"I've seen diapers, and my mother is right. 'What's in the poo-poo is like the Bible: The truth is in there.'"
—**Celine Dion**

"My mom said the only reason men are alive is for lawn care and vehicle maintenance."
—**Tim Allen**

"My grandfather always said that living is like licking honey off a thorn."
—**Louis Adamic**

"I'd asked my mother what she did during the war when her flat was blown up. She remembered taking a bottle of Shocking perfume, by Schiaparelli. She said, 'When there's nothing left, you stick to the superfluous.'"
—**Jane Birkin**

# UNCLE JOHN'S QUOTATIONARY

*Here's Part 3 of our quotation dictionary.*
*(Part 2 begins on page 70.)*

**FAILURES:** fingerposts on the road to achievement. (C. S. Lewis)

**FAMILY:** a unit composed not only of children but of men, women, an occasional animal, and the common cold. (Ogden Nash)

**FASHION:** what you adopt when you don't know who you are. (Quentin Crisp)

**FETTUCCINE ALFREDO:** macaroni and cheese for adults. (Mitch Hedberg)

**FILM:** truth, 24 times a second. (Jean-Luc Godard)

**FINE QUOTATION:** a diamond on the finger of a man of wit and a pebble in the hand of a fool. (Joseph Roux)

**FIRST LADY:** an unpaid public servant elected by one person—her husband. (Lady Bird Johnson)

**FLYING:** hours and hours of boredom sprinkled with a few seconds of sheer terror. (Gregory "Pappy" Boyington)

**FORCE:** the weapon of the weak. (Ammon Hennacy)

**FOOSBALL:** a combination of soccer and shish kabobs. (Mitch Hedberg)

**FORGIVENESS:** the key to action and freedom. (Hannah Arendt)

**FREELANCE WRITER:** a man who is paid per piece or per word or perhaps. (Robert Benchley)

**FRIEND:** one before whom I may think aloud. (Ralph Waldo Emerson)

**FRIENDSHIP:** one mind in two bodies. (Mencius)

**GAMBLER:** a man who makes his living out of hope. (William Bolitho)

**GARLIC:** one of the five elements. The other four are earth, air, fire, and water. (Louis Diat)

**GENIUS:** another word for magic…and the whole point of magic is that it is inexplicable. (Margot Fonteyn)

**GENTLEMAN:** any man who wouldn't hit a woman with his hat on. (Fred Allen)

**GLUTTON:** one who digs his grave with his teeth. (French proverb)

**GLUTTONY:** an emotional escape, a sign something is eating us. (Peter De Vries)

**GOALS:** dreams with deadlines. (Diana Scharf Hunt)

**GOD:** the last fading smile of a cosmic Cheshire cat. (Julian Huxley)

**GOLF:** a poolroom moved outdoors. (Barry Fitzgerald)

**GOSSIP:** the opiate of the oppressed. (Erica Jong)

**GOVERNMENT DEFICIT:** the difference between the amount of money the government spends and the amount it has the nerve to collect. (Sam Ewing)

**GRANDCHILDREN:** the only people who can get more out of you than the IRS. (Gene Perret)

**GRATITUDE:** happiness doubled by wonder. (G. K. Chesterton)

**GRAY HAIR:** God's graffiti. (Bill Cosby)

**GROW OLD:** to pass from passion to compassion. (Albert Camus)

**GUILT:** the pledge drive constantly hammering in our heads that keeps us from fully enjoying the show. (Dennis Miller)

**HAPPINESS:** when what you think, what you say, and what you do are in harmony. (Mahatma Gandhi)

**HARDWARE:** where the people in your company's software section will tell you the problem is. (Dave Barry) *See "Software"—page 304*

**HEALTH FOOD:** the food they serve in hell. (Henry Beard)

**HERO:** someone who understands the responsibility that comes with his freedom. (Bob Dylan)

**HIP-HOP:** an urban cultural reaction to the experience of being overtly and covertly marginalized by a fully enfranchised white American majority. (Carol Cooper)

**HISTORIAN:** a deaf person who goes on answering questions that no one has asked him. (Leo Tolstoy)

**HISTORY:** the only laboratory we have in which to test the consequences of thought. (Etienne Gilson)

**HOCKEY:** a form of disorderly conduct in which the score is kept. (Doug Larson)

**HOLLYWOOD:** a place where they'll pay you $50,000 for a kiss and 50 cents for your soul. (Marilyn Monroe)

**HONEST POLITICIAN:** one who, when he is bought, will stay bought. (Simon Cameron)

**HORSE SENSE:** the thing a horse has which keeps it from betting on people. (W. C. Fields)

**HOUSEWORK:** a treadmill from futility to oblivion with stop-offs at tedium and counterproductivity. (Erma Bombeck)

**HUMOR:** the pursuit of a gentle grin, usually in solitude. (Frank Muir)

**HUNCH:** creativity trying to tell you something. (Frank Capra)

*For more, see page 164.*

"Michael Moore and I actually have a lot in common—we both appreciate living in a country where there's free expression. But, Michael, if you ever show up at my front door with a camera, I'll kill you. I mean it."

—Clint Eastwood

Ralph Teetor, the man who invented cruise control for cars, was blind.

# :( TROUBLED SOULS :(

*Sometimes it feels really good to wallow in self-pity.*

"Every year spring comes, with nasty little birds yapping their fool heads off."
—**Dorothy Parker**

"The more you stay in this job, the more you realize that a public figure, a major public figure, is a lonely man."
—**Richard Nixon**

"Being a sex symbol is a heavy load to carry, especially when one is tired, hurt, and bewildered."
—**Marilyn Monroe**

"Most of the time I don't have much fun. The rest of the time I don't have any fun at all."
—**Woody Allen**

"Oh, God, I struggle with low self-esteem all the time! I think everyone does. I have so much wrong with me, it's unbelievable!"
—**Angelina Jolie**

"I fell off stage and bruised some ribs. The worst part was that the audience didn't realize I was gone."
—**Richard Marx**

"There's something about me that makes a lot of people want to throw up."
—**Pat Boone**

"I have so many different personalities in me and I still feel lonely."
—**Tori Amos**

"I have no idea where my pathetic nature comes from. If I thought about it too long, it would depress me."
—**Steve Carell**

"Why does a person even get up in the morning? You have breakfast, you floss your teeth so you'll have healthy gums in your old age, and then you get in your car and drive down I-10 and die. Life is so stupid I can't stand it."
—**Barbara Kingsolver**

"I have flabby thighs, but fortunately my stomach covers them."
—**Joan Rivers**

"My depression is the most faithful mistress I have known—no wonder, then, that I return the love."
—**Søren Kierkegaard**

---

"Somebody's boring me...I think it's me." —Dylan Thomas

# NEW YORK, NEW YORK

*Start spreading the news—here's a mix of Big Apple quotes.*

"If you're inclined to leave the nest, New York is where most people think they have to go."
—**Griffin Dunne**

"New York has a trip-hammer vitality which drives you insane with restlessness if you have no inner stabilizer."
—**Henry Miller**

"New York has always been going to hell…but somehow it never gets there."
—**Robert Pirsig**

"I think my favorite sport in the Olympics is the one in which you make your way through the snow, you stop, you shoot a gun, and then you continue on. In most of the world, it's known as the Biathlon, except in New York City, where it's known as winter."
—**Michael Ventre**

"New Yorkers like to boast that if you can survive in New York, you can survive anywhere. But if you can survive anywhere, why live in New York?"
—**Edward Abbey**

"Every great wave of popular passion that rolls up on the prairies is dashed to spray when it strikes the hard rocks of Manhattan."
—**H. L. Mencken**

"There is something about New York City that is so theatrical. I used to feel when I walked out of my apartment on the way to school that I was walking out on stage."
—**Dabney Coleman**

"I love New York City; I've got a gun."
—**Charles Barkley**

"New York needs no explanation. I mean, if you come from Ohio or New Jersey, you have to start explaining."
—**Jason Alexander**

"I come from New York, where, if you fall down, someone will pick you up by your wallet."
—**Al McGuire, NBA coach**

"I love how people talk to you in New York—just assault you and tell you what they think of your jacket."
—**Madonna**

---

"New York is a sucked orange." —Ralph Waldo Emerson

# LAW & DISORDER

*We asked our attorney what he thought of this page.*
*He sent us a "cease and desist" letter.*

"We all know that the law is the most powerful of schools for the imagination. No poet ever interpreted nature as freely as a lawyer interprets the truth."
—Jean Giraudoux

"It is the trade of lawyers to question everything, yield nothing, and talk by the hour."
—Thomas Jefferson

"Ignorance of the law excuses no man…from practicing it."
—Adison Mizner

"No brilliance is required in law, just common sense and relatively clean fingernails."
—John Mortimer

"An incompetent attorney can delay a trial for months or years. A competent attorney can delay one even longer."
—Evelle J. Younger

"A lawyer starts life giving $500 worth of law for $5 and ends giving $5 worth for $500."
—Benjamin H. Brewster

"A lawyer will do anything to win a case. Sometimes he will even tell the truth."
—Patrick Murray

"Lawyers are always more ready to get a man into troubles than out of them."
—William Goldsmith

"I always wait until a jury has spoken before I anticipate what they will do."
—Janet Reno

"The power of the lawyer is in the uncertainty of the law."
—Jeremy Bentham

"I don't want to know what the law is, I want to know who the judge is."
—Roy Cohn

"A lawyer with a briefcase can steal more than a thousand men with guns can."
—Mario Puzo

"The only thing a lawyer won't question is the legitimacy of his mother."
—W. C. Fields

More than 60% of the world's lawyers live in the United States.

"Make crime pay.
Become a lawyer."

**—Will Rogers**

# JESSICA SIMPSON

*She's the quintessential dumb blond...or is she? Some claim
the ditziness is just a ruse to get more endorsements.
Either way, her quotes are funny.*

"On my first day of junior high, I was in geography class and the teacher asked us if anybody knew the names of the continents. So I raised my hand and I said 'A-E-I-O-U!'"

"I stuttered as a kid, but I think it was because I had too much in my head. Too much to sort."

"Twenty-three is old. It's almost 25, which is like almost mid-20s."

"All I have to say is: Jessica Simpson is the most beautiful woman on the planet."

"Is this chicken or is this fish? I know it's tuna. But it says chicken. By the sea."

"I'm not anorexic, I'm from Texas! Are there anorexics in Texas?"

"You've done a nice job decorating the White House."
—*to Secretary of the Interior Gale Norton*

"Platypus? I thought it was pronounced platymapus. Has it always been pronounced platypus?"

"Is that weird, taking my Louis Vuitton bag camping?"

"I think there's a difference between ditzy and dumb. Dumb is just not knowing. Ditzy is having the courage to ask."

"I don't really care what I'm famous for."

"My whole life I've played the role of the blonde. It's always worked for me. It's a good thing, but it can also be a bad thing if you get labeled as the 'blonde' all the time."

"It's fun putting it in, but then you have to fold it."
—*on laundry*

"I want to be a diva, like 'people-totally-respect-my-music' diva, not diva like 'carry-my-Diet-Coke-around.'"

# COCKY JOCKS

*Are they grossly arrogant or merely confident?*

"I'll watch the highlights every now and then but, as far as watching the game, I feel like I am the game."
—Terrell Owens

"They say Elvis is dead. I say, no, you're looking at him. Elvis isn't dead; he just changed color."
—Dennis Rodman

"I don't listen to the refs. I don't listen to anyone who makes less money than I do."
—Charles Barkley

"I'm glad you're doing this story on us and not on the WNBA. We're so much prettier than all the other women in sports."
—Martina Hingis, tennis star, in *Detour* magazine

"Unstoppable, baby!"
—Marc Jackson, NBA rookie, after he made a lay-up during a 29-point loss

"If there was ever a man born to be a hitter, it was me."
—Ted Williams

"I am the most ruthless, brutal champion ever. There is no one who can match me. I want your heart. I want to eat your children."
—Mike Tyson

"If I am to be a chauvinist pig, I want to be the number-one pig."
—Bobby Riggs, before losing a tennis match to Billie Jean King

"I already believe I am the best linebacker in the game. Now, I have to show one more thing—that I am the most dominating, influential person in the game and the best football player to ever put on a pair of cleats."
—Ray Lewis

"It's called talent. I just have it. I can't explain it. You either have it or you don't."
—Barry Bonds

"Yeah, I'm arrogant. But that doesn't mean I'm not a nice person."
—Jeremy Roenick

"Confidence is a very fragile thing." —Joe Montana

# HELLO DAHLY

*Roald Dahl wrote about the important stuff in life—friendly giants, evil witches, eccentric chocolate makers, and giant magical peaches. Here is some of his wit, wisdom...and weirdness.*

"A little nonsense now and then is relished by the wisest men."

"A writer of fiction lives in fear. Each new day demands new ideas, and he can never be sure whether he is going to come up with them or not."

"Homesickness is a bit like seasickness. You don't know how awful it is until you get it, and when you do, it hits you right in the top of the stomach and you want to die."

"How simple life could be if one had a regular routine to follow with fixed hours, a fixed salary, and very little original thinking to do."

"Watch with glittering eyes the whole world around you because the greatest secrets are always hidden in the most unlikely places."

"Some children are spoiled and it is not their fault; it is their parents'."

"Great excitement is probably the only thing that really interests a six-year-old boy."

"Nowadays you can go anywhere in the world in a few hours. Nothing is fabulous anymore."

"A person is a fool to become a writer. His only compensation is absolute freedom."

"Fairy tales have always got to have something a bit scary for children...as long as you make them laugh as well."

"Watch with glittering eyes the whole world around you, because the greatest secrets are always hidden in the most unlikely places. Those who don't believe in magic will never find it."

"Don't forget about what happened to the man who suddenly got everything he ever wanted. He lived happily ever after."

—*Charlie and the Chocolate Factory*

# QUIPPY COMEBACKS

*How cool is it when someone asks you a question and you come up with a smart-aleck response right on the spot? These people know.*

**John Lennon** *in a late-1960s interview.*

**Q:** John, do you think Ringo is the best drummer in the world?

**A:** In the world? He's not even the best drummer in The Beatles!

**Pope John XXIII** *during an interview in the 1950s.*

**Q:** How many people work in the Vatican?

**A:** About half.

*NASCAR pit crew member* **Jeff Clark**, *speaking to his driver,* **Dale Earnhardt, Jr.**, *over the radio during a race.*

**Q:** How do the gauges look?

**A:** Nice. They're silver and they all have nice little red needles.

*At a congressional session in Georgia, Rep.* **Anne Mueller's** *microphone wasn't working. So she asked Speaker* **Tom Murphy** *for assistance.*

**Q:** Mr. Speaker, will you please turn me on?

**A:** Thirty years ago, I would have tried.

*During* **Adlai Stevenson's** *1956 presidential campaign, a woman called out to him:*

**Woman:** Senator, you have the vote of every thinking person!

**Stevenson:** That's not enough, madam, we need a majority.

*An interviewer asked* **Zsa Zsa Gabor** *how many husbands she'd had. Her response:* "You mean, other than my own?"

**Jay Leno:** How do you feel being treated like a movie star?

**Al Gore:** Well, it's not all easy. For example, I'm in this huge feud with Lindsay Lohan now.

**Leno:** Really? Can you give us a little more?

**Gore:** No, she knows what she did.

*B-movie star* **Bruce Campbell**, *when asked what he would want with him if marooned on a deserted island:* "A continent."

"A graceful taunt is worth a thousand insults." —Louis Nizer

# MITCH HEDBERG

*Sadly, stand-up comedian Mitch Hedberg died of a drug overdose in 2005 at age 37. But, thankfully, he left us with a treasure trove of witty observations about the mundane things in life. He didn't make them interesting, just funny.*

"I can whistle with my fingers, especially if I have a whistle."

"I bought a seven-dollar pen because I always lose pens, and I got sick of not caring."

"I bought myself a parrot. The parrot talked. But it did not say, 'I'm hungry'...so it died."

"I'd like to get four people who do cartwheels very good, and make a cart."

"An escalator can never break; it can only become stairs."

"If I had nine of my fingers missing, I wouldn't type any slower."

"I like to hold the microphone cord like this: I pinch it together, then I let it go, then you hear a whole bunch of jokes at once."

"I remixed a remix; it went back to normal."

"I used to be a hot-tar roofer. Yeah, I remember that day."

"My fake plants died because I did not pretend to water them."

"Rice is great if you're really hungry and want to eat two thousand of something."

"I would imagine the inside of a bottle of cleaning fluid is really clean. I would imagine a vodka bottle is really drunk."

"I like refried beans. That's why I wanna try *fried* beans, because maybe they're just as good and we're just wasting time. You don't have to fry them again after all."

"I have an underwater camera, just in case I crash my car into a river, and at the last minute I have a chance to take a picture of a fish that I've never seen."

"My sister wanted to be an actress. She got halfway: She does live in a trailer, but she never gets called to the set."

# POWER, INCORPORATED

*Corporations provide us with all the essentials: skimpy paychecks, watered-down news, and funny beer commercials. Love them or hate them, they're a fact of life.*

"A corporation cannot be ethical; its only responsibility is to turn a profit."
—Milton Friedman

"Naturally, corporations say they would never suppress speech. But it's not their intentions that matter; it's their capabilities."
—Ted Turner

"You don't want another Enron? Here's your law: If a company cannot explain in one sentence exactly what it does, it's illegal."
—Lewis Black

"Corporations are worms in the body politic."
—Thomas Hobbes

"The corporate grip on opinion in the United States is one of the wonders of the Western world. No first-world country has ever managed to eliminate so entirely from its media all objectivity."
—Gore Vidal

"I find rebellion packaged by a major corporation a little hard to take seriously."
—David Byrne

"Corporation: An ingenious device for obtaining profit without individual responsibility."
—Ambrose Bierce

"Nothing is illegal if a hundred businessmen decide to do it."
—Andrew Young

"The corporations don't need power. They already have it."
—Jose Luis Rodriguez

"When a business decides that success has been attained, progress stops."
—Thomas Watson

"I don't know that I want a lawyer to tell me what I cannot do. I hire him to tell me how to do what I want to do."
—J. P. Morgan

"The jean! The jean is the destructor, a dictator! It is destroying creativity."

—**Pierre Cardin**

"Jeans are the most beautiful things since the gondola."

—**Diana Vreeland**

# FASHION SENSES

*Some insights on inseams and such from fashion experts…
and from some who are wanted by the fashion police.*

"A woman's dress should be like a barbed-wire fence: serving its purpose without obstructing the view."
—**Sophia Loren**

"Fashion can be bought. Style one must possess."
—**Edna Woolman Chase, former *Vogue* fashion editor**

"Fashion is the science of appearance, and it inspires one with the desire to seem rather than to be."
—**Henry Fielding**

"The leading cause of death among fashion models is falling through street grates."
—**Dave Barry**

"Fashion is born by small facts, trends or even politics; never by the shortening or lengthening of the skirt."
—**Elsa Schiaparelli**

"When in doubt, wear red."
—**Bill Blass**

"Fashion changes. Style remains."
—**Coco Chanel**

"I don't design clothes. I design dreams."
—**Ralph Lauren**

"Good design is always on a tightrope of bad taste."
—**Elsa Schiaparelli**

"Bored with red? It would be like becoming bored with the person you love."
—**Diana Vreeland**

"I despise simplicity. It is the negation of all that is beautiful."
—**Norman Hartnell, dress designer for Queen Elizabeth II**

"Art produces ugly things which frequently become more beautiful with time. Fashion, on the other hand, produces beautiful things which always become ugly with time."
—**Jean Cocteau**

"Fashion matters considerably more than horoscopes, rather more than dog shows, and slightly more than hockey."
—**Roy Blount, Jr.**

**"Beauty is not caused. It is." —Emily Dickinson**

# THE ARTIST'S WAY

*These famous artists paint word pictures
of what it means to be an artist.*

"The true artist is known by the use he makes of what he annexes, and he annexes everything."
—Oscar Wilde

"An artist is a creature driven by demons. He doesn't know why they choose him, and he's usually too busy to wonder why."
—William Faulkner

"No artist is ahead of his time. He is his time. It is just that others are behind the time."
—Martha Graham

"We should talk less and draw more."
—Goethe

"If to the viewer's eyes, my world appears less beautiful than his, I'm to be pitied and the viewer praised."
—Rockwell Kent

"Drawing is the honesty of the art. There is no possibility of cheating. It is either good or bad."
—Salvador Dali

"If only we could pull out our brain and use only our eyes."
—Pablo Picasso

"Great art picks up where nature ends."
—Mark Chagall

"Where the spirit does not work with the hand, there is no art."
—Leonardo da Vinci

"If you could say it in words, there would be no reason to paint."
—Edward Hopper

"I have always believed that art should be a deep pleasure. I think there is a contradiction in an art of total despair, because the very fact that the art is made seems to contradict despair."
—David Hockney

"If you know something well, you can always paint it, but people would be better off buying chicken."
—Grandma Moses

# MEET WILSON MIZNER

*Wilson Mizner (1876–1933) never achieved the same level of fame as Mark Twain or Oscar Wilde, but this Broadway playwright, Hollywood screenwriter, prizefight manager, and Klondike gold seeker could match wits with the best of them.*

"Life's a tough proposition, and the first hundred years are the hardest."

"I respect faith, but doubt is what gets you an education."

"A fellow who is always declaring he's no fool usually has his suspicions."

"I've had several years in Hollywood, and I still think the real movie heroes are in the audience."

"A good listener is not only popular everywhere, but after a while he gets to know something."

"The most beautiful sentence I have ever heard is, 'Have one on the house.'"

"Some of the greatest love affairs I've known involved one actor, unassisted."

"The gent who wakes up and finds himself a success hasn't been asleep."

"I never saw a mob rush across town to do a good deed."

"Insanity is considered a ground for divorce, though by the same token it's the shortest mental detour to marriage."

"Hollywood is a trip through a sewer in a glass-bottomed boat."

"Don't talk about yourself. It will be done when you leave."

"To my embarassment, I was born in bed with a lady."

"The life of the party almost always winds up in a corner with an overcoat over him"

"The worst-tempered people I've met were people who knew they were wrong."

*Mizner, on his deathbed, had just awakened from a coma to find a priest by his bed...*
"Why should I talk to you? I've just been talking to your boss."

"Life is a foreign language; all men mispronounce it." —Christopher Morley

# AGING

*Because we're not getting any younger…*

"Growing old is like being increasingly penalized for a crime you haven't committed."
—Pierre Teilhard de Chardin

"Some people say, 'Who would want to be 90?' And I say, 'Anyone who is 89.'"
—Phyllis Diller

"By the time you know what to do, you're too old to do it."
—Ted Williams

"Back then I was skinnier. I hit it better, I putted better, and I could see better. Other than that, everything's the same."
—Homero Blancas, *PGA Senior Tour player*

"No wise man ever wished to be younger."
—Jonathan Swift

"So much has been said and sung of beautiful young girls, why don't somebody wake up to the beauty of old women?"
—Harriet Beecher Stowe

"I'm saving that rocker for the day when I feel as old as I really am."
—Dwight D. Eisenhower

"Retire? I can't spell the word. I'd play in a wheelchair."
—Keith Richards

"From age to age, nothing changes, and yet everything is completely different."
—Aldous Huxley

"If you think 40 is old, picture George Burns when he was 40, and you'll think, 'My God, look how *young* he is!'"
—Jay Newman

"I'd go out with women my age, but there are no women my age."
—George Burns

"In youth we learn; in age we understand."
—Marie Ebner-Eschenbach

"He who is of a calm and happy nature will hardly feel the pressure of age, but to him who is of an opposite disposition, youth and age are equally a burden."
—Plato

"When you're over the hill, that's when you pick up speed."
—Quincy Jones

"Anyone who stops learning is old, whether at 20 or 80. The greatest thing…

# RANDOM QUOTES

*Here are some quotations about all sorts of things that seemed to make a nice stew all by themselves. Leftovers…mmmmm…*

"You never realize how the human voice can change until a woman stops yelling at her husband and answers the phone."
—**Neal O'Hara**

"It is not love that makes the world go around, but rather those mutually supportive alliances through which partners recognize their dependence on each other for the achievement of shared and private goals."
—**Fred Allen**

"For 15 minutes I got to be a rock star. After 20 minutes, it turned into Spinal Tap."
—**Mark Mothersbaugh, lead singer of Devo**

"The more seriously someone takes themselves, the more likely they'll have a humiliating public scandal."
—**Tom Arnold**

"It is useless to hold a person to anything he says while he's in love, drunk, or running for office."
—**Shirley MacLaine**

"No day is so bad it can't be fixed with a nap."
—**Carrie Snow**

"Nothing astonishes men so much as common sense and plain dealing."
—**Ralph Waldo Emerson**

"Never settle with words what you can accomplish with a flamethrower."
—**Bruce Feirstein**

"You may not be able to change the world, but at least you can embarrass the guilty."
—**Jessica Mitford**

"It's not how you pick your nose, it's where you put that booger that counts."
—**Tre Cool**

"He who limps is still walking."
—**Joan Rivers**

"The salvation of this human world lies nowhere else than in the human heart, in the human power to reflect, in human meekness and human responsibility."
—**Václav Havel**

# OVERCOMING ADVERSITY

*Longtime BRI friend Jennifer Massey sent us these quotations she collected for her book* Marley Rides, *which chronicles her teenage son's three-year battle with cancer. We're still missing you, Mars!*

"The problem is not that there are problems. The problem is expecting other-wise and thinking that having problems is a problem."
—**Theodore Rubin**

"Challenges are what make life interesting; overcoming them is what makes life meaningful."
—**Joshua J. Marine**

"What is to give light must endure burning."
—**Viktor Frankl**

"Most of the important things in the world have been accom-plished by people who have kept on trying when there seemed to be no hope at all."
—**Dale Carnegie**

"Problems are only opportuni-ties in work clothes."
—**Henry Kaiser**

"It is not true that life is one damned thing after another—it is one damn thing over and over."
—**Edna St. Vincent Millay**

"Pure and complete sorrow is as impossible as pure and complete joy."
—**Leo Tolstoy**

"Life is thickly sown with thorns, and I know no other remedy than to pass quickly through them. The longer we dwell on our misfortunes, the greater is their power to harm us."
—**Voltaire**

"The more we relax into the contractions, the less pain we feel."
—**Gloria Karpinski**

"When written in Chinese, the word 'crisis' is composed of two characters. One repre-sents danger, and the other represents opportunity."
—**John F. Kennedy**

"If you are distressed by any-thing external, the pain is not due to the thing itself, but to your own estimate of it; and this you have the power to revoke at any moment."
—**Marcus Aurelius**

# EXERCISE

*Let's see...the treadmill, or the couch? Here
are some thoughts to help us decide.*

"If you're working out in front of a mirror and watching your muscles grow, your ego has reached a point where it is now eating itself. That's why I believe there should be a psychiatrist at every health club, so that when they see you doing this, they will take you away for a little chat."
—Lewis Black

"It's been about two months since I've worked out. I just don't have the time. Which is odd, because I have the time to go out to dinner. And watch TV. And get a bone-density test. And try to figure out what my phone number spells in words."
—Ellen DeGeneres

"I'm cute in gym shorts! I'm slim and trim, and you'd be impressed—I've got good calves."
—Larry King

"An hour of basketball feels like 15 minutes. An hour on a treadmill feels like a weekend in traffic school."
—David Walters

"If it weren't for the fact that the TV set and the refrigerator are so far apart, some of us wouldn't get any exercise at all."
—Joey Adams

"The belly is the reason why man does not so readily take himself for a god."
—Friedrich Nietzsche

"A man who drinks in a healthy, fit, and self-approving manner will mix vodka with yogurt and get tangled in the Nautilus machine trying to kiss his own ass."
—P. J. O'Rourke

"[Arnold Schwarzenegger] had this 20-foot gym trailer, and he said I could use it any time. He invited me in, but after one look at all this gym equipment, I declined and went outside for a cigarette."
—Nick Stahl, who co-starred in *Terminator 3*

"I have to exercise in the morning, before my brain figures out what I'm doing."
—Marsha Doble

# SUSAN B. ANTHONY

*Susan B. Anthony was the first woman ever to appear on an American coin. Reason: in the latter half of the 19th century, she spearheaded the women's rights movement.*

"I always distrust people who know so much about what God wants them to do to their fellows."

"Independence is happiness."

"The older I get, the greater power I seem to have to help the world; I am like a snowball—the further I am rolled, the more I gain."

"Modern invention has banished the spinning wheel, and the same law of progress makes the woman of today a different woman from her grandmother."

"Cautious, careful people, always casting about to preserve their reputation and social standing, never can bring about a reform. Those who are really in earnest must be willing to be anything or nothing in the world's estimation, and publicly and privately, in season and out, avow their sympathy with despised and persecuted ideas, and bear the consequences."

"It was we, the people; not we, the white male citizens; but we, the whole people, who formed the Union."

"It would be ridiculous to talk of male and female atmospheres, male and female springs or rains, male and female sunshine....How much more ridiculous is it in relation to mind, to soul, to thought, where there is as undeniably no such thing as sex, to talk of male and female education and of male and female schools."

"So long as society says a woman is incompetent to be a lawyer, minister, or doctor, but has ample ability to be a teacher, every man of you who chooses this profession tacitly acknowledges that he has no more brains than a woman?"

"Resolved, that the women of this nation in 1876 have greater cause for discontent, rebellion, and revolution than the men of 1776."

# FATHERS

*A page for Dad.*

"Fatherhood is pretending the present you love most is soap-on-a-rope."
—**Bill Cosby**

"The fundamental defect of fathers, in our competitive society, is that they want their children to be a credit to them."
—**Bertrand Russell**

"To be as good as our fathers we must be better."
—**Wendell Phillips**

"Fathers like to have children good-natured, well-behaved, and comfortable, but how to put them in that desirable condition is out of their philosophy."
—**Ernestine Rose**

"My father was frightened of his father, I was frightened of my father, and I am damned well going to see to it that my children are frightened of me."
—**King George V of England**

"It is not flesh and blood but the heart which makes us fathers and sons."
—**Johann Schiller**

"I talk and talk and talk, and I haven't taught people in 50 years what my father taught me by example in one week."
—**Mario Cuomo**

"Blessed indeed is the man who hears many gentle voices call him father."
—**Lydia M. Child**

"It doesn't matter who my father was; it matters who I remember he was."
—**Anne Sexton**

"A soldier destroys in order to build; the father only builds, never destroys. The one has the potentiality of death; the other embodies creation and life. And while the hordes of death are mighty, the battalions of life are mightier still. It is my hope that my son, when I am gone, will remember me not from the battlefield but in the home repeating with him our simple daily prayer."
—**Douglas MacArthur**

"It is impossible to please all the world and one's father."
—**Jean de La Fontaine**

"My father worked for the same firm for 12 years. They replaced him with a gadget that does...

"To be a dad in real life, you have to improvise 24 hours a day."

—Tom Bosley

"I've had a hard life, but my hardships are nothing against the hardships that my father went through in order to get me to where I started."

—Bartrand Hubbard

"That is the thankless position of the father in the family: the provider for all, and the enemy of all."

—August Strindberg

"Never raise your hand to your kids. It leaves your groin unprotected."

—Red Buttons

"By the time a man realizes that maybe his father was right, he usually has a son who thinks he's wrong."

—Charles Wadsworth

# ALL THAT JAZZ

*Hey, cats. Put on your shades, sit back, and read
some smooth quotations on jazz—or, as Anaïs Nin
defined it, "the music of the body."*

"Jazz is the big brother of the blues. If a guy's playing blues, he's in high school. When he starts playing jazz it's like going on to college, to a school of higher learning."
—B. B. King

"The word 'jazz' in its progress toward respectability has meant first sex, then dancing, then music."
—F. Scott Fitzgerald

"I think there are only three things America will be known for 2,000 years from now when they study this civilization: the Constitution, jazz music, and baseball."
—Gerald Early

"If they act too hip, you know they can't play!"
—Louis Armstrong

"There's more bad music in jazz than any other form. Maybe that's because the audience doesn't really know what's happening."
—Pat Metheny

"Only play what you hear. If you don't hear anything, don't play anything."
—Chick Corea

"It's like an act of murder. You play with intent to commit something."
—Duke Ellington

"What is jazz? It's almost like asking, What is French? Jazz is a musical language—a dialect that actually embodies the spirit of America."
—Branford Marsalis

"Jazz will endure just as long people hear it through their feet instead of their brains."
—John Philip Sousa

"Master your instrument. Master the music. And then forget all that bullsh*t and just play."
—Charlie Parker

"Jazz is not dead...it just smells funny."
—Frank Zappa

Louis Armstrong, a cool cat with great chops, coined the slang terms "cat" and "chops."

# QUOTABLE MUPPETS

*Jim Henson and Frank Oz—along with a team of talented writers and performers—brought life to a bunch of fabric, fake hair, and plastic eyes.*

**Statler:** I like this show so far.
**Waldorf:** It hasn't started yet.
**Statler:** That's what I like about it!

"Only time can heal your broken heart, just as only time can heal his broken arms and legs."
—Miss Piggy

**Loretta Swit:** You can't just pick Miss Piggy up and throw her out in the snow!
**Kermit:** Not without a forklift, I can't!

**Nurse Piggy:** But I love him.
**Dr. Bob:** How could you love him? You're a nurse.
**Nurse Piggy:** That may be true, but I am a woman first.
**Dr. Bob:** No, you're not. You're a pig first. Nurse second. I don't think "woman" made the top 10.

"Kermit, cancel my bread impersonation act! They didn't deliver my poppy seeds. You wouldn't want me to walk out there *naked*, would you?"
—Gonzo

"Aaah, a marriage made in heaven. A frog and a pig. We can have bouncing baby figs!"
—Kermit

**Statler:** Well, Waldorf, they finally made it to Broadway.
**Waldorf:** Yes, and I already bought tickets.
**Statler:** Are they good seats?
**Waldorf:** Sure are. They're on the next train out of town!

"Who's Jim Henson, for God sakes? I'm up here working my tail off! I hear his name bandied about a lot around here, but I don't know him. He seems to have his hand in a lot of things around here, but I don't particularly know what that means."
—Kermit

**Dancer:** I hear you come from a broken home.
**Animal:** Yeah, I broke it myself!

"Someday we'll find it, that rainbow connection/ The lovers, the dreamers, and me."
—Kermit

# SEX SEX SEX SEX SEX SEX

*Is our modern society obsessed with sex? Nahh...*

"Sex is like art. Most of it is pretty bad, and the good stuff is out of your price range."
—**Scott Roeben**

"Nothing in our culture is more overrated than the epidermal felicity of two featherless bipeds in desperate congress."
—**Quentin Crisp**

"It's not that sex is the primary element of the universe, it's just that when it's unfulfilled, it will affect you."
—**Jack Nicholson**

"If insemination were the sole biological function of sex, it could be achieved far more economically in a few seconds. Indeed, the least social of mammals mate with scarcely more ceremony. The species that have evolved long-term bonds are also, by and large, the ones that rely on elaborate courtship rituals. Love and sex do indeed go together."
—**Edward O. Wilson**

"There is nothing safe about sex. There never will be."
—**Norman Mailer**

"Kissing is the most delicious, most beautiful and passionate thing that two people can do. Better than sex, hands down.
—**Drew Barrymore**

"Sex follows love, it never precedes it."
—**Sophia Loren**

"Nine-tenths of that which is attributed to sexuality is the work of our magnificent ability to imagine, which is no longer an instinct, but exactly the opposite: a creation."
—**José Ortega y Gasset**

"In America, sex is an obsession. In other parts of the world, it's a fact."
—**Marlene Dietrich**

"There are a number of mechanical devices that increase sexual arousal, particularly in women. Chief amongst these is the Mercedes-Benz 380L convertible."
—**P. J. O'Rourke**

"There's people making babies to my music. That's nice."
—**Barry White**

The Duke of Orleans is believed to have made the first valentine card.

# HISTORY LESSONS

*What happened yesterday can teach us a lot
about what to do—or not to do—today.*

"History is a relentless master. It has no present, only the past rushing into the future. To try to hold fast is to be swept aside."
—**John F. Kennedy**

"History is a vast early warning system."
—**Norman Cousins**

"The only thing new in the world is the history you don't know."
—**Harry S. Truman**

"History doesn't repeat itself, but it rhymes."
—**Will Rogers**

"God cannot alter the past, though historians can."
—**Samuel Butler**

"When will our consciences grow so tender that we will act to prevent human misery rather than avenge it?"
—**Eleanor Roosevelt**

"History is philosophy teaching by example."
—**Dionysius**

"History is the sum total of things that could have been avoided."
—**Konrad Adenauer**

"We live in a world where amnesia is the most wished-for state. When did history become a bad word?"
—**John Guare**

"American history is longer, larger, more various, more beautiful, and more terrible than anything anyone has ever said about it."
—**James A. Baldwin**

"The past is our definition. We may strive, with good reason, to escape it, or to escape what is bad in it, but we will escape it only by adding something better to it."
—**Wendell Berry**

"One of the lessons of history is that nothing is often a good thing to do and always a clever thing to say."
—**Will Durant**

# THE SIMMMMMMPSONS

*For nearly two decades, Homer, Marge and family—along with
the strange array of characters in Springfield, USA—have
been satirizing modern society with a combination of
acerbic wit and absurd slapstick. Woo-hoo!*

"Brothers and sisters are natural enemies. Like Englishmen and Scots. Or Welshmen and Scots. Or Japanese and Scots. Or Scots and other Scots. Damn Scots! They ruined Scotland!"
—**Groundskeeper Willie**

"There's no shame in being a pariah."
—**Marge**

"Call this an unfair generalization if you want to, but old people are no good at everything."
—**Moe**

"Science is like a blabbermouth who ruins the movie by telling you how it ends. Well, I say there are some things we don't want to know. Important things."
—**Ned Flanders**

"Shoplifting is a victimless crime. Like punching someone in the dark."
—**Nelson Muntz**

"Remember, you can always find East by staring directly at the sun."
—**Bart**

"Lisa, normally, I would say that you should stand up for what you believe in, but you've been doing that an awful lot lately."
—**Marge**

"Loneliness and cheeseburgers are a dangerous mix."
—**Comic Book Guy**

"To be loved, you have to be nice to others *every day*! To be hated, you don't have to do squat."
—**Homer**

"I hope this has taught you kids a lesson: kids never learn."
—**Chief Wiggum**

"Family. Religion. Friendship. These are the three demons you must slay if you wish to succeed in business."
—**Mr. Burns**

Hiya Brendan!

"What good is money if it can't inspire terror in your fellow man?"
—Mr. Burns

"I'm no theologian. I don't know who or what God is. All I know is He's more powerful than Mom and Dad put together."
—Lisa

"You go through life, you try to be nice to people, you struggle to resist the urge to punch 'em in the face, and for what?"
—Moe

"You should listen to your heart, and not the voices in your head."
—Marge

"We will not negotiate with terrorists. Is there a nearby city who will?"
—Mayor Quimby

"Fire can be our friend; whether it's toasting marsh-mallows, or raining down on Charlie."
—Principal Skinner

"I'm not a nerd, Bart. Nerds are smart."
—Milhouse

"Marge, promise me you'll put me in a home. It's like being a baby, only you're old enough to appreciate it."
—Homer

"Once the government approves something, it's no longer immoral!"
—Reverend Lovejoy

"It's like my dad always said: eventually, everybody gets shot."
—Moe

"Honor-roll students will be rewarded by a trip to an archaeological dig. Also, all detention students will be punished with a trip to an archaeological dig."
—Principal Skinner

"The answer to life's problems aren't at the bottom of a bottle, they're on TV!"
—Homer Simpson

"War is neither glamorous nor fun. There are no winners, only losers. There are no good wars, with the following exceptions: The American Revolution, World War II, and the *Star Wars* trilogy."
—Bart

# TO WIT

*Clevah quotes from clevah folks!*

"If all the world's a stage, I want to operate the trap door."
—**Paul Beatty**

"I like Beethoven, especially the poems."
—**Ringo Starr**

"My brothers and sisters all hated me 'cause I was an only child."
—**Weird Al Yankovic**

"I'd love to see Christ come back to crush the spirit of hate and make men put down their guns. I'd also like just one more hit single."
—**Tiny Tim**

"In life, it's not who you know that's important, it's how your wife found out."
—**Joey Adams**

"Nostalgia is like a grammar lesson: you find the present tense, but the past perfect."
—**Owens Lee Pomeroy**

"The only reason some people get lost in thought is because it's unfamiliar territory."
—**Paul Fix**

"I never made a mistake in grammar but once in my life, and as soon as I done it, I seen it."
—**Carl Sandburg**

"If people are having trouble communicating, the least they could do is shut up about it."
—**Tom Lehrer**

"I saw a woman wearing a sweatshirt with the word 'Guess' on it. I said, 'Thyroid problem?'"
—**Arnold Schwarzenegger**

"Do you think that every time someone has acupuncture there's a voodoo doll out there having a really bad day?"
—**Caryn Leschen**

"When I finished school, I took one of those career-aptitude tests, and based on my verbal ability score, they suggested I become a mime."
—**Tim Cavanagh**

"There's nothing wrong with being shallow as long as you're insightful about it."
—**Dennis Miller**

"Indecision may or may not be my problem." —Jimmy Buffett

# WE ARE FAMILY

*Here we ponder the experience that is our closest relatives.*

"If you ever start feeling like you have the goofiest, craziest, most dysfunctional family in the world, all you have to do is go to a state fair. Because five minutes at the fair, you'll be going, 'You know, we're alright. We are dang near royalty.'"
—**Jeff Foxworthy**

In every dispute between parent and child, both cannot be right, but they may be, and usually are, both wrong. It is this situation which gives family life its peculiar hysterical charm."
—**Isaac Rosenfeld**

"Why do grandparents and grandchildren get along so well? They have the same enemy—the mother."
—**Claudette Colbert**

"A family is a little kingdom, torn with factions and exposed to revolutions."
—**Samuel Johnson**

"If you cannot get rid of the family skeleton, you may as well make it dance."
—**George Bernard Shaw**

"A happy family is but an earlier heaven."
—**John Bowring**

"If Vincent Price were to co-star with Bette Davis in a story by Edgar Allan Poe directed by Roger Corman, it could not fully express the pent-up violence and depravity of a single day in the life of the average family."
—**Quentin Crisp**

"Family love is messy, clinging, and of an annoying and repetitive pattern, like bad wallpaper."
—**Friedrich Nietzsche**

"The family is one of nature's masterpieces."
—**George Santyana**

"Families are about love overcoming emotional torture."
—**Matt Groening**

"Call it a clan, call it a network, call it a tribe, call it a family: Whatever you call it, whoever you are, you need one."
—**Jane Howard**

President Martin Van Buren was born in his father's tavern.

# CHIASMUS

*What's a chiasmus? It's a statement where the second half reverses the first half, resulting in an elegant play on words. Here are some favorites.*

"It's nice to be important, but it's more important to be nice."
—Roger Federer

"In the case of good books, the point is not how many of them you can get through, but rather how many can get through to you."
—Mortimer J. Adler

"There is nothing wrong with men possessing riches. The wrong comes when riches possess men."
—Billy Graham

"One should eat to live, not live to eat."
—Cicero

"It's better to spend money like there's no tomorrow than to spend tonight like there's no money."
—P. J. O'Rourke

"In America, you can always find a party. In Soviet Russia, the Party can always find you!"
—Yakov Smirnoff

"You can give without loving, but you cannot love without giving."
—Amy Carmichael

"Is man one of God's blunders, or is God one of man's blunders?"
—Nietzsche

"In peace sons bury their fathers, but in war fathers bury their sons."
—Croesus

"The two most engaging powers of an author are to make new things familiar, and familiar things new."
—Samuel Johnson

"It is better to deserve honors and not have them than to have honors and not deserve them."
—Mark Twain

"When they are alone they want to be with others, and when they are with others they want to be alone. After all, human beings are like that."
—Gertrude Stein

How romantic: Charles Dickens nicknamed his wife "Dearest Darling Pig."

# PRIMETIME PROVERBS

*Television can teach us all sorts of things about life, love, and what it means to be human. (At least that's what we told Uncle John when we wanted to go home and do "research" for these quotations.)*

## ON FRIENDS

**Lucille:** Today at lunch, you were ashamed to be with me.
**Gob:** No, I was ashamed to be seen with you. I like being with you.
—*Arrested Development*

"Good friends support each other after something bad has happened. Great friends act as if nothing has happened."
—Gabrielle,
*Desperate Housewives*

## ON BAD HABITS

"I was gonna quit smoking, but it turns out quitting smoking is stressful. And when I'm stressed out, I smoke."
—Earl, *My Name is Earl*

"I like being a mess. It's who I am."
—Ally, *Ally McBeal*

## ON SMALL TALK

**Sean:** Why are you answering questions with questions?
**Eddie:** Why does that concern you?
—*Grounded for Life*

## ON SEARCHING

**Locke:** I used to get angry all the time. Frustrated, too.
**Sun Kwon:** You're not frustrated any more?
**Locke:** I'm not lost any more.
**Sun Kwon:** How did you do that?
**Locke:** The same way anything lost gets found. I stopped looking.
—*Lost*

## ON ADOLESCENCE

**Sam:** Cindy's kind of boring. I mean, all she wants to do is make out and stuff.
**Neal:** I'd kill to be that bored.
—*Freaks and Geeks*

## ON RELATIONSHIPS

**Paris:** What if I fall for him and he doesn't like me?
**Rory:** Then you'll find someone else.
**Paris:** But what if there is no one else?
**Rory:** Then you'll buy some cats.
—*Gilmore Girls*

## ON THE WORK ETHIC

"The thing about Jim is, when he's excited about something, he gets really into it and he does a really great job. But the problem with Jim is that he works here, so that hardly ever happens."

—Pam, *The Office*

## ON EVIL

"Villains who twirl their moustaches are easy to spot. Those who clothe themselves in good deeds are well camouflaged."

—Jean-Luc Picard,
*Star Trek: The Next Generation*

## ON GROWING UP

"You want to know the best part about childhood? At some point, it stops."

—Malcolm,
*Malcolm in the Middle*

## ON DATING

**Sharona:** How was the date?
**Monk:** It was hell. Thank God I'm not single.
**Sharona:** But you are single.
**Monk:** Oh yeah.

—*Monk*

# WE'LL ALWAYS HAVE PARIS

*Who would have thought Paris Hilton*
*was so quotable? Whatever.*

"People think I'm stupid, but I'm smarter than most people."

"People are going to judge me: 'Paris Hilton, she uses money to get what she wants.' Whatever. I haven't accepted money from my parents since I was 18. I've worked my ass off. I have things no heiress has. I've done it all on my own…like a hustler."

"A true heiress is never mean to anyone—except a girl who steals your boyfriend."

"I take my dog Tinkerbell seriously. I take my job seriously. But I don't take myself all that seriously."

"I'm totally normal. I think it's obnoxious when people demand limos or bodyguards. I eat at McDonald's or Taco Bell. My parents taught me to be humble."

"Every woman should have four pets in her life. A mink in her closet, a jaguar in her garage, a tiger in her bed, and a jackass who pays for everything."

"The only rule is don't be boring, and dress cute wherever you go. Life is too short to blend in."

"The way I see it, you should live everyday like its your birthday."

"No matter what a woman looks like, if she's confident, she's sexy."

"One of my heroes is Barbie. She may not do anything, but she always looks great doing it."

"I don't think there's ever been anyone like me that's lasted. And I'm going to keep lasting."

---

Paris Hilton's feet are so big (size 11) that she has designers custom-make her shoes.

# AMERICAN INDIAN PROVERBS

*"The Great Spirit raised both the white man and the Indian. I think he raised the Indian first."* —Mahpiua Luta (Red Cloud), Oglala Lakota

Truth does not happen; it just is.
—Hopi

He who is present at a wrongdoing and does not lift a hand to prevent it is as guilty as the wrongdoers.
—Omaha

Before eating, always take a little time to thank the food.
—Arapaho

Only when the last tree has withered, and the last fish caught, and the last river been poisoned, will we realize we cannot eat money.
—Cree

After dark, all cats are leopards.
—Zuni

We should be as water, which is lower than all things yet stronger even than the rocks.
—Ogalala Sioux

The rain falls on the just and the unjust.
—Hopi

Those who have one foot in the canoe and one foot in the boat are going to fall into the river.
—Tuscarora

Thoughts are like arrows: once released, they strike their mark. Guard them well, or one day you may be your own victim.
—Navajo

See how the boy is with his sister and you can know how the man will be with your daughter.
—Plains Sioux

We stand somewhere between the mountain and the ant.
—Onondaga

Creation is ongoing.
—Lakota

What is life? It is the flash of a firefly in the night. It is the breath of a buffalo in the wintertime. It is the little shadow which runs across the grass and loses itself in the sunset.
—Blackfoot

# POLITICIANSPEAK

*Yes, these words actually came out of the mouths
of people in public office.*

"Everything has been said, but not everyone has said it yet."
—Rep. Morris Udall (D–AZ)

"Eight more days, and I can start telling the truth again."
—Sen. Chris Dodd (D–CT), eight days before an election

"I know you believe you understand what you think I said, but I am not sure you realize that what you heard is not what I meant."
—Alan Greenspan, before a Congressional committee

"If guns are outlawed, how can we shoot the liberals?"
—Mike Gunn, Mississippi state senator (R)

"Every American should have above average income, and my administration is going to see they get it."
—Bill Clinton

"We are not disorganized. We just have a kind of organization that transcends understanding."
—Jacques Barzaghi, campaign aide to Jerry Brown

"I'm all for Lawrence Welk. Lawrence Welk is a wonderful man. He used to be, or was, or, wherever he is now, bless him."
—George H. W. Bush

"You work three jobs? Uniquely American, isn't it? I mean, that is fantastic that you're doing that."
—George W. Bush, to a divorced mother of three

"*La Prensa* accused us of suppressing freedom of expression. This was a lie and we could not let them publish it."
—Nelba Blandon, Nicaraguan Interior Ministry Director of Censorship

"Well, I really think he shatters the myth of white supremacy once and for all."
—Rep. Charles Rangel, when asked what he thought of President George W. Bush

"I don't mind not being President. I just mind that someone else is."
—Sen. Ted Kennedy (D–MA)

# GOOD VS. EVIL

*It's a fight to the finish!*

"The line separating good and evil passes not through states, nor between classes nor between parties either—but right through the human heart."
—**Alexandr Solzhenitzyn**

"The devil never comes offering you something evil. The devil comes offering you a larger audience."
—**Murray Kempton**

"Evil always turns up in this world through some genius or other."
—**Denis Diderot**

"Because everyone knows that good is good, bad exists."
—**Lao Tzu**

"There are dark shadows on the earth, but its lights are stronger in the contrast."
—**Charles Dickens, *The Pickwick Papers***

"It is in the solitary mind and soul of the individual that the battle between good and evil is waged and ultimately won or lost."
—**M. Scott Peck**

"The wicked are wicked, no doubt, and they go astray and they fall, and they come by their desserts: but who can tell the mischief which the very virtuous do?"
—**William Makepeace Thackeray, *The Newcomes***

"Evil is not absolute, and good is often an occasion more than a condition."
—**Gilbert Parker**

"The sad truth is that most evil is done by people who never make up their minds to be good or evil."
—**Hannah Arendt**

"No one ever became extremely wicked suddenly."
—**Juvenal**

"Good has but one enemy, the evil; but the evil has two enemies, the good and itself."
—**Johannes von Muller**

"The belief in a supernatural source of evil is not necessary. Men alone are quite capable of every wickedness."
—**Joseph Conrad**

"Hate the sin, love the sinner." —**Mahatma Gandhi**

# WHAT'S SO FUNNY?

*Some serious thoughts from some funny folks on
what it takes to make people laugh.*

"Comedy is simply a funny
way of being serious."
　　　—Peter Ustinov

"The way I approach comedy
is to commit to everything as
if it's a dramatic role, meaning
you play it straight."
　　　—Will Ferrell

"Comedy is unusual people in
real situations; farce is real
people in unusual situations."
　　　—Chuck Jones

"The duty of comedy is to
correct men by amusing them."
　　　—Molière

"Humor is reason gone mad."
　　　—Groucho Marx

"If you find a funny story and
just tell it like it is, it's funny.
If you try to make a so-so story
funny by inserting your own
humor into it, it's tacky."
　　　—Uncle John

"Good humor is one of the
preservatives of our peace and
tranquility"
　　　—Thomas Jefferson

"God writes a lot of comedy.
The trouble is, He's stuck with
so many bad actors who don't
know how to play funny."
　　　—Garrison Keillor

"Humor is a rubber sword—
it allows you to make a point
without drawing blood."
　　　—Mary Hirsch

"The more you learn about
the world, the more opportunities there are to laugh at it."
　　　—Bill Nye

"All I need to make a comedy
is a park, a policeman, and a
pretty girl."
　　　—Charlie Chaplin

"You cannot be mad at
somebody who makes you
laugh, it's as simple as that."
　　　—Jay Leno

"Among those whom I like
or admire, I can find no
common denominator, but
among those whom I love,
I can: All of them make me
laugh."
　　　—W. H. Auden

"He deserves Paradise who makes his companions laugh." —The Koran

# HOKEY HOCKEY

*Professional hockey players are strange creatures*
*(but don't tell them that to their face).*

"I can wear my face shield one day, then not wear it the next day. It's like a pair of glasses, some days I wear it, some days I don't. I'm not wearing any underwear either. There is no reason."
—**Alexander Mogilny**

"I grabbed it and squeezed it back into place. It gave a little crunch and popped right in."
—**Jay Wells, on how he fixed his broken nose after being hit with a high stick**

"One was on the ice and we put that one back in. Another was up my nose and they had to pull it down."
—**Sami Kapanen, on finding his teeth after a collision**

"One road trip we were stuck on the runway for seven hours. The plane kept driving and driving until we arrived at the rink...and I realized we were on a bus."
—**Glenn Healy, on playing in the minor leagues**

"How would you like a job where, every time you make a mistake, a big red light goes on and 18,000 people boo?"
—**Jacques Plante, goalie**

"They do a lot of talking, but I'm not sure they actually understand each other."
—**Darren McCarty, on Vladimir Konstantinov and Claude Lemieux**

"I had to pinch myself seeing the grassy knoll and the book suppository building."
—**Trevor Linden, after visiting John F. Kennedy's assassination site in Dallas**

"There's a thousand theories, but theories are for scientists. We're too stupid for that. We've just got to get back to the X's and O's."
—**Mike Ricci, on a losing streak**

"I'd drink more."
—**Bobby Hull, when asked how he would handle his career all over again**

---

Title of the movie *Slapshot* in Japan: *Roughhouse Hockey Players Who Curse a Lot and Play Dirty.*

# STERN RANTS

*Howard Stern has been shocking the airwaves since the 1980s.*

"I'm sickened by all religions. Religion has divided people. I don't think there's any difference between the pope wearing a large hat and parading around with a smoking purse and an African painting his face white and praying to a rock."

"I believe in God—I'm afraid not to."

"Writing a book just might be the hardest thing I've ever done, besides trying to get laid in college."

"I like music that makes me want to kill myself."

"I'm for legalizing marijuana. Why pick on those drugs? Valium is legal. You just go to a doctor and get it and overdose on it—what's the difference? Prozac, all that stuff, so why not marijuana? Who cares? It's something that grows out of the ground—why not? Go smoke a head of cabbage. I don't care what you smoke."

"Standards have gone to an all-time low, and I'm here to represent them."

"You have to make a decision about what you want to do in life—because you can be gone tomorrow. Soon as you leave, you will be forgotten."

"The United States has too many freedoms."

"I still feel like I've got to prove something. There are a lot of people hoping I fail. But I like that. I need to be hated."

"I worry about going too far. I'm not going to do that, not because I'm a prude, but because it becomes mind-numbing and it doesn't make you laugh."

"I'm a supporter of *my* free speech."

"Waving a flag is easy. Paying your taxes is hard."

"The world scares me."

---

**Howard Stern practices Transcendental Meditation.**

# DON'T

*Don't even think of skipping this page.*

"Don't go around saying the world owes you a living. The world owes you nothing. It was here first."
—**Mark Twain**

"Don't misinform your Doctor nor your Lawyer."
—**Benjamin Franklin**

"Don't be afraid to see what you see."
—**Ronald Reagan**

"Don't go to the grave with life unused."
—**Bobby Bowden**

"Don't play dumb and don't play dirty."
—**Marv Levy**

"Don't think, just do."
—**Horace**

"Don't find fault, find a remedy."
—**Henry Ford**

"Don't ever prophesy; for if you prophesy wrong, nobody will forget it; and if you prophesy right, nobody will remember it."
—**Josh Billings**

"If you don't like something, change it. If you can't change it, change your attitude. Don't complain."
—**Maya Angelou**

"Don't take tomorrow to bed with you."
—**Norman Vincent Peale**

"Don't be afraid of mistakes. There aren't any."
—**Miles Davis**

"Don't fear failure so much that you refuse to try new things. The saddest summary of a life contains three descriptions: could have, might have, and should have."
—**Louis E. Boone**

"Don't divide the world into 'them' and 'us'."
—**Donald Rumsfeld**

"Don't do drugs, don't have unprotected sex, don't be violent. Leave that to me."
—**Eminem**

"Don't let one cloud obliterate the whole sky."
—**Anaïs Nin**

---

**Crosswalk misspelling:** The "Don't" in "DONT WALK" signs is missing the apostrophe.

"Don't be too timid and squeamish about your actions. All life is an experiment. The more experiments you make, the better."

—Ralph Waldo Emerson

# FOOD OF THE GODS

*Our salute to chocolate, invented by the Aztecs more than 2,500 years ago...and we never even got the chance to thank them.*

"Cocoa is the divine drink, which builds up resistance and fights fatigue. A cup of this precious drink permits a man to walk for a whole day without food."
—**Montezuma**

"Nothing can match chocolate for drama, dazzle, and deep-down allure."
—**Nancy Baggett**

"If in fact you are what you eat, I am a 114-pound bar of bittersweet chocolate."
—**Lora Brody**

"Some say women are addicted to chocolate. I say we're merely loyal."
—**Cathy Guisewite**

"Chocolate makes otherwise normal people melt into strange states of ecstasy."
—**John West**

"Always serve too much hot fudge sauce on hot fudge sundaes. It makes people overjoyed, and puts them in your debt."
—**Judith Olney**

"Chocolate is more than a food, but less than a drug."
—**R. J. Huxtable, pharmacologist**

"Caramels are a fad. Chocolate is a permanent thing."
—**Milton Hershey**

"There is a simple memory aid to determine whether it is the correct time to order chocolate dishes: Any month whose name contains the letter A, E, or U is the proper time for chocolate."
—**Sandra Boynton**

"There's no metaphysics on Earth like chocolates."
—**Fernando Pessoa**

"I am not strict vegan, because I'm a hedonist pig. If I see a big chocolate cake that is made with eggs, I'll have it."
—**Grace Slick**

"Strength is the capacity to break a chocolate bar into four pieces with your bare hands—and then eat just one of the pieces."
—**Judith Viorst**

# THE "DOCTOR" IS IN

*Real wisdom from fake doctors.*

"Before we start, did anyone lose a bunch of twenties rolled up in a rubber band? Because we found the rubber band."
—**Dr. Otto Octavius,** *Spider-man 2*

"Boundaries don't keep other people out. They fence you in. Life is messy; that's how we're made. So, you can waste your lives drawing lines. Or you can live your life crossing them."
—**Dr. Grey,** *Grey's Anatomy*

"The best rewards come when you risk the most. Sometimes the risk is its own reward."
—**Doogie Howser, M.D.**

"The secret of survival: Always expect the unexpected."
—**Doctor Who**

"Don't pick at your food. It won't heal."
—**Dr. Hawkeye Pierce,** *M\*A\*S\*H*

"I think as a matter of principle one should always try to avoid eating one's friends."
—**Dr. Doolittle,** on being a vegetarian

**Dr. Cameron:** Men should grow up.
**Dr. House:** Yeah. And dogs should stop licking themselves. It's not gonna happen.
—*House, M.D.*

"People who are popular when they're young often grow up to have very dull lives. People who are different go on to be successful and make wonderful contributions."
—**Dr. Quinn,** *Dr. Quinn Medicine Woman*

"Lady, people aren't chocolates. Do you know what they are mostly? Bastards. Bastard-coated bastards with bastard fillings. But I don't find them half as annoying as I find naive bubble-headed optimists who walk around vomiting sunshine."
—**Dr. Cox,** *Scrubs*

"The knee bone's connected to the…something! The something's connected to the…red thing! The red thing's connected to my…wristwatch! Uh-oh."
—**Dr. Nick Riviera,** *The Simpsons*

The word "electric" was first used in 1600 by William Gilbert, Queen Elizabeth I's doctor.

# WRITERS ON WRITING

*They sit in a room, usually alone, and bang away at a keyboard for hours on end, trying to communicate something to rest of us. Why do they do it? And how can they do it better? Read on.*

"Many people hear voices when no one is there. Some of them are called mad and are shut up in rooms where they stare at the walls all day. Others are called writers and they do pretty much the same thing."
—**Margaret Chittenden**

"The most difficult thing about being a poet is knowing what to do with the other 23 ½ hours of the day."
—**Max Beerbohm**

"Science fiction writers, I am sorry to say, really do not know anything. We can't talk about science, because our knowledge of it is limited and unofficial, and usually our fiction is dreadful."
—**Philip K. Dick**

"There is creative reading as well as creative writing."
—**Ralph Waldo Emerson**

"I love being a writer. What I can't stand is the paperwork."
—**Peter DeVries**

"The faster I write, the better my output. If I'm going slow, I'm in trouble. It means I'm pushing the words instead of being pulled by them."
—**Raymond Chandler**

"If you're going to have a complicated story, you must work to a map; otherwise you'll never make a map of it afterwards."
—**J. R. R. Tolkien**

"It's just a matter of writing the kind of book I enjoy reading. Something better be happening at the beginning, and then on every page after, or I get irritated."
—**Jonathan Franzen**

"Wanting to meet a writer because you like their books is like wanting to meet a duck because you like pâté."
—**Margaret Atwood**

"To me, the greatest pleasure of writing is not what it's about, but the music the words make."
—**Truman Capote**

# TALKIN' 'BOUT COUNTRY MUSIC

*Yee ha!*

"Country music has always been the best shrink that 15 bucks can buy."
—**Dierks Bentley**

"You got to have smelt a lot of mule manure before you can sing like a hillbilly."
—**Hank Williams**

"A lot of people say you've got all the loving in the world when you walk out onstage. But hell, that applause don't help you any when you're laying in that bed at night being totally ignored."
—**Patsy Cline**

"Country music is still your grandpa's music, but it's also your daughter's music."
—**Shania Twain**

"I don't know what it's like for a book writer or a doctor or a teacher as they work to get established in their jobs. But for a singer, you've got to continue to grow or else you're just like last night's cornbread—stale and dry."
—**Loretta Lynn**

"Country music is the people's music. It just speaks about real life and about truth and it tells things how they really are."
—**Faith Hill**

"Country music to me is heartfelt music that speaks to the common man. It is about real life stories with simple melodies. Country music speaks directly and simply about the highs and lows of life. Something that anyone can relate to."
—**George Jones**

"I just wake up and say, 'You're a bum—go do something worthwhile today.'"
—**Garth Brooks**

"After about three lessons, the voice teacher said, 'Don't take voice lessons, Johnny. Do it your way.'"
—**Johnny Cash**

"Ninety-nine percent of the world's lovers aren't with their first choice. That's what makes the jukebox play."
—**Willie Nelson**

# THE GOVERNATOR

*This page of Arnold Schwarzenegger quotes is even more fun if you read it out loud while doing your best Ahh-nold impression.*

"The public doesn't care about figures."
   **—asked if he would provide details on budget cuts**

"I have a love interest in every one of my films—a gun."

"My own dreams fortunately came true in this great state [California]. I became Mr. Universe. I became a successful businessman. And even though some people say I still speak with a slight accent, I have reached the top of the acting profession."

"I just use my muscles as a conversation piece, like someone walking a cheetah down 42nd Street."

"I will not change. Because if you are successful and you change, you are an idiot."

"I think that the only way that you really keep a secret is by not telling anyone."

"I have inhaled, exhaled everything."

"I am very fortunate to have some cameramen say of me, 'Arnold, you were born for the camera to love you.'"

"I told Warren if he mentions Prop. 13 one more time, he has to do 500 push-ups."

"I think that gay marriage should be between a man and a woman."

"It's simple, if it jiggles, it's fat."

"To those critics who are so pessimistic about our economy, I say, Don't be economic girlie men!"

"My body is like breakfast, lunch, and dinner. I don't think about it, I just have it."

"I can promise you that when I go to Sacramento, I will pump up Sacramento."

"For me life is continuously being hungry. The meaning of life is not simply to exist, to survive, but to move ahead, to go up, to achieve, to conquer."

# "I'D LIKE TO THANK…"

*About 99% of all acceptance speeches are boring.*
*These excerpts celebrate the other 1%.*

## PAUL WILLIAMS
**Award:** The 1977 Oscar for Best Song, "Evergreen." The five-foot-tall songwriter walked up to the podium…
**Excerpt:** "I was going to thank all of the little people, but then I remembered—I am the little people."

## JUSTIN TIMBERLAKE
**Award:** International Album award ("Justified") and the International Male Solo Artist award at the 2004 Brit Awards
**Excerpt:** "This is only my first record, so you guys stick with me. We've still got depression and drug addiction to go through."

## JIM CARREY
**Award:** Golden Globe for Best Actor in a Comedy, *Man on the Moon* (2000)
**Excerpt:** "I am now the Establishment I once rejected."

## SHIRLEY MACLAINE
**Award:** The Oscar for Best Actress in *Terms of Endearment* (1983)
**Excerpt:** "I deserve this."

## NICOLE KIDMAN
**Award:** A star on the Hollywood Walk of Fame
**Excerpt:** "I've never been so excited to have people walk all over me for the rest of my life!"

## DIANNE WIEST
**Award:** The Oscar for Best Supporting Actress for *Hannah and Her Sisters* (1987)
**Excerpt:** "Gee, this isn't like I imagined it would be in the bathtub."

## JESSICA YU

**Award:** The Oscar for Best Documentary Short Subject for *Breathing Lessons* (1997)

**Excerpt:** "What a thrill! You know you've entered new territory when you realize that your outfit cost more than your film."

## KANYE WEST

**Award:** At the 2006 MTV Europe Music Awards in Denmark, Kanye West was thrilled to win Best Hip-Hop Artist of the Year. But he was much less thrilled when his video, "Touch the Sky," lost the Best Video award to an obscure British band called Justice vs. Simian. As they were receiving their award, West crashed the stage.

**Tirade:** "F*ck this! 'Touch the Sky' cost a million dollars! Pamela Anderson was in it! I was jumping across canyons and sh*t! If I don't win, this awards show loses credibility!"

Backstage, West continued to fume: "I haven't seen their video. Possibly it could have been quite good, but no way better than 'Touch the Sky.' That is complete bullsh*t, I paid a million! Obviously it's not all about the money, but the response it got transcended everything, it really made great TV. It took a month to film. I stood on a mountain. I flew a helicopter over Vegas. I did it to be the king of all videos and I wanted to walk home with that award!"

## YOUR GOVERNMENT AT [DELETED]

"The [DELETED] is a key element of the World Military Command Control System (WWMCCS) warning network....[DELETED] currently consists of [DELETED] satellite; two [DELETED] satellites; an [DELETED] for [DELETED] from the [DELETED] satellite; a [DELETED] for [DELETED] and the [DELETED] satellites; and a [DELETED] which provides [DELETED] for the [DELETED]....Using these data, [DELETED] can be inferred."

> —**from an arms control impact statement submitted to Congress by the Pentagon**

# PAINTERS OF LIGHT

*Photographers come and go…but their images live on forever.*

"Sometimes I get to places just when God's ready to have somebody click the shutter."
—Ansel Adams

"In photography there is a reality so subtle that it becomes more real than reality."
—Alfred Stieglitz

"I really believe there are things nobody would see if I didn't photograph them."
—Diane Arbus

"The moment an emotion or fact is transformed into a photograph, it is no longer a fact but an opinion. All photographs are accurate, but none of them is the truth."
—Richard Avedon

"A camera, by arresting motion, gives permanence to the impermanent."
—Freeman Patterson

"In a photograph, a person's eyes tell much; sometimes they tell all."
—Alfred Eisenstaedt

"My own eyes are no more than scouts, for the camera's eye may entirely change my idea."
—Edward Weston

"Most things in life are moments of pleasure and a lifetime of embarrassment; photography is a moment of embarrassment and a lifetime of pleasure."
—Tony Benn

"The photographer's primary subject is light. What that light illuminates are just props."
—Jay Newman

"Best wide-angle lens? Two steps backward. Look for the 'ah-ha.'"
—Ernst Haas

"While there is perhaps a province in which the photograph can tell us nothing more than what we see with our own eyes, there is another in which it proves to us how little our eyes permit us to see."
—Dorothea Lange

# DIRECTORS ON DIRECTING

*Lights…Camera…Action!*

"The way to make a film is to begin with an earthquake and work up to a climax."
—**Cecil B. DeMille**

"The camera is so refined that it makes it possible for us to shed light on the human soul, to reveal it more brutally and thereby add to our knowledge new dimensions of the 'real.'"
—**Ingmar Bergman**

"There are no rules in film-making. Only sins. And the cardinal sin is dullness."
—**Frank Capra**

"The closer you get to the bull's-eye of how life is, the better."
—**Albert Brooks**

"As a director you get to create a world with its own special logic. You get to play God. It's like the view from Olympus."
—**Tim Burton**

"I don't like scary films. I wouldn't go see my films."
—**Brian De Palma**

"For every person who seeks fear in the real or personal sense, millions seek it vicariously, in the cinema. Give them the same pleasure they have when they wake up from a nightmare."
—**Alfred Hitchcock**

"My films are not the way I think things should be, but the way things are."
—**Robert Altman**

"The most memorable scenes in the best films are those which are built predominantly of images and music."
—**Stanley Kubrick**

"For a director, each work he completes is like a whole lifetime."
—**Akira Kurosawa**

"He doesn't really understand the nature of acting. He's like, 'It's right there on the page, it's right there. I wrote it, it's there, just do *that*.' But you can't just do *that* that easily."
—**Harrison Ford,
on George Lucas**

**"A wide screen just makes a bad film twice as bad."** —Samuel Goldwyn

# THAT'S LIFE

*Some thoughts on the grand adventure that is living.*

"The tragedy of life is not that it ends so soon, but that we wait so long to begin it."
—W. M. Lewis

"Life is a rollercoaster. Try to eat a light lunch."
—David A. Schmaltz

"Life is one grand, sweet song, so start the music."
—Ronald Reagan

"Life may have no meaning. Or even worse, it may have a meaning of which I disapprove."
—Ashleigh Brilliant

"Life is not so bad if you have plenty of luck, a good physique, and not too much imagination."
—Christopher Isherwood

"It is not length of life, but depth of life."
—Ralph Waldo Emerson

"When I hear somebody sigh that 'Life is hard,' I am always tempted to ask, 'Compared to what?'"
—Sidney J. Harris

"Life is 10 percent what happens to you and 90 percent how you respond to it."
—Lou Holtz

"Every action of our lives touches on some chord that will vibrate in eternity."
—Edwin Hubbel Chapin

"Life is a zoo in a jungle."
—Peter De Vries

"I came into this world black, naked and ugly. And no matter how much I accumulate, it's a short journey. I will go out of this world black, naked and ugly. So I enjoy life."
—Screamin' Jay Hawkins

"Life is a mirror, and what you see out there, you must first see inside of you."
—Wally "Famous" Amos

"Life is like stepping onto a boat which is about to sail out to sea and sink."
—Shunryu Suzuki-roshi

"The art of living is more like wrestling than dancing."
—Marcus Aurelius

"One-half the troubles of this life can be traced to saying yes too quickly and not saying no soon enough."
—Josh Billings

"I love living. I have some problems with my life, but living is the best thing they've come up with so far."
—Neil Simon

"Every man and woman is born into the world to do something unique and distinctive, and if he or she does not do it, it will never be done."
—Benjamin E. Mays

"Everything has been figured out, except how to live."
—Jean-Paul Sartre

"There ain't no answer. There ain't going to be any answer. There never has been an answer. That's the answer."
—Gertrude Stein

"We have to live our lives as if we are dying of a fatal disease. Because we are."
—Phineas Narco

"It's a very short trip. While alive, live."
—Malcolm Forbes

"The most unfair thing about life is the way it ends. I mean, life is tough. What do you get at the end of it? Death! What's that, a bonus? I think the life cycle is all backwards. You should die first, get it out of the way. Then you live in an old age home. You get kicked out when you're too young, you get a gold watch, you go to work. You work forty years until you're young enough to enjoy your retirement. You do drugs, alcohol, you party, you get ready for high school. You go to grade school, you become a kid, you play, you have no responsibilities, you become a little baby, you go back into the womb, you spend your last nine months floating...and you finish off as an orgasm."
—George Carlin

"Success and failure are equally disastrous." —Tennessee Williams

# ERMA BOMBECK

*Erma Bombeck (1927–96) was an author and nationally syndicated columnist whose humor and insights into modern home life helped make her one of the most quotable people in Bathroom Reader history.*

"In two decades I've lost a total of 789 pounds. I should be hanging from a charm bracelet."

"It goes without saying that you should never have more children than you have car windows."

"Marriage has no guarantees. If that's what you're looking for, go live with a car battery."

"It is not until you become a mother that your judgment slowly turns to compassion and understanding."

"When mothers talk about the depression of the empty nest, they're not mourning the passing of all those wet towels on the floor, or the music that numbs your teeth, or even the bottle of capless shampoo dribbling down the shower drain. They're upset because they've gone from supervisor of a child's life to a spectator. It's like being the vice president of the United States."

"Graduation day is tough for adults. They go to the ceremony as parents. They come home as contemporaries. After twenty-two years of child-raising, they are unemployed."

"My theory on housework is, if the item doesn't multiply, smell, catch fire, or block the refrigerator door, let it be. No one else cares. Why should you?"

"One thing they never tell you about child-raising is that for the rest of your life, at the drop of a hat, you are expected to know your child's name and how old he or she is."

"In general, my children refuse to eat anything that hasn't danced on television."

"I haven't trusted polls since I read that 62% of women had affairs during their lunch hour. I've never met a woman in my life who would give up lunch for sex."

# EPITAPHS

*Tombstone inscriptions: Some are homey, some are philosophical…
and some kind of make you scratch your head.*

Liberty, Humanity, Justice,
Equality
—**Susan B. Anthony**

So we beat on, boats against
the current, borne back
ceaselessly into the past
—**F. Scott & Zelda Fitzgerald**

Beloved Father
—**Bela Lugosi**

Everybody Loves Somebody
Sometime
—**Dean Martin**

Workers of all lands unite.
The philosophers have only
interpreted the world in
various ways; the point is
to change it.
—**Karl Marx**

Nothing of him that doth fade
But doth suffer a sea-change
Into something rich
and strange
—**Percy Bysshe Shelley**

I am ready to meet my Maker.
Whether my Maker is prepared
for the great ordeal of meeting
me is another matter.
—**Winston Churchill**

The Cowboy's Prayer
Oh Lord, I reckon I'm not
much just by myself. I fail to
do a lot of things I ought to
do. But Lord, when trails are
steep and passes high, Help
me to ride it straight the
whole way through. And
when in the falling dusk I
get the final call, I do not
care how many flowers they
send— Above all else the
happiest trail would be for
You to say to me, "Let's
ride, My friend."
Amen
—**Roy Rogers**

In loving memory from the
Family
—**Benjamin "Bugsy" Siegel**

*kata ton daimona eay toy*
{True to his own spirit.}
—**Jim Morrison**

Cast a cold eye  On life, on
death  Horseman, pass by!
—**William Butler Yeats**

Murdered by a traitor and a
coward whose name is not
worthy to appear here.
—**Jesse James**

# PUNK ROCK!

*The anti-music of the 1970s and '80s has been sliced, diced, and dissected by critics and fans. But can anybody really explain it?*

"You just pick a chord, go twang, and you've got music."
—**Sid Vicious, Sex Pistols**

"You can't consciously create something that's important. It's a combination of chemistry, conditions, the environment, everything."
—**Siouxsie Sioux, Siouxsie and the Banshees**

"When punk rock came along, the one thing you were not supposed to be was musical."
—**Nick Lowe**

"I like music that's offensive. I like it to sound like nails on a blackboard, to get me wild."
—**Iggy Pop**

"We didn't sell a lot of records, but somehow we left an impression."
—**Johnny Ramone**

"Punk is saying, doing, and playing what you want. In Webster's, 'nirvana' means freedom from pain, suffering, and the external world, and that's my definition of punk rock."
—**Kurt Cobain, Nirvana**

"I think punk rock, especially for me, was a big middle finger to talent."
—**Mike Watt, the Minutemen**

"Punk isn't dead. It will only die when corporations can exploit and mass produce it."
—**Jello Biafra, Dead Kennedys**

"A guy walks up to me and asks 'What's punk?' So I kick over a garbage can and say 'That's punk!' So he kicks over a garbage can and says 'That's punk?' and I say 'No, that's trendy."
—**Billie Joe Armstrong, Green Day**

"Punk is defined by an attitude rather than a musical style."
—**David Byrne**

"Sometimes the most positive thing you can be in a boring society is absolutely negative."
—**Johnny Rotten, Sex Pistols**

"I would say that punk rock has non-terminal cancer. It's got a lot of growths on it, but it's not gonna die from it."
—**Mike Burkett, NOFX**

# INDIANA SOLO

*Harrison Ford is one of the most famous actors of our time. He's pretty low-key, but he's said a few things about movies, his craft, his politics, and how to stay happy.*

"At my first screen test, the studio guy told me, 'Kid, you have no future in this business.' I said, 'Why?' He said, 'When Tony Curtis first walked onscreen carrying a bag of groceries—a bag of groceries!—you took one look at him and said, "THAT'S a movie star!"' I said, 'Weren't you supposed to say, "That's a grocery delivery boy"?'"

"I used to shake my head, as in, 'No, I just look like him.' But that's not fair. So I said to those little old ladies at Trenton airport, 'Yes, I am Harrison Ford.' And they still didn't believe it was me."

"I grew up in the Midwest. You don't ask what a person's religion is, you don't ask what their politics are, you don't ask how much money they make, and I pretty much still have that attitude about it. It's none of anybody's business and I don't advantage anyone by telling them what my personal politics are."

"Being happy is something I had to learn. I often surprise myself by saying, 'Wow, this is it. I guess I'm happy. I got a home I love. A career that I love. I'm even feeling more and more at peace with myself.' If there's something else to happiness, let me know."

"I don't think I've mastered anything. I'm still wrestling with the same frustrations, the same issues, the same problems as I always did. That's what life is like."

"I think American films right now are suffering from an excess of scale. Lots of movies we're seeing now are more akin to video games than stories about relationships."

"I'm like a fireman. When I go out on a call, I want to put out a big fire; I don't want to put out a fire in a dumpster."
**—on why he likes starring in blockbuster films**

In 1971 Harrison Ford was offered the part of Mike "Meathead" Stivic on *All in the Family*...

"It's a little-known fact, but I wanted Han Solo to die at the end of *Return of the Jedi*. I thought it would give more weight and resonance. But George Lucas didn't want me killed by those teddy-bear guys."

"If real emotion is available, use it, otherwise I follow what I think is an Alcoholics Anonymous rule: 'Fake it 'til you make it.' Emotions are an interesting language. Sometimes they sneak up on you when you're not expecting, when you are available to it."

"I had no expectation of the level of adulation that would come my way. I just wanted to make a living with a regular role in a television series."

"What does that mean when a director says 'trust me'? Does that mean I should obviate all of my experience? Should I replace a certain knowledge with belief? Where does that get you? I have had experience in my life. I am 63 years old. Why should I be trusting a director?"

"Whoever had the bright idea of putting Indiana Jones in a leather jacket and a fedora in the jungle ought to be dragged into the street and shot."

"Han Solo is not a cardboard character to me at all. I never thought of the character as having only two dimensions until the critics said so. And they're wrong. The third dimension is me."

"I think that has to be the biggest mistake of my career. I blame my agent."

**—Burt Reynolds, on not being chosen to play Han Solo in *Star Wars***

...but turned it down because he felt Archie Bunker was too racist. (Rob Reiner got the part.)

# SHAKESPEAREAN WISDOM

*All's well that's said well.*

"Love sought is good, but given unsought is better."
—*Twelfth Night*

"We know what we are, but know not what we may become."
—*Hamlet*

"Our doubts are traitors, and make us lose the good we oft might win, by fearing to attempt."
—*Measure for Measure*

"Have more than thou showest, speak less than thou knowest, lend less than thou owest."
—*King Lear*

"The common curse of mankind—folly and ignorance."
—*Troilus and Cressida*

"Some rise by sin, and some by virtue fall."
—*Measure for Measure*

"The worst is not/ So long as we can say, 'This is the worst.'"
—*King Lear*

"Virtue is bold, and goodness never fearful."
—*Measure for Measure*

"Speak low if you speak love."
—*Much Ado About Nothing*

"How poor are they that have not patience."
—*Othello*

"'Tis better to be brief than tedious."
—*Richard III*

"Love all, trust few. Do wrong to none."
—*All's Well That Ends Well*

"We are such stuff as dreams are made on, rounded with a little sleep."
—*The Tempest*

"Everyone can master a grief but he that has it."
—*Much Ado About Nothing*

"Cowards die many times before their deaths; The valiant never taste of death but once."
—*Julius Caesar*

# UNCLE JOHN'S QUOTATIONARY

*Here's Part 4 of our quotation dictionary.*
*(Part 3 begins on page 103.)*

**IDEA:** a point of departure and no more. As soon as you elaborate it, it becomes transformed by thought. (Pablo Picasso)

**IMPOSSIBLE:** a word to be found only in the dictionary of fools. (Napoleon Bonaparte)

**IMPRESSIONISM:** the newspaper of the soul. (Henri Matisse)

**INDIFFERENCE:** the only sure defense. (Jody Powell)

**INFLUENCE:** what you think you have until you try to use it. (Joan Welsh)

**INSANITY:** knowing that what you're doing is completely idiotic, but still, somehow, you just can't stop it. (Elizabeth Wurtzel)

**INSOMNIA:** a gross feeder. It will nourish itself on any kind of thinking, including thinking about not thinking. (Clifton Fadiman)

**INSPIRATION:** a peculiar effect of divine flatulence emitted by the Holy Spirit which hisses into the ears of a few chosen of God. (Voltaire)

**INSULTS:** the arguments employed by those who are in the wrong. (Jean-Jacques Rousseau)

**INTELLECTUAL:** someone who has found something more interesting than sex. (Edgar Wallace)

**IRONY:** a state of affairs that is the reverse of what was to be expected; a result opposite to and in mockery of the appropriate result. For instance: A diabetic, on his way to buy insulin, is killed by a runaway truck. He is the victim of an accident. If the truck was delivering sugar, he is the victim of an oddly poetic coincidence. But if the truck was delivering insulin, ah! Then he is the victim of an irony. (George Carlin)

**JAZZ MUSICIAN:** a juggler who uses harmonies instead of oranges. (Benny Green)

**JEALOUSY:** the tribute mediocrity pays to genius. (Fulton J. Sheen)

**JOURNALISM:** a profession whose business it is to explain to others what it personally does not understand. (Lord Northcliffe)

**JUGGLING:** the art of controlling patterns in time and space. (Ronald Graham)

**JURY:** a group of 12 people, who, having lied to the judge about their health, hearing, and business engagements, have failed to fool him. (H. L. Mencken)

**JUSTICE:** truth in action. (Benjamin Disraeli)

**KANSAS:** a state of mind, a neurotic condition, a psychological phase, a symptom, indeed, something undreamed of in your philosophy, an inferiority complex against the tricks and manners of plutocracy—social, political and economic. (William Allen White)

**KIDS:** ones who dance before they learn there is anything that isn't music. (William Stafford)

**KILT:** a costume sometimes worn by Scotsmen in America and Americans in Scotland. (Ambrose Bierce)

**KISS:** a lovely trick designed by nature to stop speech when words become superfluous. (Ingrid Bergman)

**KISSING:** a means of getting two people so close together that they can't see anything wrong with each other. (Rene Yasenek)

**KLEENEX:** what men should be like; soft, strong, and disposable. (Cher)

**KLEPTOMANIAC:** A rich thief. (Ambrose Bierce)

**KNOWLEDGE:** knowing that we cannot know. (Ralph Waldo Emerson)

*For more, see page 203.*

# THE VILLAINS SPEAK

*Hollywood bad guys (and gals) are often the
most interesting characters in the movies.*

"This "Superman" is nothing of the kind—I've discovered his weakness already. He cares."
　　—General Zod (Terence Stamp), *Superman II*

"I'm a killer. A murdering bastard, you know that. And there are consequences to breaking the heart of a murdering bastard."
　　—Bill (David Carradine) *Kill Bill, Vol. 2*

"You want this, don't you? The hate is swelling in you now. Take your Jedi weapon. Use it. I am unarmed. Strike me down with it! Give in to your anger. With each passing moment you make yourself more my servant."
　　—The Emperor (Ian McDiarmid) *Return of the Jedi*

"Pop quiz, hotshot: There's a bomb on a bus. Once the bus goes 50 miles an hour, the bomb is armed. If it drops below 50, it blows up. What do you do? What do you do?"
　　—Howard Payne (Dennis Hopper) *Speed*

Holly McClane: After all your posturing, all your speeches, you're nothing but a common thief.
Hans Gruber: I am an exceptional thief, Mrs. McClane. And since I'm moving up to kidnapping, you should be more polite.
　　—Bonnie Bedelia and Alan Rickman, *Die Hard*

"Free will. It's like butterfly wings: once touched, they never get off the ground. No, I only set the stage; you pull your own strings."
　　—John Milton (Al Pacino) *The Devil's Advocate*

Max: You killed him!
Vincent: No, I shot him. The bullets and the fall killed him.
　　—Jamie Foxx and Tom Cruise, *Collateral*

"Say a word about this over the radio, and the next wings you see will belong to the flies buzzing over your rotting corpse!"
　　—Cyrus Grissom (John Malkovich) *Con Air*

Vlad the Impaler, the inspiration for Dracula, studied for the priesthood.

# DAVID LETTERMAN

*The funniest former Indiana weatherman on late-night TV.*

"Everyone has a purpose in life. Perhaps yours is watching television."

"Charlton Heston admitted he had a drinking problem, and I said to myself, 'Thank God this guy doesn't own any guns!'"

"Everyone has this sense of togetherness right now. For example, one guy on the subway today, he wanted to share my pants."

"Today is Friday the 13th. Down in Washington, a confused George W. Bush lit a menorah."

"Today is Earth Day, or, as the Bush administration calls it, Monday."

"I had no idea this thing was televised. Boy, is my face red."

"That National Rifle Association theme restaurant in Times Square is offering 10% off your steak if you can locate the exit wound. The other special is Chicken on a Deathbed of Rice."

"Thanksgiving is the day when…my mom, after six Bloody Marys, looks at the turkey and goes: 'Here kitty, kitty.'"

"You can tell it's the Christmas season. Stores are selling off their expired milk as eggnog."

"The National Council on Psychic Research has officially designated this to be true: The experience of changing planes in New York now counts as a near-death experience."

"You can e-mail me, but I prefer letters that come through conventional mail. I like letters that have been licked by strangers."

"7-Eleven now has edible straws to go with their Slurpees. If they want something edible, why not start with the hot dogs?"

"I was in the polling place today, and honest to God, I see a guy stick his head out of the curtains. And he's holding a pair of pants and he says, 'Can I get these in a 46?'"

Coincidence? Indiana ranks #1 in both "danger from tornadoes" and mobile-home sales.

# RHYME TYME

*We're very proud of this page we've done,*
*'cause quotes that rhyme are really fun!*

"Early to bed, early to rise,
work like hell and advertise."
——**Laurence J. Peter**

"Everything comes too late
for those who only wait."
——**Elbert Hubbard**

"Good, better, best.
Never let it rest.
Until your good is better
and your better is your best."
——**Tim Duncan**

"I had the blues
because I had no shoes
until upon the street,
I met a man who had no feet."
——**Denis Waitley**

"If the ride is fly,
then you must buy!"
——**Snoop Dogg**

"If a nation expects
to be ignorant and free,
it expects what never was
and never shall be."
——**Thomas Jefferson**

"I'd rather drink a beer
than win 'Father of the Year.'"
——**Homer Simpson**

"Like a death at a birthday
party, you ruin all the fun.
Like a sucked and spat-out
Smartie, you're no use to
anyone."
——**John Cooper Clarke**

"Whoever hopes
a faultless tax to see,
hopes what ne'er was, is not,
and ne'er shall be."
——**Alexander Pope**

"Love is lost
in men's capricious minds,
but in women's,
it fills all the room it finds."
——**John Crowne**

"I didn't do the crime.
I'm not going to pay them a
dime."
——**O. J. Simpson**

"I would rather get spanked
by my poor old daddy
than kill some dude
in a damn rice paddy."
——**Muhammad Ali**

"Forty for you, sixty for me.
And equal partners we will be."
——**Joan Rivers**

Vizzini: "No more rhymes, I mean it!" Fezzik: "Anybody want a peanut?" —*The Princess Bride*

"Anything white is sweet;
anything brown is meat;
anything grey, don't eat."
—Stephen Fry,
on airplane food

"Be kind, O Bacchus,
take this empty pot
offered to thee
by Xenophon, the sot,
Who, giving this,
gives all that he has got!"
—Eratosthenes

"Our blood will turn from red
to blue, although our money is
but new."
—Walter Annenberg

"Too much truth is uncouth."
—Franklin P. Adams

"Every time you win, it
diminishes the fear a little bit.
You never really cancel the
fear of losing; you keep chal-
lenging it."
—Arthur Ashe

"What you believe,
remember, you can achieve."
—Mary Kay Ash

"You only require two things
in life: your sanity and your
wife."
—Tony Blair

"But who forgives
the senior's ceaseless verse,
Whose hairs grow hoary
as his rhymes grow worse?"
—Lord Byron

## HOMER GETS THE BAD NEWS

**Dr. Hibbert:** Now, a little death anxiety is normal. You can expect to go through five stages. The first is denial.

**Homer:** No way! Because I'm not dying!

**Dr. Hibbert:** The second is anger.

**Homer:** Why you little...!

**Dr. Hibbert:** After that comes fear.

**Homer:** What's after fear?! What's after fear?!

**Dr. Hibbert:** Bargaining.

**Homer:** Doc, you gotta get me out of this! I'll make it worth your while!

**Dr. Hibbert:** Finally, accept-ance.

**Homer:** Well, we all gotta go sometime.

**Dr. Hibbert:** Mr. Simpson, your progress astounds me.

# MONEY TALKS

*And we always listen.*

"I really don't like talking about money. All I can say is that the Good Lord must have wanted me to have it."
—**Larry Bird**

"I get so tired listening to one million dollars here, one million dollars there, it's so petty."
—**Imelda Marcos**

"I, Joan Crawford, believe in the dollar. Everything I earn, I spend."
—**Joan Crawford**

"I'd asked around 10 or 15 people for suggestions. Finally one lady friend asked the right question. 'Well what do you love most?' That's how I started painting money."
—**Andy Warhol**

"We can tell our values by looking at our checkbook stubs."
—**Gloria Steinem**

"What difference does it make how much you have? What you do not have amounts to much more."
—**Seneca**

"I know of nothing more despicable and pathetic than a man who devotes all of the hours of the waking day to the making of money for money's sake."
—**John D. Rockefeller**

"You aren't wealthy until you have something money can't buy.
—**Garth Brooks**

"Life is a game. Money is how we keep score."
—**Ted Turner**

"The person who does not know how to live while they are making a living is a poorer person after their wealth is won than when they started."
—**Josiah Gilbert Holland**

"Riches do not consist in the possession of treasures, but in the use made of them."
—**Napoleon Bonaparte**

"Money never made a man happy yet, nor will it. The more a man has, the more he wants. Instead of filling a vacuum, it makes one."
—**Benjamin Franklin**

# "BREAKING UP...

*...is hard to do."* —*Neil Sedaka*

"Love knows not its own depth until the hour of separation."
—**Khalil Gibran**

"Breaking up is like trying to tip over a Coke machine. You can't do it in one push. You have to rock it back and forth a couple of times."
—**Jerry Seinfeld**

"The hottest love has the coldest end."
—**Socrates**

"Take me or leave me, or, as is the usual order of things, both."
—**Dorothy Parker**

"Love begins with a smile, grows with a kiss, and ends with a teardrop."
—**Anonymous**

"Love is unconditional, relationships are not."
—**Grant Gudmundson**

"What is broken is broken, and I'd rather remember it as it was at its best than mend it and see the broken places as long as I lived."
—**Margaret Mitchell**

"Sometimes, when one person is missing, the whole world seems depopulated."
—**Alphonse de Lamartine**

"The best way to mend a broken heart is time and girlfriends."
—**Gwyneth Paltrow**

"All discarded lovers should be given a second chance, but with somebody else."
—**Mae West**

"Nothing takes the taste out of peanut butter quite like unrequited love."
—**Charlie Brown**

"Love is never lost. If not reciprocated, it will flow back and purify the heart."
—**Washington Irving**

"Let no one who loves be unhappy...even love unreturned has its rainbow."
—**J. M. Barrie**

"I thought when love for you died, I should die. It's dead. Alone, most strangely, I live on."
—**Rupert Brooke**

"Life is a relationship between molecules." —**Linus Pauling**

# REAGAN'S WISDOM

*They didn't call Ronald Reagan (1911–2004)*
*"The Great Communicator" for nothing...*

"They say the world has become too complex for simple answers. They are wrong."

"We must reject the idea that every time a law is broken, society is guilty rather than the lawbreaker. It is time to restore the American precept that each individual is accountable for his actions."

"A people free to choose will always choose peace."

"Freedom must be fought for, protected, and handed on for the next generation to do the same, or one day we will spend our sunset years telling our children and our children's children what it was once like in the United States where men were free."

"Peace is not the absence of conflict, it is the ability to handle conflict by peaceful means."

"We can't help everyone, but everyone can help someone."

"Concentrated power has always been the enemy of liberty."

"To sit back hoping that someday, some way, someone will make things right is to go on feeding the crocodile, hoping he will eat you last— but eat you he will."

"Above all, we must realize that no arsenal, or no weapon in the arsenals of the world, is so formidable as the will and moral courage of free men and women. It is a weapon our adversaries in today's world do not have."

"If you're afraid of the future, then get out of the way, stand aside. The people of this country are ready to move again."

"I never thought it was my style or the words I used that made a difference: It was the content. I wasn't a great communicator; I communicated great things."

# REAGAN'S WISDOM?

*...but he still had a communicator malfunction now and then.*

"Well, I learned a lot—I went down to Latin America to find out from them and their views. You'd be surprised. They're all individual countries."

"You know, if I listened to Michael Dukakis long enough, I would be convinced that people are homeless and going without food and medical attention and that we've got to do something about the unemployed."

"How are you, Mr. Mayor? I'm glad to meet you. How are things in your city?"
**—to Samuel Pierce, Reagan's secretary of Housing and Urban Development, during a White House reception for mayors**

"Approximately 80% of our air pollution stems from hydrocarbons released by vegetation, so let's not go overboard in setting tough emission standards from man-made sources."

"Facts are stupid things."

"If you've seen one redwood, you've seen them all."

**Ronald Reagan:** My name is Ronald Reagan. What's yours?
**Mike Reagan:** I'm your son.
**Ronald Reagan:** Oh, I didn't recognize you.
**—after delivering a commencement address at Mike's prep school**

"The best minds are not in government. If any were, business would hire them away."

"Why should we subsidize intellectual curiosity?"

"I never drink coffee at lunch. I find it keeps me awake for the afternoon."

"We are trying to get unemployment to go up, and I think we're going to succeed."

"It's silly talking about how many years we will have to spend in the jungles of Vietnam when we could pave the whole country and put parking stripes on it and still be home by Christmas."

"I favor the Civil Rights Act of 1964, and it must be enforced at gunpoint if necessary."

# BABY BOOMERS

*Why is it that most of the quotes from and about baby boomers seem to be long-winded? Hmm...*

"Maybe it isn't surprising that the first big menopause books to greet the baby boomers are so morbid and alarmist. A book titled *Menopause: No Big Deal* might better describe the experience of a generation of busy, high-achieving women. But it probably wouldn't leap off the shelves."
—**Barbara Ehrenreich**

"If we want an image to sum up the spirit of the age, it would be this: a middle-aged man playing air guitar."
—**Michael Bywater**

"As an official member of the boomer generation, I do not believe it was intended for us to die. We were special right from the get-go; dying wasn't part of our script."
—**Dr. Terry Grossman**

"Surveyed baby boomers were asked when they believe old age begins. The most common answer was 85—three years after the average American can expect to be dead and buried."
—**Kay S. Hymowitz**

"Boomers always struck me as very self-centered and self-important, because there are so many of us. We're always in the middle of the next fun moment at some everlasting party, unable to defer the gratification to tackle the long-term problems."
—**Michael Franc**

"Gilding the lily—casting the everyday and unexceptional in the most grandiose terms—has always been a weakness of Boomers, who sometimes compare Captain Marvel comic books to the Sistine Chapel or call Yoko Ono an artist."
—**Andrew Ferguson**

"We did change the world, but we stopped short. We joined the Democrats and organized religion, got paid off and ripped off, and became a part of the status quo—a by-line in history. We should have held out, changed the agenda, and started our own political party."
—**Winston Burton**

# THE COMPUTER AGE

*This page is dedicated to Uncle John. If he had his way, we'd still be using typewriters to punch out Bathroom Readers.*

"After growing wildly for years, the field of computing appears to be reaching its infancy."
—**John Pierce**

"The thing with high tech is that you always end up using scissors."
—**David Hockney**

"Computers are like Old Testament gods; lots of rules and no mercy."
—**Joseph Campbell**

"Programming today is a race between software engineers striving to build bigger and better idiot-proof programs, and the universe trying to produce bigger and better idiots. So far, the universe is winning."
—**Rich Cook**

"Think? Why think? We have computers to do that for us."
—**Jean Rostand**

"Humanity is acquiring all the right technology for all the wrong reasons."
—**R. Buckminster Fuller**

"One of the problems the Internet has introduced is that in the electronic village all the village idiots have Internet access."
—**Peter Nelson**

"Computers make it easier to do a lot of things, but most of the things they make it easier to do don't need to be done."
—**Andy Rooney**

"Any sufficiently advanced technology is indistinguishable from magic."
—**Arthur C. Clarke**

"The real danger is not that computers will begin to think like men, but that men will begin to think like computers."
—**Sydney J. Harris**

"There is unexpected beauty hidden everywhere in this world—one just has to be open to seeing it. Remember that the next time you sneeze on your monitor."
—**Nathan Walton**

"The Internet is not something you just dump something on. It's not a truck. It's a series of tubes. If you don't understand, those tubes can be filled and if they are filled, when you put your message in, it gets in line and it's going to be delayed by anyone that puts into that tube enormous amounts of material."

—Sen. Ted Stevens (R–AK)

# KURT VONNEGUT

*Here are some thoughts from a man who dropped out of college because his professor told him that his stories weren't any good. So what did Vonnegut do? He went on to be one of the 20th century's most celebrated novelists.*

"I want to stay as close to the edge as I can without going over. Out on the edge you see all kinds of things you can't see from the center."

"People have to talk about something just to keep their voiceboxes in working order in case there's ever anything really meaningful to say."

"Just because some of us can read and write and do a little math, that doesn't mean we deserve to conquer the universe."

"I'd rather have written one episode of *Cheers* than anything I've written."

"We're terrible animals. I think that the Earth's immune system is trying to get rid of us, as well it should."

"I was taught that the human brain was the crowning glory of evolution so far, but I think it's a very poor scheme for survival."

"True terror is to wake up one morning and discover that your high school class is running the country."

"If you really want to disappoint your parents, and don't have the heart to be gay, go into the arts."

"Life is no way to treat an animal, not even a mouse."

"If you can do a half-assed job of anything, you're a one-eyed man in a kingdom of the blind."

"I still believe that peace and happiness can be worked out some way. I am a fool."

"Beware of the man who works hard to learn something, learns it, and finds himself no wiser than before."

"Laughter and tears are both responses to frustration and exhaustion. I myself prefer to laugh, since there is less cleaning up to do afterward."

"We are here on Earth to fart around. Don't let anybody tell you different." —Kurt Vonnegut

# THE COACH'S LAMENT

*Being head coach of a prominent sports team is a tough job.*
*Win or lose, you have to stand in front of a gaggle of reporters*
*after the game and explain what happened out there.*

"We can't run. We can't pass. We can't stop the run. We can't stop the pass. We can't kick. Other than that, we're just not a very good football team right now."
—**Bruce Coslet,**
**Cincinnati Bengals**

"I don't think any coach really knows where they are on opening day. It's kind of like the story about the guy falling off the building and he's waving to everybody on the way down thinking everything is great until he hits the pavement."
—**Bill Belichick,**
**New England Patriots**

"It's a terrible thing to have to tell your fans that their team won't win it this year. But it's better than lying to them."
—**Sparky Anderson,**
**Detroit Tigers**

"On this team, we're all united in a common goal: to keep my job."
—**Lou Holtz, Notre Dame**

"They say you're not a coach in the league 'til you've been fired. I must be getting pretty good."
—**Terry Simpson, after being**
**fired from his third NHL team**

"If you make every game a life-and-death proposition, you're going to have problems. For one thing, you'll be dead a lot."
—**Dean Smith,**
**North Carolina Tarheels**

"The man who complains about the way the ball bounces is likely the one who dropped it."
—**Lou Holtz, Notre Dame**

"No matter how much you've won, no matter how many games, no matter how many championships, no matter how many Super Bowls, you're not winning now, so you stink."
—**Bill Parcells,**
**Dallas Cowboys**

"Can't anybody here play this game?"
—**Casey Stengel,**
**baseball manager**

---

**"All managers are losers...the most expendable pieces of furniture on Earth." —Ted Williams**

# A NUMBERS GAME

*We admit it: Numbers are not our strong suit here at
the BRI. We leave that to the experts: bank tellers,
professional poker players, and these people.*

"The concept of numbers is
the obvious distinction
between beast and man.
Thanks to numbers, the cry
becomes a song, noise acquires
rhythm, the spring is transformed into a dance, force
becomes dynamic, and out-
lines become figures."
—Joseph-Marie de Maistre

"The generation of random
numbers is too important to
be left to chance."
—Robert Coveyou

"If you're a good numbers
person, you're a bad language
person."
—Frank Luntz

"The creator of the universe
works in mysterious ways.
But He uses a base ten count-
ing system and likes round
numbers."
—Scott Adams

"Although he may not always
recognize his bondage, modern
man lives under a tyranny of
numbers."
—Nicholas Eberstadt

"I know that 2 and 2 make
4—and should be glad to
prove it too if I could—
though I must say if by any
sort of process I could convert
2 and 2 into 5 it would give
me much greater pleasure."
—Lord Byron

"If people do not believe that
mathematics is simple, it is
only because they do not realize how complicated life is."
—John Louis von Neumann

"Mathematics is the supreme
judge; from its decisions there
is no appeal."
—Tobias Dantzig

"Pure mathematics is the
poetry of logical ideas."
—Albert Einstein

"The laws of nature are but
the mathematical thoughts
of God."
—Euclid

"The hardest arithmetic to
master is that which enables
us to count our blessings."
—Eric Hoffer

"It is known that there are an infinite number of worlds, simply because there is an infinite amount of space for them to be in. However, not every one of them is inhabited. Any finite number divided by infinity is as near nothing as makes no odds, so the average population of all the planets in the Universe can be said to be zero. From this it follows that the population of the whole Universe is also zero, and that any people you may meet from time to time are merely products of a deranged imagination."

—Douglas Adams

# CLASSICAL GAS

*They were the rock stars of their time—adored by some, loathed by others. But the fact that we still know their names today means their music lived on.*

"I never hear in my imagination the parts successively, I hear them all at once. What a delight this is! All this inventing, this producing, takes place in a pleasing, lively dream."
—Wolfgang Amadeus Mozart

"What is best in music is not to be found in the notes."
—Gustav Mahler

"Music is the one incorporeal entrance into the higher world of knowledge which comprehends mankind but which mankind cannot comprehend."
—Ludwig van Beethoven

"Any composer who is gloriously conscious that he is a composer must believe that he receives his inspiration from a source higher than himself."
—John Philip Sousa

"A creative artist works on his next composition because he is not satisfied with his previous one."
—Dmitri Shostakovich

"True music must repeat the thought and inspirations of the people and the time. My people are Americans and my time is today."
—George Gershwin

"The twelve notes in each octave and the variety of rhythm offer me opportunities that all of human genius will never exhaust."
—Igor Stravinsky

"Music embodies feeling without forcing it to contend and combine with thought, as it is forced in most arts and especially in the art of words."
—Franz Liszt

"One supreme fact which I have discovered is that it is not willpower, but imagination that creates. Imagination creates reality."
—Richard Wagner

"It is not hard to compose, but what is fabulously hard is to leave the superfluous notes under the table."
—Johannes Brahms

---

When Beethoven died in 1827, more than 20,000 people attended his funeral.

# THE 9/11 "CONSPIRACY"

*The tragic events of September 11, 2001, shook the nation. The culprits were the terrorist organization al-Qaeda, headed by Osama Bin Laden. As with most major events, conspiracy theorists have come out and made extraordinary claims.*

"There's something wrong here. The American people, the families, the country and the Congress need to know the truth, the whole truth, the complete truth. And so far we haven't gotten it…Somebody's got to connect the dots and answer the questions. If the 9/11 Commission won't do it, then Congress has to do it."
—**Rep. Curt Weldon**

"President Kennedy, known for separating his life into compartments, would enclose words and numbers inside circles and boxes. Events long after his death give one doodle an unintended chill: A small circle with the numbers '9-11' contained within. Just to the lower left on the page, the word 'conspiracy' is underlined."
—**Hillel Italie,**
***Associated Press***

"Were there contacts over time between Iraq and al-Qaeda? Yes, there were efforts made to communicate. We found no evidence of collabo-ration in any effort to mount any kind of operation against the United States' interests."
—**Richard Ben-Veniste,**
**9/11 Commission**

"Bin Laden was completely protected by the oil companies in this country who told President Bush not to go after him because it would p*ss off the Saudis."
—**Oliver Stone**

"The current junta in charge of our affairs, one not legally elected, but put in charge of us by the Supreme Court in the interests of the oil and gas and defense lobbies, have used first Oklahoma City and now September 11 to further erode things."
—**Gore Vidal**

"Bin Laden, deeply misguided as he may be, is no more responsible for what happened this week than I am. His name was introduced with the most obvious co-ordination immediately after the disaster unfolded in the same way that

the background to Lee Harvey Oswald was being circulated BEFORE President Kennedy was even dead."
—David Icke, British author

"If the events of September 11, 2001, have proven anything, it's that the terrorists can attack us, but they can't take away what makes us American—our freedom, our liberty, our civil rights. No, only Attorney General John Ashcroft can do that."
—Jon Stewart

"To those who scare peace-loving people with phantoms of lost liberty, my message is this: Your tactics only aid terrorists."
—John Ashcroft, Attorney General

"Do you think that Osama bin Laden planned 9-11 from a cave in Afghanistan? I can't get a cell-phone signal from here to Queens. I think our government knows where he is and I don't think we're going to be capturing him or killing him any time soon."
—Michael Moore

"If the decision [to limit access to White House docu-

ments] stands, I, as a member of the 9-11 commission, cannot look any American in the eye, especially family members of victims, and say the commission had full access. This investigation is compromised."
—Sen. Max Cleland

"I first began to suspect that 9/11 was in inside job when the Bush-Cheney Administration invaded Iraq. We can prove that the government's story is false."
—Morgan Reynolds, Ph.D.

"The official story of what actually took place on 9-11 is a lie."
—Philip J. Berg, Former Deputy Attorney General

"The official story is so inadequate and far-fetched that there must be another one."
—Andreas von Buelow, Former State Secretary of West Germany

"Let us never tolerate outrageous conspiracy theories concerning the attacks of September the 11th; malicious lies that attempt to shift the blame away from the terrorists themselves, away from the guilty."
—George W. Bush

# SHALLOW STARLETS

*Hollywood's leading ladies chime in on the important things in life.*

"I believe in love, but I don't sit around waiting for it. I buy houses."
—**Renee Zellweger**

"I couldn't stand that my husband was being unfaithful. I am Raquel Welch! Understand?"
—**Raquel Welch**

"I'd like to change my butt. It hangs a little too long. God forbid what it will look like when I'm older. It will probably be dragging along on the ground behind me."
—**Teri Hatcher**

"If you act like you know what you're doing, you can do anything you want...except neurosurgery."
—**Sharon Stone**

"After a while, you have no idea how old you are because you've lied so many times."
—**Sandra Bullock**

"I think the most important thing a woman can have next to talent, of course—is her hairdresser."
—**Joan Crawford**

"What's the point of doing something good if nobody's watching?"
—**Nicole Kidman**

"I can match bottoms with anyone in Hollywood."
—**Mia Farrow**

"Whoever said money can't buy happiness simply didn't know where to go shopping."
—**Bo Derek**

"I definitely believe in plastic surgery. I don't want to be an old hag. There's no fun in that."
—**Scarlett Johansson**

"One realizes how we take water for granted and how important it is to have it in order to stay alive. Beyond the drinking of it, let's not forget the hygiene."
—**Kim Basinger**

"I have perfected the art of putting my feet on my husband's lap during awards ceremonies so he can rub them."
—**Annette Bening**

# PRO BONO

*The lead singer of U2 wants to change the world. Can he do it?*

"Pop music tells you that everything is OK; rock music tells you that it's not, but that you can change it."

"Music can change the world because it can change people."

"To be one, to be united is a great thing. But to respect the right to be different is maybe even greater."

"The less you know, the more you believe."

"Painters, novelists, poets just can't be too cool. That's what fashion people are supposed to be. If your definition of art is breaking open the breastbone and pulling open the ribcage and, you know, a blood transfusion—you can't be cool like that."

"I've never thought of myself as cool. Irish people are not cool—they're hot."

"Celebrity is ridiculous and silly. But celebrity is currency, so I wanted to use mine effectively."

"We thought that we had the answers, it was the questions we had wrong."

"As a rock star, I have two instincts, I want to have fun, and I want to change the world. I have a chance to do both."

"The reason why there's operas and novels and pop tunes written about love is because it's such an extraordinary thing, not because it's commonplace, and yet that's what you're told. You grow up with this idea that it's the norm."

"Overcoming my dad telling me that I could never amount to anything is what has made me the megalomaniac that you see today."

"The world is more malleable than you think. We can bend it into a better shape. Ask big questions, demand big answers."

"Look, I'm sick of Bono and I *am* Bono."

"Bono is chairman and founding member of Overachievers Anonymous." —The Edge

# BOREDOM

*You write an intro.*

"Boredom is a vital problem for the moralist, since at least half the sins of mankind are caused by the fear of it."
—**Bertrand Russell**

"You'll find boredom where there is an absence of a good idea."
—**Earl Nightingale**

"Immunity to boredom gives the computer an edge."
—**Alan Lakein**

"I begin with the principle that all men are bores. Surely no one will prove himself so great a bore as to contradict me in this."
—**Søren Kierkegaard**

"All kinds are good except the kind that bores you."
—**Voltaire**

"It's a sad truth that everyone is a bore to someone."
—**Llewellyn Miller**

"There's no excuse to be bored. Sad, yes. Angry, yes. Depressed, yes. Crazy, yes. But bored? Never."
—**Viggo Mortensen**

"The life of the creative person is led, directed, and controlled by boredom. Avoiding boredom is one of our most important purposes."
—**Saul Steinberg**

"The biggest bore is the person who is bored by everything."
—**Frank Tyger**

"Boredom is like a pitiless zooming-in on the epidermis of time. Every instant is dilated and magnified like the pores of the face."
—**Charlotte Whitton**

"I am never bored anywhere. Being bored is an insult to oneself."
—**Jules Renard**

"Boredom is rage spread thin."
—**Paul Tillich**

"'I am bored' generally means 'I am boring.'"
—**Dennis Prager**

"I fell asleep reading a dull book and dreamed I kept on reading, so I awoke from sheer boredom."
—**Heinrich Heine**

"Chaos often breeds life, when order breeds habit." —**Henry Adams**

# BUGS

*Insects outnumber humans by more than a billion to one,*
*so we should probably be saying nicer things about them.*

"Anyone who thinks that they are too small to make a difference has never tried to fall asleep with a mosquito in the room."
—**Christie Todd Whitman**

"We hope that, when the insects take over the world, they will remember with gratitude how we took them along on all our picnics."
—**Richard Vaughan**

"If all mankind were to disappear, the world would regenerate back to the rich state of equilibrium that existed ten thousand years ago. If insects were to vanish, the environment would collapse into chaos."
—**Edward O. Wilson**

"I always felt that insects are the general rule, and everything else is a special case."
—**Paul Bystrak**

"If you step on people in this life, you're going to come back as a cockroach."
—**Willie Davis**

"Time flies like an arrow. Fruit flies like a banana."
—**Groucho Marx**

"I dreamed I was a butterfly, flitting around in the sky; then I awoke. Now I wonder: Am I a man who dreamt of being a butterfly, or am I a butterfly dreaming that I am a man?"
—**Chuang Tsu**

"Teaching a child not to step on a caterpillar is as valuable to the child as it is to the caterpillar."
—**Bradley Miller**

"Some days you're a bug, some days you're a windshield."
—**Price Cobb**

"Human knowledge will be erased from the world's archives before we possess the last word that a gnat has to say to us."
—**Jean-Henri Fabre**

"The butterfly counts not months but moments, and has time enough."
—**Rabindranath Tagore**

# PUNCTUATION MARKS

*Too best understand language and writting you need good
grammar spellin and puntuation. That way its easyer
for people to undderstand what your trying to say.*

"The hyphen, that's the most un-American thing in the world."
—Woodrow Wilson

"An excessive use of exclamation marks is a certain indication of an unpracticed writer or of one who wants to add a spurious dash of sensation to something unsensational."
—H. W. Fowler

"English usage is sometimes more than mere taste, judgement, and education—sometimes it's sheer luck, like getting across the street."
—E. B. White

"Arguments over grammar and style are often as fierce as those over IBM versus Mac, and as fruitless as Coke versus Pepsi."
—Jack Lynch

"The older I grow, the less important the comma becomes. Let the reader catch his own breath."
—Elizabeth Clarkson Zwart

"Grammar is a piano I play by ear. All I know about grammar is its power."
—Joan Didion

"When a thought takes one's breath away, a grammar lesson seems an impertinence."
—Thomas W. Higginson

"When there is a gap between one's real and one's declared aims, he turns instinctively to long words and exhausted idioms, like a cuttlefish spurting out ink."
—George Orwell

"I will not go down to posterity talking bad grammar."
—Benjamin Disraeli

"I demand that my books be judged with utmost severity, by knowledgeable people who know the rules of grammar and of logic, and who will seek beneath the footsteps of my commas the lice of my thought in the head of my style."
—Louis Aragon

"If the English language made any sense, 'lackadaisical' would have something to do with a shortage of flowers."
—**Doug Larson**

"Only presidents, editors, and people with tapeworm have the right to use the editorial 'we'."
—**Mark Twain**

Real headline: "Woman Born Feb. 29 Has Baby Same Day"

# HANGIN' WITH TJ!

*When President John F. Kennedy hosted several Nobel Prize winners at a 1962 White House dinner, he remarked, "This is probably the greatest concentration of talent and genius in this house, except for perhaps those times when Thomas Jefferson dined alone." Here are a few quotes from Jefferson (1743–1826).*

"Every generation needs a new revolution."

"Where the press is free and every man able to read, all is safe."

"We in America do not have government by the majority. We have government by the majority who participate."

"The will of the people is the only legitimate foundation of any government, and to protect its free expression should be our first object."

"All tyranny needs to gain a foothold is for people of good conscience to remain silent."

"Do not bite at the bait of pleasure till you know there is no hook beneath it."

"In matters of style, swim with the current; in matters of principle, stand like a rock."

"Never trouble another for what you can do for yourself."

"Nothing gives one person so much advantage over another as to remain always cool and unruffled under all circumstances."

"We confide in our strength, without boasting of it; we respect that of others, without fearing it."

"We often repent of what we have said, but never, never, of that which we have not."

"When angry, count ten before you speak; if very angry, a hundred."

"Do you want to know who you are? Don't ask. Act! Action will delineate and define you."

"Rebellion to tyrants is obedience to God."

"He who receives ideas from me, receives instruction himself without lessing mine; as he who lights his taper at mine receives light without darkening me."

# CHEESY QUOTES

*This is as gouda quote page as we could put together about cheese, Jack.*

"The early bird gets the worm, but the second mouse gets the cheese."
—Jon Hammond

"Well, and what's cheese? Corpse of milk."
—James Joyce

"McDonald's double cheese-burgers are a weapon of mass destruction."
—Ralph Nader

"Swiss cheese is a rip-off. It's the only cheese I can bite into and miss."
—Mitch Hedberg

"Right now, I'm as single as a slice of American cheese."
—Nick Cannon

"When cheese gets its picture taken, what does it say?"
—George Carlin

"I went into a French restaurant and asked the waiter, 'Have you got frog's legs?' He said, 'Yes,' so I said, 'Well, hop into the kitchen and get me a cheese sandwich.'"
—Tommy Cooper

"Poets have been mysteriously silent on the subject of cheese."
—G. K. Chesterton

"What happens to the hole when the cheese is gone?"
—Bertolt Brecht

"The ancient poets ne'er did dream / That Canada was land of cream, / They ne'er imag-ined it could flow / In this cold land of ice and snow, / Where everything did solid freeze, / They ne'er hoped or looked for cheese."
—James McIntyre, poet, a.k.a. "The Chaucer of Cheese"

"How can one conceive of a one-party system in a country that has over two hundred varieties of cheese?"
—Charles de Gaulle

"A meal without cheese is like a beautiful woman who lacks an eye."
—Jean Anthelme Brillat-Savarin

"Cheese: milk's leap toward immortality."
—Cliff Fadiman

Do you really, really love cheese? If so, then you are a *turophile*.

# THE WRITTEN WORD

*At some point in your life, you may have to write something.*
*Here are some pointers from old pros to help ease the way.*

"Do not copy my style! The first rule of writing: write about what you know, not what you think you know. So, think about what you've done in your life and write about that."
—**Jackie Collins**

"An author in his book must be like God in the universe: present everywhere and visible nowhere."
—**Gustave Flaubert**

"A story must have a beginning, a middle, and an end, but not necessarily in that order."
—**Jean Luc Godard**

"Anybody who likes writing a book is an idiot. Because it's impossible—it's like having a homework assignment every stinking day until it's done. And when it's done and you're sitting there reading it, you realize the 12,000 things you didn't do. And when people read it, they tell you, 'Well, gee, I'm not interested.' 'Great, I'm glad I wrote this!'"
—**Lewis Black**

"The writing process is fantastic psychotherapy—if you can survive."
—**Joni Mitchell**

"Don't use words too big for the subject. Don't say 'infinitely' when you mean 'very'; otherwise you'll have no word left when you want to talk about something really infinite."
—**C. S. Lewis**

"There's nothing to writing. All you do is sit down at a typewriter and open a vein."
—**Walter Wellesley Smith**

"Writing is like getting married. One should never commit oneself until one is amazed at one's luck."
—**Iris Murdoch**

"There are thousands of thoughts lying within a man that he does not know till he takes up the pen and writes."
—**William Thackeray**

"If you wish to be a writer, write."
—**Epictetus**

---

"You can't write poetry on the computer." —**Quentin Tarantino**

# HONOR THY MOTHER

*Some quotes from people giving credit where credit is due.*

"My mother was the most beautiful woman I ever saw. I attribute all my success in life to the moral, intellectual, and physical education I received from her."
—George Washington

"The memory of my mother and her teachings were the only capital I had to start life with, and on that capital I have made my way."
—Andrew Jackson

"My mother was very involved with me. We had a dialogue constantly, like an umbilical cord. And I probably grew up very afraid of losing that connection."
—Howard Stern

"The most remarkable thing about my mother is that for 30 years she served the family nothing but leftovers. The original meal has never been found."
—Calvin Trillin

"To describe my mother would be to write about a hurricane in its perfect power."
—Maya Angelou

"The reason why I took the name Queen was that my mother told me that all women were queens and should be treated as such."
—Queen Latifah

"The heart of a mother is a deep abyss at the bottom of which you will always find forgiveness."
—Honoré de Balzac

"Mama exhorted her children at every opportunity to 'jump at de sun.' We might not land on the sun, but at least we would get off the ground."
—Zora Neale Hurston

"Neurotics build castles in the air; psychotics live in them. My mother cleans them."
—Rita Rudner

"My mother was so true and so sure of me, I felt that I had someone to live for—someone I must not disappoint."
—Thomas Edison

"You never get over being a child, long as you have a mother to go to."
—Sarah Orne Jewett

# THE DAILY GRIND

*It's tough to complain about your job when you work at a place as great as the Bathroom Readers' Institute...but we still do.*

"Oh, you hate your job? Why didn't you say so? There's a support group for that. It's called EVERYBODY, and they meet at the bar."
—**Drew Carey**

"My father taught me to work; he did not teach me to love it. I never did like to work, and I don't deny it. I'd rather read, tell stories, crack jokes, talk, laugh—anything but work."
—**Abraham Lincoln**

"Work is a necessary evil to be avoided."
—**Mark Twain**

"If hard work were such a wonderful thing, surely the rich would have kept it all to themselves."
—**Lane Kirkland**

"Work is accomplished by those employees who have not yet reached their level of incompetence."
—**Laurence J. Peter**

"Beware of all enterprises that require new clothes."
—**Henry David Thoreau**

"Personally, I have nothing against work, particularly when performed, quietly and unobtrusively, by someone else."
—**Barbara Ehrenreich**

"Work expands so as to fill the time available for its completion."
—**C. Northcote Parkinson**

"It's a shame that a man can't eat for eight hours; he can't drink for eight hours; he can't make love for eight hours. The only thing a man can do for eight hours is work."
—**William Faulkner**

"Unemployment is of vital importance, particularly to the unemployed."
—**Edward Heath**

"People who work sitting down get paid more than people who work standing up."
—**Ogden Nash**

"The best way to appreciate your job is to imagine yourself without one."
—**Oscar Wilde**

# MR. T

*If you're a fool, don't read this page, as you will likely end up being pitied.*

"'T' stands for 'tender' for the ladies and the kids. For the bad guys and thugs, 'T' stands for 'tough.'"

"As a kid, I got three meals a day. Oatmeal, miss-a-meal, and no meal."

"I believe in the Golden Rule. The man with the gold rules."

"When I was growing up, my family was so poor we couldn't afford to pay attention."

"It takes a smart guy to play dumb."

"Anger: use it, but don't lose it."

"I was born and raised in the ghetto, but the ghetto was not born and raised in me."

"For five years, Mr. T disappeared. Fools went unpitied!"
   **—on his bout with cancer**

"When you see me now, I'm nothing but a big overgrown tough mama's boy. And I speak with that glee because the problem with society is we don't have enough mama's boys."

"Calvin Klein and Gloria Vanderbilt don't wear clothes with your name on it, so why should you wear their name?"

"Pity is between sorry and mercy. See, if you pity him, you won't have to beat him up. So that's why you gotta give fools another chance because they don't know any better."
   **—on pitying fools**

"I thought about my father being called 'boy,' my uncle being called 'boy,' my brother being called 'boy.' What does a black man have to do before he's given respect as a man?' So when I was 18 years old, I said I was old enough to be called a man. I self-ordained myself 'Mr. T' so the first word out of everybody's mouth is 'Mister.' That's a sign of respect that my father didn't get."

**As a bodyguard, Mr. T protected Muhammad Ali, Michael Jackson, and Steve McQueen.**

# THE AMERICAN INDIAN EXPERIENCE

*Wisdom from the First Peoples.*

"One does not sell the land upon which people walk."
—**Crazy Horse, Oglala Sioux**

"I am poor and naked but I am the chief of a nation. We do not want riches but we do want to train our children right. Riches would do us no good. We could not take them with us to the other world. We do not want riches. We want peace and love."
—**Red Cloud, Oglala Sioux**

"Treat all men alike. Give them all the same law. Give them all an even chance to live and grow. All men were made by the same Great Spirit Chief. They are all brothers."
—**Chief Joseph, Nez Perce**

"We did not think of the great open plains, the beautiful rolling hills and winding streams with tangled growth as 'wild.' To us it was tame. Earth was bountiful and we were surrounded with the blessings of the Great Mystery."
—**Luther Standing Bear, Rosebud Sioux**

"When it comes time to die, be not like those whose hearts are filled with the fear of death, so when their time comes they weep and pray for a little more time to live their lives over again in a different way. Sing your death song, and die like a hero going home."
—**Chief Aupumut, Mohican**

"Silence is the cornerstone of character."
—**Ohiyesa, Wahpeton Santee Sioux**

"The old Indian teaching was that it is wrong to tear loose from its place on the earth anything that may be growing there. It may be cut off, but it should not be uprooted."
—**Wooden Leg, Cheyenne**

"May the stars carry your sadness away, may the flowers fill your heart with beauty, may hope forever wipe away your tears, and, above all, may silence make you strong."
—**Chief Dan George, Salish**

---

**Any American citizen may name any unnamed mountain or hill in the United States.**

# WRONG, WRONG, WRONG

*Next time you feel like making a bold statement about what will happen, remember these dumb predictions.*

## ON POLITICS

"Democracy will be dead by 1950."

—John Langdon-Davies,
*A Short History of The Future*, 1936

"Reagan doesn't have the presidential look."

—United Artists executive, on Ronald Reagan, 1964

"By the year 1982, the graduated income tax will have practically abolished major differences in wealth."

—Irwin Edman, professor of philosophy,
Columbia University, 1932

"Left-handed incumbents have never been reelected...so look for a one-term Clinton presidency."

—*Time* magazine, on left-handed Bill Clinton, 1992

## ON INTERNATIONAL RELATIONS

"In all likelihood world inflation is over."

—Per Jacobsson, Managing Director,
International Monetary Fund, 1959

"We will bury you."

—Nikita Khrushchev, Soviet Premier, predicting the victory of Soviet communism over U.S. capitalism, 1958

"Four or five frigates will do the business without any military force."

—British prime minister Lord North,
on dealing with the rebellious American colonies, 1774

"We will be greeted as liberators in Iraq."

—Vice President Dick Cheney, 2003

**"I don't need bodyguards." —Jimmy Hoffa, 1975**

## ON MEDICINE

"Louis Pasteur's theory of germs is ridiculous fiction."
> —Pierre Pachet, professor of physiology
> at the University of Toulouse, 1872

"If excessive smoking actually plays a role in the production of lung cancer, it seems to be a minor one."
> —W. C. Heuper, National Cancer Institute, 1954

"We can close the books on infectious diseases."
> —William H. Stewart, U.S. Surgeon General, 1969

"That virus is a pussycat."
> —Dr. Peter Duesberg, molecular-biology
> professor at UC Berkeley, on HIV, 1988

## ON BUSINESS

"The concept is interesting and well-formed, but in order to earn better than a 'C,' the idea must be feasible."
> —Yale University management professor,
> on Fred Smith's term paper proposing reliable overnight
> delivery service. (Smith later founded Federal Express.)

"Drill for oil? You mean drill into the ground to try and find oil? You're crazy."
> —Drilling company manager, refusing to provide
> service to Edwin L. Drake, who told them they could
> all get rich drilling for oil in Pennsylvania, 1859

"I have travelled the length and breadth of this country and talked with the best people, and I can assure you that data processing is a fad that won't last out the year."
> —Editor in charge of business books
> for Prentice Hall, 1957

"With over 15 types of foreign cars already on sale here, the Japanese auto industry isn't likely to carve out a big share of the market for itself."
> —*Business Week*, 1968

"There is no reason anyone would want a computer in their home."

—Ken Olsen, President, Chairman and founder of Digital Equipment Corp., 1977

## ON EXPLORATION

"So many centuries after the Creation it is unlikely that anyone could find hitherto unknown lands of any value."

—Committee advising King Ferdinand and Queen Isabella of Spain regarding a proposal by Christopher Columbus, 1486

"Ours has been the first expedition, and doubtless to be the last, to visit this profitless locality."

—Lt. Joseph Ives, after exploring the Grand Canyon in 1861

"Man will never reach the moon regardless of all future scientific advances."

—Lee De Forest, Ph.D., pioneer of radio, 1967

## ON TECHNOLOGY

"You would make a ship sail against the winds and currents by lighting a bonfire under her deck...I have no time for such nonsense."

—Napoleon Bonaparte, commenting on Robert Fulton's steamship, 1803

"Within the next few decades, autos will have folding wings that can be spread when on a straight stretch of road so that the machine can take to the air."

—Eddie Rickenbacker, *Popular Science*, 1924

"I confess that in 1901, I said to my brother Orville that man would not fly for fifty years. Ever since, I have distrusted myself and avoided all predictions."

—Wilbur Wright, 1908

# C.S. LEWIS

*Clive Staples Lewis (1898–1963) wrote* The Chronicles of Narnia.
*He was also one of the 20th century's most esteemed philosophers.*

"An explanation of cause is not a justification by reason."

"Courage is not simply one of the virtues, but the form of every virtue at the testing point."

"Experience: that most brutal of teachers. But you learn, my God do you learn."

"Affection is responsible for nine-tenths of whatever solid and durable happiness there is in our lives."

"You don't have a soul. You are a Soul. You have a body."

"The real problem is not why some pious, humble, believing people suffer, but why some do not."

"Aim at heaven and you will get earth thrown in. Aim at earth and you get neither."

"You are never too old to set another goal or to dream a new dream."

"Friendship is unnecessary, like philosophy, like art. It has no survival value; rather it is one of those things that give value to survival."

"It may be hard for an egg to turn into a bird: It would be a sight harder for it to learn to fly while remaining an egg. We are like eggs at present. And you cannot go on indefinitely being just an ordinary, decent egg. We must be hatched or go bad."

"Nothing that you have not given away will ever be really yours."

"This is one of the miracles of love: It gives a power of seeing through its own enchantments and yet not being disenchanted."

"What saves a man is to take a step. Then another step."

"With the possible exception of the equator, everything begins somewhere."

# HIP-HOP CULTURE

*One of the youngest forms of popular music, hip-hop has transcended the streets and become a major part of modern society. And it's just getting started.*

"Hip-hop is colorless. Hip-hop music is made from black, brown, yellow, red and white."
—**Afrika Bambaataa**

"I think that hip-hop should be a pulpit for the people. All you are really doing is talking in rap form. It can always be transformed into an avenue of information."
—**Slick Rick**

"I think that Dante was hip-hop culture because he wrote in vernacular Italian, and at the time that was unheard of; people wrote in Latin or Petrach wrote in high Italian, and so Dante was talking street stuff."
—**Jim Jarmusch**

"Big shout-out to everybody with sleep apnea, high blood pressure, congestive heart failure! I do that too."
—**D12 rapper Bizarre's father, on MTV**

"Sometimes I feel like rap music is almost the key to stopping racism."
—**Eminem**

"If I'm more of an influence to your son as a rapper than you are as a father, you got to look at yourself as a parent."
—**Ice Cube**

"Hip-hop isn't just music, it is also a spiritual movement of the blacks."
—**Lauryn Hill**

"Rap is something you do, hip-hop is something you live."
—**KRS One**

"I want kids of this generation to see that there's unity in hip-hop. We all found something that's important to us, and music is all we've really got."
—**Missy Elliot**

"Hip-hop is supposed to uplift and create, to educate people, and to make a change."
—**Doug E. Fresh**

"I love hip-hop, because you ain't gotta hold your tongue."
—**Busta Rhymes**

"As long as it has soul to it, hip hop can live on."
—**Tupac Shakur**

# RED'S GOT OUR BACK

*When longtime Boston Celtics coach and team president Red Auerbach died at the age of 89 in 2006, professional sports lost one of its most beloved mentors…and some great one-liners.*

"If you're keeping score, win."

"If you're comfortable in a situation, stick with it."

"I never had a set of rules. Every situation is different."

"If they think we got an edge, we got an edge."

"The hardest thing to do is win it the second time."

"Loyalty is a two-way street."

"If you get up in the morning and you say, 'I got to go to work. How can I get out of this?' you're not happy."

"Power is ego."

"You play as you practice."

"He who believes in nobody knows that he himself is not to be trusted."

"The only correct actions are those that demand no explanation and no apology"

"An acre of performance is worth a world of promise."

"You must be a man of integrity. Never break your word. Don't have two sets of standards."

"Natural abilities are like natural plants: To grow, they need pruning."

"If you want to be a champion, feel like one, and then act like one."

"What makes a winner as much as anything: luck."

"If you want to get people to listen, don't talk so much."

"Show me a good loser, and I'll show you a loser."

A first-aid kit was found in King Tut's tomb.

# UNCLE JOHN'S QUOTATIONARY

*Here's Part 5 of our quotation dictionary.*
*(Part 4 begins on page 164.)*

**LANGUAGE:** the blood of the soul into which thoughts run, and out of which they grow. (Oliver Wendell Holmes)

**LAW:** a sort of hocus-pocus science that smiles in your face while it picks your pocket. (H. L. Mencken)

**LAWYERS:** men whom we hire to protect us from lawyers. (Elbert Hubbard)

**LEADERSHIP:** the art of getting someone else to do something you want done because he wants to do it. (Dwight D. Eisenhower)

**LEGAL:** used to mean lawful; now it means some kind of loophole. (Leo Kessler)

**LEISURE:** the mother of philosophy. (Thomas Hobbes)

**LIBERAL:** someone who feels a great debt to his fellow man, which debt he proposes to pay off with your money.

(G. Gordon Liddy)

**LIES:** the great lubricant of our way of life. They sell products, flatter the powerful, appease the electorate, and save vast sums from the IRS. (Barbara Ehrenreich)

**LIFE:** a long lesson in humility. (J. M. Barrie)

**LISTENING:** a willingness to let the other person change you. (Alan Alda)

**LOSER:** anyone too incompetent to master the ways of the world, or too proud. (Rick Bayan)

**LOVE:** an exploding cigar we willingly smoke. (Linda Barry)

**LULLABY:** the spell whereby the mother attempts to transform herself back from an ogre to a saint. (James Fenton)

**MAGNETISM:** a powerful force that causes certain items to be attracted to

refrigerators. (Dave Barry)

**MALE:** a domestic animal which, if treated with firmness and kindness, can be trained to do most things. (Jilly Cooper)

**MAN:** a being in search of meaning. (Plato)

**MARRIAGE:** our last, best chance to grow up. (Joseph Barth)

**MIDDLE CLASS:** the wimpiest term in the lexicon of social taxonomy, meaning little more than not rich, not poor. (Barbara Ehrenreich)

**MIND:** the most capricious of insects—flitting, fluttering. (Virginia Woolf)

**MIRACLES:** a retelling in small letters of the very same story which is written across the whole world in letters too large for some of us to see. (C. S. Lewis)

**MISOGYNIST:** a man who hates women as much as women hate one another. (H. L. Mencken)

**MISTAKES:** the dues one pays for a full life. (Sophia Loren)

**MOTHER:** a person who, seeing there are only four pieces of pie for five people, promptly announces she never did care for pie. (Tenneva Jordan)

**MOTORCYCLE:** a system of concepts worked out in steel. (Robert M. Pirsig)

**MOSQUITO:** the state bird of New Jersey. (Andy Warhol)

**MOTIVATION:** when dreams put on work clothes. (Milton Berle)

**MOVIES:** the repository of myth. (John Boorman)

**MTV:** the lava lamp of the 1980s. (Doug Ferrari)

**MUSIC:** moonlight in the gloomy night of life. (Jean Paul Richter)

*For more, see page 246.*

"Luck is preparation meeting opportunity." —**Oprah Winfrey**

George Harrison's last letter: a note to Mike Myers...asking for a Mini-Me doll.

# PROCRASTINATION

*We did this page last.*

"My mother always told me I wouldn't amount to anything because I procrastinate. I said, 'Just wait!'"
—**Judy Tenuta**

"Don't fool yourself that important things can be put off till tomorrow; they can be put off forever, or not at all."
—**Mignon McLaughlin**

"How does a project get to be a year behind schedule? One day at a time."
—**Fred Brooks**

"Procrastination is the art of keeping up with yesterday."
—**Don Marquis**

"Things may come to those who wait, but only the things left by those who hustle."
—**Abraham Lincoln**

"Don't put off till tomorrow what can be enjoyed today."
—**Josh Billings**

"Defer no time, delays have dangerous ends."
—**William Shakespeare**

"Procrastination is like a credit card: it's a lot of fun until you get the bill."
—**Christopher Parker**

"I love deadlines. I like the whooshing sound they make as they fly by."
—**Douglas Adams**

"Procrastination is, hands down, our favorite form of self-sabotage."
—**Alyce Cornyn-Selby**

"Procrastination is opportunity's assassin."
—**Victor Kiam**

"One of the greatest labor-saving inventions of today is tomorrow."
—**Vincent T. Foss**

"One thing that's good about procrastination is that you always have something planned for tomorrow."
—**Gil Stern**

"Only put off until tomorrow what you are willing to die having left undone."
—**Pablo Picasso**

**"Meet the sun every day as if it could cast a ballot." —Henry Cabot Lodge**

# NAPOLEON BONAPARTE: NAUGHTY OR NICE?

*Napoleon I (1769–1821) is best known for conquering most of Europe. But when reading through his words (he talked a lot), we've found that aside from the warmongering, there was a wisdom there as well. So here are some not-so-nice quotes, followed by some kind-of-nice ones.*

**NOT SO NICE:**

"I am sometimes a fox and sometimes a lion. The whole secret of government lies in knowing when to be the one or the other."

"If you wish to be a success in the world, promise everything, deliver nothing."

"I can no longer obey; I have tasted command, and I cannot give it up."

"I have only one counsel for you—be master."

"Power is my mistress. I have worked too hard at her conquest to allow anyone to take her away from me."

"A man like me troubles himself little about the lives of a million men."

"I should have conquered the world."

**KIND OF NICE:**

"A leader is a dealer in hope."

"All men have the same dose of happiness. I would have been no less happy as Monsieur Bonaparte than as the Emperor Napoleon."

"Great ambition is the passion of a great character. Those endowed with it may perform very good or very bad acts. All depends on the principles which direct them."

"The human race is governed by its imagination."

"Nothing is more difficult, and therefore more precious, than to be able to decide."

"In the long run, the sword will always be conquered by the spirit."

"Glory is fleeting, but obscurity is forever."

---

**Myth-conception:** Napoleon was actually slightly *taller* than the average Frenchman.

# TAXING QUOTES

*Ah, tax season…that time of year when we drink too much coffee,
stay up late, and cry a little. Maybe some funny quotes
will help. Dang it, where are those receipts?*

"Like mothers, taxes are often misunderstood, but seldom forgotten."
—**Lord Bramwell**

"You don't pay taxes—they take taxes."
—**Chris Rock**

"A tax loophole is 'something that benefits the other guy.' If it benefits you, it is tax reform."
—**Sen. Russell B. Long**

"Did you ever notice that when you put the words 'The' and 'IRS' together, it spells 'THEIRS'?"
—**Anonymous**

"There are two systems of taxation in our country: one for the informed, and one for the uninformed."
—**Learned Hand,**
*U.S. Appeals Court Justice*

"This is too difficult for a mathematician. It takes a philosopher."
—**Albert Einstein,**
*while filing his tax return*

"There may be liberty and justice for all, but there are tax breaks only for some."
—**Martin A. Sullivan**

"I'm proud to pay taxes in the United States; the only thing is, I could be just as proud for half the money."
—**Arthur Godfrey**

"The power to tax involves the power to destroy."
—**Justice John Marshall**

"There is one difference between a tax collector and a taxidermist—the taxidermist leaves the hide."
—**Mortimer Caplin,**
*former IRS Commissioner*

"I admit that if the point of taxation is so-called fairness and redistribution, then my plan will not be your cup of tea."
—**Sen. Richard Lugar**

"I owed the government $3,400 in taxes. So I sent them two hammers and a toilet seat."
—**Michael McShane**

"A government big enough to give you everything you want is strong enough to take everything you have."
—**Thomas Jefferson**

"We try to cooperate fully with the IRS, because, as citizens, we feel a strong patriotic duty not to go to jail."
—**Dave Barry**

"The Declaration of Independence, the words that launched our nation—1,300 words. The Bible, the word of God—773,000 words. The Tax Code, the words of politicians—7,000,000 words—and growing!"
—**Steve Forbes**

"I just wanted to read you something from the Internal Revenue Code. It is the last sentence of section 509A of the code: 'For purposes of paragraph 3, an organization described in paragraph 2 shall be deemed to include an organization described in section 501C-4, 5, or 6, which would be described in paragraph 2 if it were an organization described in section 501C-3.' And that's just one sentence out of those fifty-seven feet of books!"
—**Ronald Reagan**

"In the future, they'll be taxing you by the atom."
—**Tony Follari**

"Worried about an IRS audit? Avoid what's called a 'red flag,' something the IRS always looks for. For example, say you have some money left in your bank account after paying taxes. That's a red flag."

—**Jay Leno**

# FROM THE 4077th

*It's a mish-mash of M\*A\*S\*H quotes! This Korean War sitcom ran from 1972 to '83. Over the years, the show evolved from slapstick farce to poignant "dramedy"—but it never lost its flair for clever language.*

"The way I see it, the army owes us so many coffee breaks, we should get 1954 off."
—**Hawkeye Pierce**

"You blow another kiss, Pierce, and those lips will never walk again."
—**Col. Sherman Potter**

"I want foxholes there, there, there and there—each one smartly dug. The kind of hole a man can throw himself into with pride."
—**Frank Burns**

"Frank, you've been pushing your stethoscope too far in your ears. I think it scratched your brain."
—**Col. Henry Blake**

"Quiet, will you? The man is trying to be dull. Go ahead, Frank, dull away."
—**Trapper John McIntyre**

"You ever had one of those wars where everything goes wrong?"
—**Hawkeye Pierce**

"Every time he tickles those ivories, the entire elephants' graveyard turns over."
—**Charles Emerson Winchester III, on Father Mulcahy's piano playing**

"This is Frank Burns, one of our best surgeons. A real killer."
—**Col. Henry Blake**

"The only thing Charles remembers fondly from his childhood is his hair."
—**Hawkeye Pierce**

"The meek may inherit the earth, but it's the grumpy who get promoted!"
—**Father Mulcahy**

"You have to give Winchester credit. He is bright, educated, and an A-1 surgeon, and with all that he still found room to be a total jerk."
—**Sherman Potter**

"We all know it's brutal up there at the front, especially those of us at the rear."
—**Frank Burns**

---

*Sesame Street's Big Bird has a teddy bear. It's named Radar.*

# DOGS

*"Did somebody say 'cookie'?"* —*Porter the Wonder Dog*

"A dog has the soul of a philosopher."
—**Plato**

"Dogs are our link to paradise. They don't know evil or jealousy or discontent,"
—**Milan Kundera**

"A boy can learn a lot from a dog: obedience, loyalty, and the importance of turning around three times before lying down."
—**Robert Benchley**

"People teach their dogs to sit; it's a trick. I've been sitting my whole life, and a dog has never looked at me as though he thought I was tricky."
—**Mitch Hedberg**

"I wonder if other dogs think poodles are members of a weird religious cult."
—**Rita Rudner**

"From the dog's point of view, his master is an elongated and abnormally cunning dog."
—**Mabel Louise Robinson**

"Dogs are my favorite people."
—**Richard Dean Anderson**

"If you think dogs can't count, try putting three dog biscuits in your pocket and then giving Fido only two of them."
—**Phil Pastoret**

"Properly trained, a man can be dog's best friend."
—**Corey Ford**

"Ever consider what they must think of us? I mean, here we come back from a grocery store with the most amazing haul—chicken, pork, half a cow. They must think we're the greatest hunters on earth!"
—**Anne Tyler**

"I've seen a look in dogs' eyes, a quickly vanishing look of amazed contempt, and I am convinced that basically dogs think humans are nuts."
—**John Steinbeck**

"Dogs' lives are too short. Their only fault, really."
—**Agnes Sligh Turnbull**

"The dog is a gentleman. I hope to go to his heaven, not man's."
—**Mark Twain**

---

**The only two dog breeds to survive the sinking of the *Titanic*: Pekingese and Pomeranian.**

# FDR

*Franklin Delano Roosevelt was president of the United States from 1933 until his death in 1945. He pulled the country out of the worst economic depression it had ever seen...and helped the Allies win World War II.*

"No man can sever the bonds that unite him to society simply by averting his eyes."

"Public office means serving the public and nobody else."

"Whoever seeks to set one religion against another seeks to destroy all religion."

"We have more faith in the collective opinion of all Americans than in the individual opinion of any one American."

"The only limit to our realization of tomorrow will be our doubts of today."

"America has always been a land of action—a land of adventurous pioneering, a land of growing and building. America must always be such a land."

"Freedom of speech is of no use to the man who has nothing to say."

"A selfish victory is always destined to be an ultimate defeat."

"There never has been—there never can be—successful compromise between good and evil. Only total victory can reward the champions of tolerance and decency and freedom and faith."

"Peace can endure only so long as humanity really insists upon it, and is willing to work for it—and sacrifice for it."

"When you see a rattlesnake poised to strike, you do not wait until he has struck to crush him."

"Eternal truths will be neither true nor eternal unless they have fresh meaning for every new social situation."

"I do not look upon these United States as a finished product. We are still in the making."

# REEL INSULTING

*You got a problem with this page, punk? Well, do ya?*

"Fat, drunk, and stupid is no way to go through life, son."
—Dean Wormer (John Vernon), *Animal House*

"There's a name for you ladies, but it isn't used in high society, outside of a kennel."
—Crystal Allen (Joan Crawford), *The Women*

"I need him like the axe needs the turkey."
—Jean Harrington (Barbara Stanwyck), *The Lady Eve*

"You aren't too bright. I like that in a man."
—Matty Walker (Kathleen Turner), *Body Heat*

"It isn't that I don't like you, Susan, because after all, in moments of quiet, I'm strangely drawn toward you. But, well, there haven't been any quiet moments."
—Dr. Huxley (Cary Grant), *Bringing Up Baby*

Princess Leia (Carrie Fisher): Why, you stuck up, half-witted, scruffy-looking nerf-herder!
Han Solo (Harrison Ford): Who's scruffy-looking?
—*The Empire Strikes Back*

Rita (Doris Belack): I'd like to make her a little more attractive. How far can you pull back?
Cameraman: How do you feel about Cleveland?
—*Tootsie*

Bruce Baldwin (Ralph Bellamy): He's not the man for you, but I sorta like him. He's got a lot of charm.
Hildy Johnson (Rosalind Russell): Well, he comes by it naturally. His grandfather was a snake.
—*His Girl Friday*

"You're uglier than a modern-art masterpiece."
—Sgt. Hartman (R. Lee Ermey), *Full Metal Jacket*

"Well, that covers a lot of ground. Say! You cover a lot of ground yourself. You'd better beat it. I hear they're gonna tear you down and put up an office building where you're standing. You know, you haven't stopped talking since I came here. You must have been vaccinated with a phonograph needle."
—Groucho Marx, *Duck Soup*

"God created man, but I could do better." —Erma Bombeck

# CHEFS DE CUISINE

*Michelangelo had the Sistine Chapel; da Vinci had the Mona Lisa. These people are also artists—but their canvas is the dinner plate.*

"The only time to eat diet food is while you're waiting for the steak to cook."
—**Julia Child**

"The discovery of a new dish does more for the happiness of mankind than the discovery of a star."
—**Jean Brillat-Savarin**

"The problem with cooking is too many rules. You don't have to have perfect squares. Who cares, you know? Like we got some architect judging us at breakfast!"
—**Emeril Lagasse**

"From an early age I understood that cooking was never going to be a job, it's a passion."
—**Gordon Ramsay**

"Make a tamale with peanut butter and jelly. Go ahead! Somebody will eat it."
—**Bobby Flay**

"Cooking is like love. It should be entered into with abandon or not at all."
—**Harriet Van Horne**

"Understand, when you eat meat, that something did die. You have an obligation to value it—not just the sirloin but also all those wonderful tough little bits."
—**Anthony Bourdain**

"You don't need a silver fork to eat good food."
—**Paul Prudhomme**

"I feel a recipe is only a theme, which an intelligent cook can play each time with a variation."
—**Madame Benoit**

"A gourmet who thinks of calories is like a tart who looks at her watch."
—**James Beard**

"When I talk about a great dish, I often get goose bumps. I'm like, whoa, I'll never forget that one."
—**Mario Batali**

"Only cook and eat food with people you like. Life's too short for bad food and bad company."
—**Rocco DiSpirito**

# LOU HOLTZ

*After coaching professional and college football for 35 years (most notably at Notre Dame), Lou Holtz has since moved on to become a college football analyst and motivational speaker. Here's why.*

"It's not the load that breaks you down, it's the way you carry it."

"Ability is what you're capable of doing. Motivation determines what you do. Attitude determines how well you do it."

"You'll never get ahead of anyone as long as you try to get even with him."

"If you burn your neighbor's house down, it doesn't make your house look any better."

"It is a fine thing to have ability, but the ability to discover ability in others is the true test."

"A bird doesn't sing because it has an answer; it sings because it has a song."

"You're never as good as everyone tells you when you win, and you're never as bad as they say when you lose."

"You might not be able to outthink, outmarket, or outspend your competition, but you can outwork them."

"No one has ever drowned in sweat."

"There's nothing is this world more instinctively abhorrent to me than finding myself in agreement with my fellow humans."

"If you try to fight the course, it will beat you."

"I can't believe that God put us on this earth to be ordinary."

"In the successful organization, no detail is too small to escape close attention."

"I think everyone should experience defeat at least once during their career. You learn a lot from it."

"When all is said and done, more is said than done."

# GOOD FOR WHAT ALES YOU

*Mmm…beeeeeer.*

"Nothing ever tasted better than a cold beer on a beautiful afternoon with nothing to look forward to than more of the same."
—**Hugh Hood**

"Not all chemicals are bad. Without chemicals such as hydrogen and oxygen, for example, there would be no way to make water, a vital ingredient in beer."
—**Dave Barry**

"If you ever reach total enlightenment while drinking beer, I bet it makes beer shoot out your nose."
—**Jack Handey**

"I'm going to buy a boat, do a little travelling, and I'm going to be drinking beer!"
—**John Welsh, Brooklyn bus driver who won $30 million in the New York lottery**

"People who drink light 'beer' don't like the taste of beer; they just like to pee a lot."
—**sign on a Wisconsin brewery**

"A meal of bread, cheese, and beer constitutes the perfect food."
—**Queen Elizabeth I**

"Filled with mingled cream and amber I will drain that glass again. Such hilarious visions clamber Through the chambers of my brain— Quaintest thoughts—queerest fancies Come to life and fade away; Who cares how time advances? I am drinking ale today."
—**Edgar Allan Poe**

"Beer speaks. People mumble."
—**Tony McGee, Lagunitas Brewing Co.**

"Beer is the center of everything. Everything revolves around beer. When you drink beer, everything revolves. Therefore beer is the center of everything."
—**University of Waterloo engineers**

"Payday came and with it beer."
—**Rudyard Kipling**

Women brewers were highly revered in ancient Babylon, assuming the role of temple priestesses.

# CHEERS AND BEERS

**Woody:** How would a beer feel, Mr. Peterson?
**Norm:** Pretty nervous, if I was in the room.

"Well ya see, Norm, it's like this: A herd of buffalo can only move as fast as the slowest buffalo. And when the herd is hunted, it is the slowest and weakest ones at the back that are killed first. This natural selection is good for the herd as a whole, because the general speed and health of the whole group keeps improving by the regular killing of the weakest members.

"In much the same way, the human brain can only operate as fast as the slowest brain cells. Excessive intake of alcohol, as we know, kills brain cells. But naturally, it attacks the slowest and weakest brain cells first. In this way, regular consumption of beer eliminates the weaker brain cells, making the brain a faster and more efficient machine. That's why you always feel smarter after a few beers."

—Cliff Clavin

**Sam:** What's new, Normie?
**Norm:** Terrorists, Sam. They've taken over my stomach and they're demanding beer.

**Woody:** How's it going, Mr. Peterson?
**Norm:** Poor.
**Woody:** I'm sorry to hear that.
**Norm:** No, I mean *pour*.

# CYNICS

*Okay, so these people aren't cynics all the time, but who among us has not wondered if this whole human adventure is really worth the trouble? These folks did...out loud.*

"Human beings will line up for miles to buy a bucket of catastrophes, but don't try selling sunshine and light; you'll go broke."
—**Chuck Jones**

"Until we stop harming all other living beings, we are still savages."
—**Thomas Edison**

"The 50-50-90 rule: Anytime you have a 50-50 chance of getting something right, there's a 90% probability you'll get it wrong."
—**Andy Rooney**

"The earth has a skin and that skin has diseases; one of its diseases is called Man."
—**Friedrich Nietzsche**

"Life's but a walking shadow, a poor player
That struts and frets
his hour upon the stage
And then is heard no more:
it is a tale told by an idiot,
full of sound and fury,
Signifying nothing."
—**William Shakespeare,**
***Macbeth***

"After one look at this planet any visitor from outer space would say, "I WANT TO SEE THE MANAGER.'"
—**William S. Burroughs**

"The trouble with the world is that the stupid are cocksure and the intelligent are full of doubt."
—**Bertrand Russell**

"To perceive is to suffer."
—**Aristotle**

"Nature is that lovely lady to whom we owe polio, leprosy, smallpox, syphilis, tuberculosis, and cancer."
—**Stanley N. Cohen**

"The earth swarms with people who are not worth talking to."
—**Voltaire**

"The end of the human race will be that it will eventually die of civilization."
—**Ralph Waldo Emerson**

"Inside every cynical person there is a disappointed idealist."
—**George Carlin**

"A cynic is a man who knows the price of everything, and the value of nothing." —Oscar Wilde

# THE PRICE OF FAME

*What would it be like to be so famous that you can't even walk down a sidewalk without being recognized by total strangers?*

"It does get old to have to always be a monkey in a zoo. I don't know what it's like anymore to be anonymous."
—**Kevin Bacon**

"There aren't many downsides to being rich, other than paying taxes and having relatives asking for money. But being famous, that's a 24-hour job right there."
—**Bill Murray**

"There is no preparation for sudden celebrity."
—**Scarlett Johannson**

"I was always indifferent to the glitter of fame. I found it troublesome, crippling, and dangerous. I detested it."
—**Marlene Dietrich**

"You use your money to buy privacy because during most of your life you aren't allowed to be normal."
—**Johnny Depp**

"I want to be so famous that drag queens will dress like me in parades when I'm dead."
—**Laura Kightlinger**

"Normally, the people who are not genuine are the ones who say: 'You know I'm not just being your friend because you're Harry Potter, right?' And it's like, 'Uh, fine, but if that's the case, why do you need to say that?'"
—**Daniel Radcliffe**

"Yeah, I love being famous. It's almost like being white."
—**Chris Rock**

"You go to school, you get a master's, you study Shakespeare, and you wind up being famous for plastic glasses."
—**Sally Jessy Raphaël**

"I love being famous. It validates that I have something to say."
—**Richard Lewis**

"Celebrity is a pretty stunning thing. At first I was like, 'They love me! Oh, I love them, too.' And suddenly, I was tap-dancing on my pedestal and then: *whack!* Face-down in the dirt."
—**Sharon Stone**

# FOOD PROVERBS

*If there is food in the office, hide it from Jay. —BRI proverb*

If ever a chef were to cook a fly, he would keep the breast for himself.
—**Poland**

The rich would have to eat money if the poor did not provide food.
—**Russia**

Worries go down better with soup.
—**Yiddish**

Laughter is brightest, in the place where the food is.
—**Ireland**

Whose bread I eat, his song I sing.
—**Germany**

When eating bamboo sprouts, remember the man who planted them.
—**China**

If you are looking for a fly in your food, it means that you are full.
—**South Africa**

Eat vegetables and fear no creditors, rather than eat duck and hide.
—**Hebrew**

The kind man feeds his cat before sitting down to dinner.
—**Hebrew**

The best food is whatever fills the belly.
—**Arab**

God never sent hunger without sending something to satisfy it.
—**Ireland**

To a good appetite there is no bad bread.
—**Spain**

A man that has had his fill is no eater.
—**Spain**

Hunger is felt by a slave and hunger is felt by a king.
—**Ashanti**

Fine words do not produce food.
—**Nigeria**

Food tastes best when you eat it with your own spoon.
—**Denmark**

You are only master of food that you haven't yet eaten.
—**Tibet**

Act, and you shall have dinner. Think, and you shall be dinner. —Klingon proverb

# MAN AND NATURE

*Uncle John spends so much time in the office reading—and "researching" in the bathroom—that we sometimes have to remind him to go outside and get some fresh air. Where does he go? To the outhouse to read some more.*

"Remember the quiet wonders. The world has more need of them than it has for warriors."
—**Charles de Lint**

"I do not know what I may appear to the world; but to myself I seem to have been only like a boy playing on the seashore, and diverting myself in now and then finding a smoother pebble or a prettier shell than ordinary, whilst the great ocean of truth lay all undiscovered before me."
—**Isaac Newton**

"Harmony with land is like harmony with a friend; you cannot cherish his right hand and chop off his left."
—**Aldo Leopold**

"No man should go through life without once experiencing healthy, even bored solitude in the wilderness, finding himself depending solely on himself and thereby learning his true and hidden strength."
—**Jack Kerouac**

"I only went out for a walk and finally concluded to stay out till sundown, for going out, I found, was really going in."
—**John Muir**

"All things are parts of one single system, which is called Nature; the individual life is good when it is in harmony with Nature."
—**Zeno (300–260 B.C.)**

"Choose only one master, Nature."
—**Rembrandt**

"If future generations are to remember us with gratitude rather than contempt, we must leave them more than the miracles of technology. We must leave them a glimpse of the world as it was in the beginning, not just after we got through with it."
—**Lyndon B. Johnson**

"Human judges can show mercy. But against the laws of nature, there is no appeal."
—**Arthur C. Clarke**

---

Isaac Newton lived for 84 years...and died a virgin.

"Why did men worship in churches, locking themselves away in the dark, when the world lay beyond its doors in all its real glory?"
—Charles de Lint

"Earth laughs in flowers."
—Ralph Waldo Emerson

"Only a people serving an apprenticeship to nature can be trusted with machines."
—Herbert Read

"Our connection to nature grounds us, it makes us more spiritually aware. We must keep the legacy of nature materially alive for future generations."
—Nelly Furtado

"We may succeed in altering the face of the earth until it is unrecognizable even to the Creator, but if we are unaffected wherein lies the meaning?"
—Henry Miller

"To see the earth as we now see it, small and beautiful in that eternal silence where it floats, is to see ourselves as riders on the earth together, brothers on that bright loveliness in the unending night—brothers who see now they are truly brothers."
—Archibald MacLeish

"The best remedy for those who are afraid, lonely, or unhappy is to go outside, somewhere where they can be quite alone with the heavens, nature, and God. Only then does one feel that all is as it should be and that God wishes to see people happy amidst the simple beauty of nature."
—Anne Frank

"It is a wholesome and necessary thing for us to turn again to the earth and in the contemplation of her beauties to know the sense of wonder and humility."
—Rachel Carson

"Like music and art, love of nature is a common language that can transcend political or social boundaries."
—Jimmy Carter

"Human subtlety will never devise an invention more beautiful, more simple or more direct than does Nature, because in her inventions, nothing is lacking and nothing is superfluous."
—Leonardo da Vinci

"I think having land and not ruining it is the most beautiful art that anybody could ever want to own."
—Andy Warhol

Every second, the rain forests are reduced by an area the size of two football fields.

# JACK KEROUAC

*What do Tom Robbins, Hunter S. Thompson, Ken Kesey,
Tom Waits, and Bob Dylan have in common? They were all
inspired by beat writer Jack Kerouac (1922–69), who
penned* On the Road *and* Dharma Bums.

"I realized either I was crazy or the world was crazy; and I picked on the world. And of course I was right."

"I saw that my life was a vast glowing empty page and I could do anything I wanted."

"Don't bother me with politics; the only thing that interests me is style."

"I had nothing to offer anybody except my own confusion."

"The only people for me are the mad ones, the ones who are mad to live, mad to talk, mad to be saved, desirous of everything at the same time, the ones who never yawn or say a commonplace thing, but burn, burn, burn."

"Offer them what they secretly want, and they of course immediately become panic-stricken."

"Let there be joy in baseball again, like in the days when Babe Ruth chased an enemy sportswriter down the streets of Boston and ended up getting drunk with him on the waterfront and came back the next day munching on hotdogs and boomed homeruns to the glory of God."

"It is not my fault that certain so-called bohemian elements have found in my writings something to hang their peculiar beatnik theories on."

"I want to work in revelations, not just spin silly tales for money. I want to fish as deep as possible into my own subconscious in the belief that once that far down, everyone will understand because they are the same that far down."

"So long and take it easy, because if you start taking things seriously, it is the end of you."

# SCHOOL DAZE

*Lyndon Johnson once said, "Education is not a problem; education is an opportunity." Wasn't he, like, a president or something?*

"I hated school. Even to this day, when I see a school bus it's just depressing to me. The poor little kids."
—Dolly Parton

"Without education, we are in a horrible and deadly danger of taking educated people seriously."
—G. K. Chesterton

"If I didn't have some kind of education, I wouldn't be able to count my money."
—Missy Elliott

"A child educated only at school is an uneducated child."
—George Santayana

"Knowledge without education is but armed injustice."
—Horace

"When you are educated, you'll believe only half of what you hear. When you're intelligent, you know which half."
—Jerome Perryman

"It was my SAT scores that led me into my present vocation in life, comedy."
—Neil Simon

"The beautiful thing about learning is that no one can take it away from you."
—B. B. King

"The difference between school and life? In school, you're taught a lesson and then given a test. In life, you're given a test that teaches you a lesson."
—Tom Bodett

"You can get all A's and still flunk life."
—Walker Percy

"High school is closer to the core of the American experience than anything else I can think of."
—Kurt Vonnegut, Jr.

"Strange as it seems, no amount of learning can cure stupidity, and higher education positively fortifies it."
—Stephen Vizinczey

# SAMUEL L. JACKSON

*Samuel L. Jackson has starred in more than 50 movies, including Goodfellas,
Pulp Fiction, and the last three Star Wars epics. His films have raked
in more than $3 billion, making him the highest-grossing actor
of all time. Lucky for us, he also has a lot of opinions.*

**On the "Biz":**
"I truly believe that in most cases people in marketing have no idea what they're trying to market."

**On Fame:**
"I love my fans and when I meet them at conventions or in the street, I make sure to stop and greet them and sign whatever they want me to sign. I really appreciate their passion and their dedication."

"Not a day goes by without someone asking me what you call a Royale with cheese in France! Now everyone's downloading my *Pulp Fiction* quotes off the Internet and I call people's houses and I'm on their answering machine!"

**On Golf:**
"The year I started golf I had a caddie, and one day I got angry with myself and threw a club. My caddie told me, 'You're not good enough to get mad.' I have never thrown a club since."

**On the Oscar Dream:**
"I have a place that's pretty much cemented in Hollywood in terms of box-office viability. The only thing an Oscar would do is jack my check up maybe $1 million."

**On Entertainment:**
"I'd rather be entertaining than poignant. People have enough drama in their lives already. They don't have enough things to make them smile."

**On Star Wars:**
"I spent a lot of time when I was a kid fighting imaginary things in my room, so when George [Lucas] puts you in that big empty green room and says you're being attacked by lots of droids, you just go in there and fight as many of them as you can. The wonderful thing is, when you go and actually see the film itself, it's amazing!"

**On being "Cool":**
"I was a square for so long and it totally amazes me that people think I'm cool."

# DO YOU BELIEVE?

*These people do…*

"I believe that a simple and unassuming manner of life is best for everyone, best both for the body and the mind."
—**Albert Einstein**

"I believe in using words, not fists."
—**Bertrand Russell**

"I believe more in the scissors than I do in the pencil."
—**Truman Capote**

"I believe everybody should have a room where they get rid of all their releases. So my room was a stage."
—**Jimi Hendrix**

"I believe in the imagination. What I cannot see is infinitely more important than what I can see."
—**Duane Michals**

"I believe that if we really want human brotherhood to spread and increase until it makes life safe and sane, we must also be certain that there is no one true faith or path by which it may spread."
—**Adlai E. Stevenson**

"I believe in equality for everyone, except reporters and photographers."
—**Mahatma Gandhi**

"I believe in luck: how else can you explain the success of those you dislike?"
—**Jean Cocteau**

"I believe in justice, maybe not in this life, but there has to be justice. And if there isn't a God, I think it would be very depressing. I'd prefer to believe there is."
—**David Zucker**

"I believe a leaf of grass is no less than the journey-work of the stars."
—**Walt Whitman**

"I believe in the brotherhood of all men, but I don't believe in wasting brotherhood on anyone who doesn't want to practice it with me. Brother-hood is a two-way street."
—**Malcolm X**

"I believe in God, only I spell it n-a-t-u-r-e."
—**Frank Lloyd Wright**

"Believe nothing, even if I have said it, unless it agrees with your own common sense." —**Buddha**

# SUPPOSEDLY SAID

*Because quoting what other people say is often like playing
a game of "telephone," what ends up in our collective
memory often isn't exactly what the speaker said.*

## TARZAN

**He supposedly said:** "Me Tarzan, you Jane."

**...But actually:** This line was never uttered in any Tarzan
film, nor in the original Edgar Rice Burroughs novel. The quote
stems from an interview in which Tarzan actor Johnny Weissmuller
made up the line as a comment on the films' simplistic dialogue.

## KARL MARX

**He supposedly said:** "Religion is the opiate of the masses."

**...But actually:** "Religion is the sigh of the oppressed creature,
the heart of a heartless world and the soul of soulless conditions.
It is the opium of the people," is what Marx really said. The
misquote implies that Marx believed religion "drugs" people. The
full quote suggests that Marx had a better understanding of why
many people flock to religion.

## JOHN KERRY

**He supposedly said:** "Who among us doesn't like NASCAR?"

**...But actually:** This quote was well circulated during the 2004
presidential election, often characterizing Senator Kerry as awkward, out of touch, and pandering to blue-collar voters. Turns out
that when *New York Times* columnist Maureen Dowd mocked
Kerry for the quote in a March 2004 column, it was the first time
the quote had ever appeared. Dowd had just made it up.

## SGT. JOE FRIDAY (Jack Webb)

**He supposedly said:** "Just the facts, ma'am."

**...But actually:** The no-nonsense cop said, "All we want are the
facts, ma'am." Satirist Stan Freberg spoofed he show on the 1953
hit record "St. George and the Dragonet," in which he says, "I just
want to get the facts, ma'am." It was Freberg's line, not Webb's,
that became synonymous with the show.

---

**"For your convenience, we will be closed Christmas Day."** —sign at a Boston supermarket

## MARIE ANTOINETTE

**She supposedly said:** "Let them eat cake."

**...But actually:** The queen was said to have made this sarcastic remark when told that many people in France had no bread to eat. In reality, French revolutionaries spread the rumor to stir up hatred for the monarch and support for overthrowing the crown.

## ADM. DAVID FARRAGUT

**He supposedly said:** "Damn the torpedoes! Full speed ahead!"

**...But actually:** According to *The Yale Book of Quotations*, the Civil War admiral never uttered this famous rallying cry at the Battle of Mobile Bay in 1864. It appeared in print in 1878, but news reports and accounts of the battle make no mention of the phrase.

## JAMES CAGNEY

**He supposedly said:** "You dirty rat!"

**...But actually:** It's commonly assumed to be a line from Cagney's film *Public Enemy Number One*, but the line isn't in that movie... nor in any others. Where the misquote originated is unknown.

## THE KING JAMES BIBLE

**It supposedly said:** "Money is the root of all evil."

**...But actually:** Money is not evil; loving it is. The full quote, misheard over the years, is: "For the love of money is the root of all evil" (1 Timothy 6-7).

## LORD ACTON

**He supposedly said:** "Power corrupts. Absolute power corrupts absolutely."

**...But actually:** The 19th-century British historian really wrote, "Power tends to corrupt. Absolute power corrupts absolutely. Great men are almost always bad men."

## WILLIAM CONGREVE

**He supposedly said:** "Hell hath no fury like a woman scorned."

**...But actually:** Close, but not quite. In his 1697 poem "The Mourning Bride," Congreve wrote: "Heaven has no rage like love to hatred turned/ Nor hell a fury like a woman scorned."

Queen Henrietta of Belgium trained a llama to spit at people.

# GROWING UP IS HARD TO DO

*Some thoughts about young people...as said by older people.*

"All children wear the sign: 'I want to be important NOW.' Many of our juvenile delinquency problem arise because nobody reads the sign."
—Don Herold

"Children in a family are like flowers in a bouquet: there's always one determined to face in an opposite direction from the way the arranger desires."
—Marcelene Cox

"I was the fattest baby in Clark County, Arkansas. They put me in the newspaper. It was like a prize turnip."
—Billy Bob Thornton

"When childhood dies, its corpses are called adults."
—Brian Aldiss

"All kids are gifted. Some just open their packages earlier than others."
—Michael Carr

"A happy childhood has spoiled many a promising life."
—Robertson Davies

"Grown-ups never understand anything for themselves, and it is tiresome for children to be always and forever explaining things to them."
—Antoine de Saint-Exupéry

"Make no mistake about why these babies are here—they are here to replace us."
—Jerry Seinfeld

"We've had bad luck with children. They've all grown up."
—Christopher Morley

"Children are like wet cement. Whatever falls on them makes an impression."
—Dr. Haim Ginott

"Adults are always asking little kids what they want to be when they grow up because they're looking for ideas."
—Paula Poundstone

"Children have never been very good at listening to their elders, but they have never failed to imitate them."
—James Baldwin

# BOO-RAY FOR HOLLYWOOD

*You wold think that people who were made famous by Hollywood
would have some nicer things to say about it. Nah.*

"I'd move to Los Angeles if New Zealand and Australia were swallowed up by a tidal wave, if there was a bubonic plague in England and if the continent of Africa disappeared from some Martian attack."
—**Russell Crowe**

"Euthanasia is legal in Hollywood. They just kill the film if it doesn't succeed immediately. If it doesn't make money, it must therefore be a bad work. I don't remember a time when there was so much respect for bad work."
—**Dustin Hoffman**

"If there's anything disgusting about the movie business, it's the whoredom of my peers."
—**Sean Penn**

"I try not to let the pressure get to me, but L.A. is a very hard place to be unless you have people here that love you. It can be very, very lonely, and it can eat you up if you don't take care of yourself."
—**Scarlett Johannson**

"I'm not swimming in the soup bowl. I'm not getting overcooked in that big stewpot."
—**Johnny Depp**

"The allure of Hollywood is huge when you don't know anything. You don't know the knives behind the smiles."
—**Steve Guttenberg**

"In Hollywood there are a lot of very insecure men running the business."
—**Rosanna Arquette**

"Whatever starts in California unfortunately has an inclination to spread."
—**Jimmy Carter**

"There are only three ages for women in Hollywood: Babe, District Attorney, and Driving Miss Daisy."
—**Goldie Hawn**

"Show business is a dream factory, Bart. The birthplace of magic and enchantment. Now go clean my toilet."
—**Krusty the Clown,**
***The Simpsons***

---

The only Best Picture Oscar nominee that was based on a TV show: *The Fugitive.*

# IT'S ABOUT TIME

*Well, what are you waiting for?*

"Yesterday is a cancelled check. Today is cash on the line. Tomorrow is a promissory note."
—**Hank Stram**

"This moment contains all moments."
—**C. S. Lewis**

"Time heals all wounds, unless you pick at them."
—**Shaun Alexander**

"Lost time is never found again."
—**Benjamin Franklin**

"They say that time changes things, but you actually have to change them yourself."
—**Andy Warhol**

"Time makes more converts than reason."
—**Thomas Paine**

"Eternity's a terrible thought. I mean, where's it all going to end?"
—**Tom Stoppard**

"If we take care of the moments, the years will take care of themselves."
—**Maria Edgeworth**

"Nothing is as far away as one minute ago."
—**Jim Bishop**

"Time enjoyed wasting was not wasted."
—**John Lennon**

"We must use time as a tool, not as a crutch."
—**John F. Kennedy**

"As if you could kill time without injuring eternity."
—**Henry David Thoreau**

"Dost thou love life? Then do not squander time; for that's the stuff life is made of."
—**Benjamin Franklin**

"Lost, yesterday, somewhere between sunrise and sunset, two golden hours, each set with sixty diamond minutes. No reward is offered, for they are gone forever."
—**Horace Mann**

"Hello! How are you doing? You think time is precious, huh? Well, I would like to tell you, you just wasted about seven seconds of your life reading this stupid thing."
—**David H. Kim**

According to an old English system of time units, a moment is one and a half minutes.

# RALPH WALDO EMERSON

*Born in Boston in 1803, Emerson was an author, philosopher, abolitionist, and one of the founders of the Transcendentalism movement, which encouraged its followers to experience spirituality through personal intuition rather than through organized religion. Here are some of his thoughts.*

"The creation of a thousand forests is in one acorn."

"Every artist was first an amateur."

"A hero is no braver than an ordinary man, but he is braver five minutes longer."

"Be an opener of doors."

"People seem not to see that their opinion of the world is also a confession of their character."

"Foolish consistency is the hobgoblin of small minds."

"Beware when the great God lets loose a thinker on this planet."

"We must be our own before we can be another's."

"The ancestor of every action is a thought."

"The world belongs to the energetic."

"Insist on yourself; never imitate. Every great man is unique."

"Truth is the property of no individual, but is the treasure of all men."

"A great man is always willing to be little."

"The years teach much which the days never knew."

"Every man supposes himself not to be fully understood or appreciated."

"No change of circumstances can repair a defect of character."

"Sometimes a scream is better than a thesis."

"This time, like all times, is a very good one, if we but know what to do with it."

"You cannot do a kindness too soon, for you never know how soon it will be too late."

"None of us will ever accomplish anything excellent or commanding except when he listens to the whisper which is heard by him alone."

"The invariable mark of wisdom is to see the miraculous in the common."

"Unless you try to do something beyond what you have already mastered, you will never grow."

—Ralph Waldo Emerson

# FIRST LADIES

*Being married to a president is no bed of roses.*

"The one thing I do not want to be called is First Lady. It sounds like a saddle horse."
—Jacqueline Kennedy

"I have sacrificed everything in my life that I consider precious in order to advance the political career of my husband."
—Pat Nixon

"When Woodrow proposed to me, I was so surprised that I nearly fell out of bed."
—Edith Galt, President Wilson's second wife

"Every politician should have been born an orphan and remain a bachelor."
—Lady Bird Johnson

"If I'm just at the White House, I have meetings in my office, I sign letters, I plan different things. Late in the afternoon, I'll quit working and wait for my husband to get home."
—Laura Bush

"I see the First Lady as another means to keep a president from becoming isolated."
—Nancy Reagan

"Always be on time. Never try to make any personal engagements. Do as little talking as humanly possible. Never be disturbed by anything. Always do what you're told to do as quickly as possible. Remember to lean back in a parade, so that people can see your husband. Don't get too fat to ride three on a seat. Get out of the way as quickly as you're not needed."
—Eleanor Roosevelt

"I have but one career, and its name is Ike."
—Mamie Eisenhower

"Now about those ghosts [in the White House]. I'm sure they're here and I'm not half so alarmed at meeting up with any of them as I am at having to meet the live nuts I have to see every day."
—Bess Truman

"Put me in a Prison."
—Louisa Catherine Adams

"Any lady who is First Lady likes being First Lady. I don't care what they say, they like it."
—Richard Nixon

---

Camp David was named for Dwight D. Eisenhower's grandson.

# MORE GENIUSES

*This book is just overflowing with intellijense!*

"Genius, in one respect, is like gold; numbers of persons are constantly writing about both, who have neither."
—**Charles Caleb Colton**

"Genius is seldom recognized for what it is: a great capacity for hard work."
—**Henry Ford**

"In the republic of mediocrity, genius is dangerous."
—**Robert G. Ingersoll**

"A man of genius makes no mistakes. His errors are the portals of discovery."
—**James Joyce**

"The thinking of a genius does not proceed logically. It leaps with great ellipses."
—**Dorothy Thompson**

"A man possesses talent; genius possesses the man."
—**Isaac Stern**

"Genius is no respecter of time, trouble, money, or persons, the four things around which human affairs turn most persistently."
—**Samuel Butler**

"Mediocrity knows nothing higher than itself, but talent instantly recognizes genius."
—**Arthur Conan Doyle**

"Genius is sorrow's child."
—**John Adams**

"A genius is one who can do anything except make a living."
—**Joey Lauren Adams**

"Talent hits a target no one else can hit; genius hits a target no one else can see."
—**Arthur Schopenhauer**

"Beware of notions like genius; they are a sort of magic wand, and should be used sparingly by anybody who wants to see things clearly."
—**José Ortega y Gasset**

"Talent shuffles the deck. Genius brings a new deck."
—**Mason Cooley**

"Doing easily what others find difficult is talent; doing what is impossible for others is genius."
—**Henri Frédéric Amiel**

# DONALD SAYS: "DON'T!"

*Former Secretary of Defense Donald Rumsfeld sure liked the "D" word.*

"Don't do or say things you would not like to see on the front page of the *Washington Post*."

"If in doubt, don't."

"Don't necessarily avoid sharp edges. Occasionally they are necessary to leadership."

"Don't automatically obey presidential directives if you disagree, or if you suspect he hasn't considered key aspects of the issue."

"Think ahead. Don't let day-to-day operations drive out planning."

"Don't be a bottleneck. If a matter is not a decision for the president or you, delegate it. Force responsibility down and out. Find problem areas, add structure and delegate. The pressure is to do the reverse. Resist it."

"Don't blame the boss. He has enough problems."

"Don't think of yourself as indispensable or infallible. As Charles De Gaulle said, 'The cemeteries of the world are full of indispensable men.'"

"Don't speak ill of your predecessors or successors. You didn't walk in their shoes."

"Don't say: 'The White House wants...' Buildings can't want."

"Don't begin to think you're the president. You're not. The Constitution provides for only one."

"Don't divide the world into 'them' and 'us.' Avoid infatuation with or resentment of the press, the Congress, rivals, or opponents. Accept them as facts. They have their jobs and you have yours."

"Learn to say, 'I don't know.' If used when appropriate, it will be often."

---

Donald Rumsfeld rarely sits down; he even had a podium in his office that he stood behind.

# SPEAKING UP WITH THE JONESES

*Here are quotes from a variety of Joneses—some you know, and some you probably don't.*

"Imagine what a harmonious world it could be if every single person, both young and old, shared a little of what he is good at doing."
—Quincy Jones

"Friends may come and go, but enemies accumulate."
—Thomas Jones, artist

"You can't be a sexy person unless you have something sexy to offer. With me, it's my voice."
—Tom Jones

"You do not suffer if you decide 'that's the way it is,' rather than 'why is it this way?'"
—Chuck Jones, animator

"One advantage of talking to yourself is that you know at least somebody's listening."
—Franklin P. Jones, American businessman

"Everyone knows we actors get paid a lot of money, so why pretend otherwise?"
—Catherine Zeta-Jones

"If I make a record I love, then somebody will like it. Maybe not everybody, but that won't matter."
—Norah Jones

"If fear is cultivated, it will become stronger. If faith is cultivated, it will achieve mastery."
—John Paul Jones, American naval hero

"We p*ss anywhere, man."
—Brian Jones, Rolling Stones guitarist

"One of the hardest things in life is having words in your heart that you can't utter."
—James Earl Jones

"Ours is the age that is proud of machines that think, and suspicious of men who try to."
—H. Mumford Jones, American educator

"There's too much reality these days."
—Shirley Jones, actor (*The Partridge Family*)

---

Brian Jones played sax on the Beatles song "You Know My Name (Look Up the Number)."

# JOAN-ZING

*We thought all the Joneses on the page to the left might want some company, so here are some Joans.*

"I like to make a lot of noise and blow bubbles. It's a good way to clear out sleeping space on airplanes."
—Joan Jett

"There are way more different character roles for men than there are for women. With women, it's usually you're the babe or you're the supportive friend, sort of brassy and obnoxious, cracking jokes. I'm not the babe."
—Joan Cusack

"I don't think I'm good in bed. My husband never said anything, but after we made love he'd take a piece of chalk and outline my body."
—Joan Rivers

"Love is a fire. But whether it is going to warm your hearth or burn down your house, you can never tell."
—Joan Crawford

"You have to say, 'I will wither if I don't do it, I'll *die* if I don't do it!' It has to be that much of a need."
—Joan Chen

"I've never had a humble opinion. If you've got an opinion, why be humble about it?"
—Joan Baez

"To free us from the expectations of others, to give us back to ourselves—there lies the great, singular power of self-respect."
—Joan Didion

"One life is all we have and we live it as we believe in living it. But to sacrifice what you are and to live without belief, that is a fate more terrible than dying."
—Joan of Arc

"The secret of having a personal life is not answering too many questions about it."
—Joan Collins

"A life of value is not a series of great things well done; it is a series of small things consciously done."
—Joan Chittister

"I succeeded by saying what everyone else is thinking."
—Joan Rivers

# WAR AND PEACE

*Some thoughts on the causes—and prevention—
of mankind's most dangerous game.*

"War is a racket. It always has been. It is possibly the oldest, easily the most profitable, surely the most vicious."
—**Gen. Smedley Butler**

"You cannot be on one hand dedicated to peace and on the other dedicated to violence. Those two things are irreconcilable."
—**Condoleezza Rice**

"Two armies that fight each other is like one large army that commits suicide."
—**Henri Barbusse**

"Peace is the only battle worth waging."
—**Albert Camus**

"Peace demands the most heroic labor and the most difficult sacrifice. It demands greater heroism than war."
—**Thomas Merton**

"The great error of nearly all studies of war has been to consider war as an episode in foreign policies, when it is an act of interior politics."
—**Simone Weil**

"Evil men, obsessed with ambition and unburdened by conscience, must be taken very seriously—and we must stop them before their crimes can multiply."
—**George W. Bush**

"If everyone demanded peace instead of another television set, then there'd be peace."
—**John Lennon**

"No war by any nation in any age has ever been declared by the people."
—**Eugene Debs**

"The best way to destroy an enemy is to make him a friend."
—**Abraham Lincoln**

"War may be only temporary, but its toll remains permanently."
—**Ramman Kenoun**

"War is an instrument entirely inefficient toward redressing wrong; and multiplies, instead of indemnifying losses."
—**Thomas Jefferson**

"The chain reaction of evil—wars producing more wars—must be broken, or we shall be plunged into the dark abyss of annihilation."
—Martin Luther King, Jr

"It is well that war is so terrible, or we should get too fond of it."
—Robert E. Lee

"Only fools seek power, and the greatest fools seek it through force."
—Lao Tzu

"War is delightful to those who have not experienced it."
—Desiderius Erasmus

"Do you know what astonished me most in the world? The inability of force to create anything."
—Napoleon Bonaparte

"There must be, not a balance of power, but a community of power; not organized rivalries, but an organized peace."
—Woodrow Wilson

"There never was a good war or bad peace."
—Benjamin Franklin

"Either war is obsolete, or men are."
—R. Buckminster Fuller

## JACK NICHOLSON PLEADS FOR PEACE

"I'm an American through and through, and I can't find any reason why anybody should be wanting to blow up everything. Saddam Hussein may have said, 'We'll win this because the West worships life and we worship death,' but I don't believe it. In my heart I know that nobody's that different that they would want what's going on now. And people can say, 'That's easy for you to say, Jack. You're one of the luckiest people on the planet.' Well, yeah. I mean, so what? I'm lucky, so because you're not, you think murdering innocent people is great? In the movie *Mars Attacks*, as the president, I'm in a condescending way trying to slip in the philosophy of Rodney King, saying to the Martians, 'Can't we all just get along?' But, I mean, can't we?"

---

...in the Hundred Years War, his ransom was 16 pounds. The English refused to pay.

# RANDOM QUOTES

*More smart things that smart people said.*

"Every man takes the limits of his own field of vision for the limits of the world."
—**Arthur Schopenhauer**

"Taking an attitude of thankfulness in all of life's circumstances will help you react as old Matthew Henry did when he was mugged. He wrote in his diary, 'Let me be thankful first because I was never robbed before; second, although they took my purse, they did not take my life; third, because although they took my all, it was not much; and fourth, because it was I who was robbed, not I who robbed.' I wonder if I could be that thankful. Could you?"
—**Billy Graham**

"The one thing that doesn't abide by majority rule is a person's conscience."
—**Harper Lee**

"Many promising reconciliations have broken down because, while both parties came prepared to forgive, neither party came prepared to be forgiven."
—**Charles Williams**

"The secret to my success is that I bit off more than I could chew and chewed as fast as I could."
—**Paul Hogan**

"The human body has two ends on it: one to create with and one to sit on. Sometimes people get their ends reversed. When this happens they need a kick in the seat of the pants."
—**Theodore Roosevelt**

"I knew we were in for a long season when we lined up for the national anthem on opening day and one of my players said, 'Every time I hear that song, I have a bad game.'"
—**Jim Leyland, baseball manager**

"To seek freedom is the only driving force I know. Freedom to fly off into that infinity out there. Freedom to dissolve; to lift off; to be like the flame of a candle, which, in spite of being up against the light of a billion stars, remains intact, because it never pretended to be more than what it is: a mere candle."
—**Carlos Castaneda**

"Even when I'm sick and depressed, I love life." —**Arthur Rubinstein**

# "IRONIC" UTTERANCES

*When famous people talk, their words are often recorded...*
*words that can come back to haunt them later.*

"If a president of the United States ever lied to the American people, he should resign."
—**Bill Clinton, 1974**

"I never stop looking for things to try and make myself better."
—**Barry Bonds**

"It's vile. It's more sad than anything else, to see someone with such potential throw it all down the drain because of a sexual addiction."
—**Rep. Mark Foley, 1998, on Bill Clinton's affair with Monica Lewinsky. In 2006 Foley resigned from Congress because of his own addictions**

"Give me liberty or give me death."
—**Patrick Henry, who owned 65 slaves when he died**

"I would not like to be a political leader in Russia. They never know when they're being taped."
—**Richard Nixon**

"We should not march into Baghdad. To occupy Iraq would instantly shatter our coalition, turning the whole Arab world against us, and make a broken tyrant into a latter-day Arab hero...It could only plunge that part of the world into even greater instability."
—**George H. W. Bush, in his 1998 book, *A World Transformed*. He later supported the 2003 Iraq war**

"I have never been a material girl. My father always told me never to love anything that cannot love you back."
—**Imelda Marcos, who owned more than 3,000 pairs of shoes**

"I don't do quagmires."
—**Donald Rumsfeld**

"And guys, if you exploit a girl, it will come back to get you. That's called 'karma.'"
—**Bill O'Reilly, who has faced sexual harassment charges at Fox News**

"Hypocrisy is the most obvious of sins." —John McCain

# ELLEN

*From stand-up comedian to sitcom star to talk-show host, Ellen DeGeneres keeps herself in the limelight. Why? Because she's funny.*

"In the beginning there was nothing. God said, 'Let there be light!' And there was light. There was still nothing, but you could see it a whole lot better."

"Want to have some fun? Go up to somebody on the street and say 'You're it!' and just run away."

"I feel like I have a hangover, without all the happy memories and mystery bruises."

"I'm a godmother, that's a great thing to be, a godmother. She calls me God for short. That's cute, I taught her that."

"Stuffed deer heads on walls are bad enough, but it's worse when they are wearing sunglasses and have streamers in their antlers because then you know they were enjoying themselves at a party when they were shot."

"Procrastination isn't the problem; it's the solution. So procrastinate now, don't put it off!"

"I'm on the patch right now. It releases small dosages of approval until I no longer crave it."

"I don't understand the sizes anymore. There's a size zero, which I didn't even know they had. It must stand for: 'Oh my God, you're thin!'"

"At the movies, we stock up on popcorn and candy like we're crossing the Sierras: 'I'll have a soft pretzel, a hot dog, milk duds, Sno-Caps. Is that the largest popcorn you've got there—that bucket? You don't have a barrel? Do you have a donkey or a pack mule or anything? Oh, and a Diet Coke.'"

"One day I was coming home from kindergarten—well, I thought it was kindergarten. It turns out I'd been working in a factory for two years. I was wondering, 'cause it was always really hot and everyone was older than me, but what did I know?"

"Go to bed in your fireplace. You'll sleep like a log."

Ellen was the 1st female comedian Johnny Carson ever invited over to the couch on the *Tonight Show.*

# I'M NOT AS THINK AS YOU DRUNK I AM

*Sober thoughts on the drunken state.*

"The hardest part about being a bartender is figuring out who is drunk and who is just stupid."
—**Richard Braunstein**

"Karaoke bars combine two of the nation's greatest evils; people who shouldn't drink, and people who shouldn't sing."
—**Tom Dreesen**

"I saw a notice that said 'Drink Canada Dry,' and I've just started."
—**Brendan Behan**

"I was so drunk last night, I fell down and missed the floor."
—**Dean Martin**

"The problem with some people is that when they aren't drunk, they're sober."
—**William Butler Yeats**

"I drink too much. The last time I gave a urine sample, it had an olive in it."
—**Rodney Dangerfield**

"Actually, it only takes one drink to get me loaded. Trouble is, I can't remember if it's the 13th or 14th."
—**George Burns**

"The best audience is one that is intelligent, well educated, and a little drunk."
—**Alben W. Barkley**

"The words a man speaks in the night of drunkenness fade like the darkness itself at the coming of day."
—**Marguerite Duras**

"I don't have a drinking problem, except when I can't find a drink."
—**Tom Waits**

"Alcohol may be man's worst enemy, but the Bible says love your enemy."
—**Frank Sinatra**

"A man's got to believe in something. I believe I'll have another drink."
—**W. C. Fields**

**Dean Martin's vanity license plate: DRUNKY**

# EVEN TOM ROBBINS GETS THE BLUES

*The author of* Jitterbug Perfume *and* Even Cowgirls Get the Blues *speaks out on politics, humanity, religion, and the Seven Dwarves.*

"Humanity has advanced not because it has been sober, responsible, and cautious, but because it has been playful, rebellious, and immature."

"To achieve the impossible, it is precisely the unthinkable that must be thought."

"Human beings were invented by water as a device for trans-porting itself from one place to another."

"If it is committed in the name of God or country, there is no crime so heinous that the public will not forgive it."

"If the world gets any smaller, I'll end up living next door to myself."

"If you want to change the world, change yourself."

"There are many things worth living for, a few things worth dying for, and nothing worth killing for."

"There is a certain Buddhistic calm that comes from having money in the bank."

"There is no such thing as a weird human being, It's just that some people require more understanding than others."

"Of the seven dwarves, only Dopey had a shaven face. This should tell us something about the custom of shaving."

"If little else, the brain is an educational toy."

"Politics is for people who have a passion for changing life but lack a passion for living it."

"The only authority I respect is the one that causes butter-flies to fly south in fall and north in springtime."

"A sense of humor, properly developed, is superior to any religion so far devised."

# AGING

*More quotes about the golden years.*

"Old age is the most unexpected of all the things that happen to a man."
—Leon Trotsky

"People do not grow old, no matter how long we live. We never cease to stand like curious children before the great mystery into which we were born."
—Albert Einstein

"Everyone desires to live long, but no one would be old."
—Abraham Lincoln

"At 20, we worry about what others think of us; at 40, we don't care what they think of us; at 60, we discover they haven't been thinking of us at all."
—Bob Hope

There's no age that isn't a good time to confront one's mortality or to consider a second adulthood."
—Barbara Ehrenreich

"How old would you be if you didn't know how old you were?"
—Satchel Paige

"You know you're getting old when all the names in your black book have 'M.D.' after them."
—Harrison Ford

"Growing old is no more than a bad habit which a busy man has no time to form."
—André Maurois

"Only from the entirely old can the entirely new be born."
—Béla Bartók

"The awful thing about getting old is that you stay young inside."
—Jean Cocteau

"I will be 83 years old on December 12 and I've decided to retire while I'm still young."
—Bob Barker

"To me, old age is always 15 years older than I am."
—Bernard M. Baruch

"I don't care how old I live; I just want to be LIVING while I am living!"
—Jack La Lanne

"Age is a very high price to pay for maturity." —Paulo Coelho

# UNCLE JOHN'S QUOTATIONARY

*Here's Part 6 of our quotation dictionary.*
*(Part 5 begins on page 203.)*

**NAP:** a brief period of sleep which overtakes superannuated persons when they endeavor to entertain unwelcome visitors or to listen to scientific lectures. (George Bernard Shaw)

**NARCISSIST:** psycho-analytic term for the person who loves himself more than his analyst. (Thomas Szasz)

**NATURAL:** a very difficult pose to keep up. (Oscar Wilde)

**NATURE:** a mutable cloud which is always and never the same. (Ralph Waldo Emerson)

**NECESSITY:** the mother of taking chances. (Mark Twain)

**NEUROSIS:** a substitute for legitimate suffering. (Carl Jung)

**NEWSPAPERS:** dead trees with information smeared on them. (Horizon, *Electronic Frontier*)

**NEW YEAR'S EVE:** the Special Olympics of inebria-tion. (P. J. O'Rourke)

**NEW YORK:** where every-one mutinies but no one deserts. (Harry Hershfield)

**NIGHT:** when words fade and things come alive. When the destructive analysis of day is done, and all that is truly important becomes whole again. When man reassembles his fragmentary self and grows with the calm of a tree. (Antoine de Saint-Exupery)

**NIRVANA:** In the Buddhist religion, a state of pleasurable annihilation awarded to the wise, particularly to those wise enough to understand it. (Ambrose Bierce)

**NOISE:** an imposition on sanity, and we live in very noisy times. (Joan Baez)

**NORMAL:** getting dressed in clothes that you buy for work and driving through traffic in a car that you are still paying for—in order to get to the job you need to pay for the clothes and the car, and the house you leave vacant all day so you can afford to live in it. (Ellen DeGeneres)

**NOSTALGIA:** a file that removes the rough edges from the good old days. (Doug Larson)

**NYMPHOMANIAC:** a woman as obsessed with sex as the average man. (Mignon McLaughlin)

**O**ATS: A grain, which in England is generally given to horses, but in Scotland supports the people. (Samuel Johnson)

**OBSTACLES:** those frightful things you see when you take your eyes off your goal. (Henry Ford)

**OBVIOUS:** the most dangerous word in mathematics. (E. T. Bell)

**OCEAN:** a body of water occupying about two-thirds of a world made for man...who has no gills. (Ambrose Bierce)

**OPTIMIST:** the human

personification of spring. (Susan J. Bissonette)

**ORIGINALITY:** the fine art of remembering what you hear but forgetting where you heard it. (Laurence J. Peter)

**OYSTERS:** the most tender and delicate of all seafoods. They stay in bed all day and night. They never work or take exercise, are stupendous drinkers, and wait for their meals to come to them. (Hector Bolitho)

**P**AINTING: The art of protecting flat surfaces from the weather and exposing them to the critics. (Ambrose Bierce)

**PARANOIA:** knowing all the facts. (William S. Burroughs)

**PARENTHOOD:** feeding the mouth that bites you. (Peter De Vries)

**PATRIOTISM:** supporting your country all the time, and your government when it deserves it. (Mark Twain)

**PHILOSOPHY:** at once the most sublime and the most trivial of human pursuits. (William James)

**PHOTOGRAPH:** a secret about a secret. The more it tells you the less you know (Diane Arbus)

**PHYSICS:** geometric proof on steroids. (Leslie S. Sachs)

**POETRY:** a theorem of a yellow-silk handkerchief knotted with riddles, sealed in a balloon tied to the tail of a kite flying in a white wind against a blue sky in in spring. (Carl Sandburg)

**POLITICALLY CORRECT:** always having to say you're sorry. (Charles Osgood)

**POLITICS:** the art of looking for trouble, finding it everywhere, diagnosing it incorrectly and applying the wrong remedies. (Groucho Marx)

**PORNOGRAPHY:** the attempt to insult sex, to do dirt on it. (D. H. Lawrence)

**POWER:** the ultimate aphrodisiac. (Henry Kissinger)

**PROMISCUOUS PERSON:** a person who is getting more sex than you are. (Victor Lownes)

**PROPHECY:** the wit of a fool. (Vladimir Nabokov)

**PSYCHOLOGY:** the Science of everything we know about what people are willing to tell us. (Tony Follari)

**PUCK:** a hard rubber disc that hockey players strike when they can't hit one another. (Jimmy Cannon)

**QUANTUM:** that embarrassing little piece of thread that always hangs from the sweater of space-time. Pull it and the whole thing unravels. (Fred Alan Wolf)

**QUEEN:** a woman by whom the realm is ruled when there is a king, and through whom it is ruled when there is not. (Ambrose Bierce)

**QUESTIONS:** the key to unlocking our unlimited potential. (Tony Robbins)

**QUEUE:** what an Englishman forms, even if he's alone. (George Mikes)

**QUOTES:** inspiration for the uninspired. (Richard Kemph)

*For more, see page 303.*

A movie theater in Atlanta, Georgia, has been showing...

# ANIMAL PROVERBS

*Let's go around the world and learn some lessons that our beastly friends have been nice enough to teach us throughout the centuries.*

Don't bargain for fish which are still in the water.
—India

If wishes were horses, then beggars would ride.
—Scotland

If you call one wolf, you invite the pack.
—Bulgaria

Use your enemy's hand to catch a snake.
—Persia

Laws, like spider webs, catch flies and let hawks go free.
—Spain

If a man be great, even his dog will wear a proud look.
—Japan

By trying often, the monkey learns to jump from the tree.
—Cameroon

In the dark, all cows are black.
—Germany

A prudent man does not make the goat his gardener.
—Hungary

It is not the cry, but the flight of the wild duck that leads the flock to fly and follow.
—China

Hunger will lead a fox out of the forest.
—Poland

You can not prevent the birds of sorrow from flying over your head, but you can prevent them from building a nest in your hair.
—China

A lame cat is better than a swift horse when rats infest the palace.
—China

One can think of life after the fish is in the canoe.
—Hawaii

When we traded the buffalo for a mare, we had no milk to drink, and we still had droppings to clean up.
—Punjab

In the ant's house, the dew is a flood.
—Denmark

# ANAÏS NIN

*French-born Anaïs Nin (1903–1977) was many things: feminist,
philosopher, model, actress, and an early female writer of erotica.
Today she is best known for her personal diaries, first published
in 1966, which spanned 60 years of her amazing life.*

"Each contact with a human being is so rare, so precious, one should preserve it."

"We don't see things as they are, we see them as we are."

"People living deeply have no fear of death."

"There are many ways to be free. One of them is to transcend reality by imagination, as I try to do."

"Dreams are necessary to life."

"I know why families were created, with all their imperfections. They humanize you. They are made to make you forget yourself occasionally, so that the beautiful balance of life is not destroyed."

"What I cannot love, I overlook. Is that real friendship?"

"When you make a world tolerable for yourself, you make a world tolerable for others."

"There is not one big cosmic meaning for all; there is only the meaning we each give to our life, an individual meaning, an individual plot, like an individual novel, a book for each person."

"When we blindly adopt a religion, a political system, a literary dogma, we become automatons. We cease to grow."

"The personal life deeply lived always expands into truths beyond itself."

"And the day came when the risk to remain tight in a bud was more painful than the risk it took to blossom."

"Dreams pass into the reality of action. From the actions stems the dream again; and this interdependence produces the highest form of living."

"The possession of knowledge does not kill the sense of wonder and mystery. There is always more mystery."

"The only abnormality is the incapacity to love." —Anaïs Nin

# FOR THE LOVE OF WINE

*This page definitely has a good bouquet and a nice oak finish, and will probably go best with a robust cheddar.*

"Wine is the sacred, symbolic, romantic beverage, the only one fittingly used to celebrate the holy Mass, to launch ships, to make the connoisseur's banquet perfect, to toast bride, beggar or king."
—Leon D. Adams

"When the wine is in, the wit is out."
—Thomas Becon

"Good wine is a necessity of life."
—Thomas Jefferson

"Name me any liquid except our own blood that flows more intimately and incessantly through the labyrinth of symbols we have conceived to make our status as human beings, from the rudest peasant festival to the mystery of the Eucharist. To take wine into our mouths is to savor a droplet of the river of human history."
—Clifton Fadiman

"Wine is the most civilized thing in the world."
—Ernest Hemingway

"Winemaking is the world's second-oldest profession and, no doubt, it has eased the burden of the world's oldest."
—Tony Aspler

"Compromises are for relationships, not wine."
—Sir Robert Scott Caywood

"Wine is the flower in the buttonhole of life."
—Werumeus Buning

"Wine makes a man more pleased with himself; I do not say it makes him more pleasing to others."
—Samuel Johnson

"Wine is a living liquid containing no preservatives. Its life cycle comprises youth, maturity, old age, and death. When not treated with reasonable respect it will sicken and die."
—Julia Child

"Milk is the drink of babies, tea the drink of women, water the drink of beasts, and Wine is the drink of the gods."
—John Stuart Blackie

Muscatel means "wine with flies in it" in Italian.

"If God forbade drinking,
would He have made wine
so good?"

—Cardinal Richelieu

Good news: You burn 3.5 calories each time you laugh.

# THAT'S DEATH

*"Life is a good play with a badly written third act."* —Truman Capote

"I'm not afraid of death because I don't believe in it. It's just getting out of one car, and into another."
—John Lennon

"Even very young children need to be informed about dying. Explain the concept of death very carefully to your child. This will make threatening him with it much more effective."
—P. J. O'Rourke

"All human things are subject to decay, and when fate summons, monarchs must obey."
—John Dryden

"Death is only an horizon, and an horizon is only the limit of our sight. Open our eyes to see more clearly."
—William Penn

"The idea is to die young as late as possible."
—Ashley Montagu

"I'm not afraid of death. It's the stake one puts up in order to play the game of life."
—Jean Giraudoux

"The timing of death, like the ending of a story, gives a changed meaning to what preceded it."
—Mary Catherine Bateson

"Dying is a very dull, dreary affair. And my advice to you is to have nothing whatever to do with it."
—W. Somerset Maugham

"All our knowledge merely helps us to die a more painful death than animals that know nothing."
—Maurice Maeterlinck

"To himself everyone is immortal; he may know that he is going to die, but he can never know that he is dead."
—Samuel Butler

"From my rotting body, flowers shall grow and I am in them and that is eternity."
—Edvard Munch

"If my doctor told me I had only six minutes to live, I wouldn't brood. I'd just type a little faster."
—Isaac Asimov

# CHRISTMAS BABIES

*All of these folks were born on December 25.*

"Everything we do, everything we are, rests on our personal power. If we have enough of it, one word is enough to change the course of our lives. If we don't, the most magnificent piece of wisdom can be revealed to us and that revelation won't make a damn bit of difference."
—Carlos Castaneda (b. 1931)

"We are the people our parents warned us about."
     —Jimmy Buffett (b. 1946)

"When you're that successful, things have a momentum, and at a certain point you can't really tell whether you have created the momentum or it's creating you."
     —Annie Lennox (b. 1954)

"I can calculate the movement of the stars, but not the madness of men."
—Sir Isaac Newton (b. 1642)

"People sometimes forget that jazz was not only built in the minds of the great ones, but on the backs of the ordinary ones."
     —Cab Calloway (b. 1907)

"There are no ugly women, only lazy ones."
     —Helena Rubinstein (b. 1870), founder of Helena Rubinstein Cosmetics

"He who cannot change the very fabric of his thought will never be able to change reality, and will never, therefore, make any progress."
     —Anwar el-Sadat (b. 1918)

"Things are never so bad they can't be made worse."
—Humphrey Bogart (b. 1899)

"I happen to think that the singular evil of our time is prejudice. It is from this evil that all other evils grow and multiply. In almost everything I've written there is a thread of this: a man's seemingly palpable need to dislike someone other than himself."
     —Rod Serling (b. 1924)

"I may be compelled to face danger, but never fear it, and while our soldiers can stand and fight, I can stand and feed and nurse them."
     —Clara Barton (b. 1821), founder of the Red Cross

---

Died on Christmas: Charlie Chaplin, Billy Martin, and Dean Martin.

# THE GANDHI WAY

*Mohandas Karamchand Gandhi (1869–1948) earned the Hindu title "Mahatma" (Great Soul) for his tireless campaigning for human rights and independence for the nation of India.*

"I am but a poor struggling soul yearning to be wholly good, wholly truthful and wholly non-violent in thought, word and deed, but ever failing to reach the ideal which I know to be true. It is a painful climb, but each step upwards makes me feel stronger and fit for the next."

"Glory lies in the attempt to reach one's goal and not in reaching it."

"To forgive is not to forget."

"An error does not become truth by reason of multiplied propagation, nor does truth become error because nobody will see it."

"There is a higher court than courts of justice and that is the court of conscience. It supercedes all other courts."

"A 'no' uttered from deepest conviction is better and greater than a 'yes' merely uttered to please, or what is worse, to avoid trouble."

"Intolerance is itself a form of violence and an obstacle to the growth of a true democratic spirit."

"If patience is worth anything, it must endure to the end of time."

"I look only to the good qualities of men. Not being faultless myself, I won't presume to probe into the faults of others.

"The moment there is suspicion about a person's motives, everything he does becomes tainted."

"An ounce of practice is worth more then tons of preaching."

"Humanity is an ocean; if a few drops of the ocean are dirty, the ocean does not become dirty."

"I do not want to foresee the future. I am concerned with taking care of the present."

Movie with the most extras: *Gandhi*, with 300,000.

# THOUGHTS ON LOVE

*"Thoughts on Love" may be an oxymoron—true love comes
from the heart, not the mind. But that doesn't mean
we should stop thinking about it.*

"I think we've got this love
thing really whacked."
—**Nick Nolte**

"If you would be loved, love
and be lovable."
—**Benjamin Franklin**

"The most precious moment
in life is when you're about to
fall in love. He's gazing at you
and you're gazing at him and
there's a sense that something
truly wondrous is about to
happen. It's a nervous moment,
but it's exhilarating."
—**Scarlett Johansson**

"Love can sometimes be
magic. But magic can sometimes just be an illusion."
—**Steven Javan Jones**

"Love never dies a natural
death. It dies because we don't
know how to replenish its
source."
—**Anaïs Nin**

"There is love, of course. And
then there's life, its enemy."
—**Jean Anouilh**

"God knows I wanted love.
But the moment I had to
choose between the man I
loved and my dresses, I chose
the dresses."
—**Coco Chanel**

"You don't love because,
you love despite; not for
the virtues, but despite the
faults."
—**William Faulkner**

"We come to love not by
finding the perfect person,
but by learning to see an
imperfect person perfectly."
—**Angelina Jolie**

"One of the best things
about love—the feeling of
being wrapped, like a gift,
in understanding."
—**Anatole Broyard**

"For everyone one who has
ever loved, one has waited."
—**Graham Greene**

"Love ain't nothing but sex
misspelled."
—**Harlan Ellison**

Cleopatra used a mixture of horse teeth, bear grease, burnt mice...

# EXERCISE

*Okay, break's over. Time for your second set of working-out quotes. And 1 and 2 and 3 and 4 and...*

"The word 'aerobics' came about when the gym instructors got together and said, 'If we're going to charge $10 an hour, we can't call it 'jumping up and down.'"
—**Rita Rudner**

"Traveling by foot can broaden your mind, while having the opposite effect on other parts of the anatomy."
—**Georgia V. Alan**

"The moment my legs begin to move, my thoughts begin to flow."
—**Henry David Thoreau**

"My idea of exercise is a good brisk sit."
—**Phyllis Diller**

"If God invented marathons to keep people from doing anything more stupid, Ironman triathlons must have taken him completely by surprise."
—**P. Z. Pearce**

"A man's health can be judged by which he takes two at a time: pills or stairs."
—**Joan Welsh**

"Whenever I feel like exercise, I lie down until the feeling passes."
—**Robert M. Hutchins**

"I consider exercise vulgar. It makes people smell."
—**Alec Yuill-Thornton**

"Melancholy is incompatible with bicycling."
—**James E. Starrs**

"People say that losing weight is no walk in the park. When I hear that, I think, 'Yeah, that's the problem.'"
—**Chris Adams**

"If you want to know if your brain is flabby, feel your legs."
—**Bruce Barton**

"The trouble with jogging is that the ice falls out of your glass."
—**Martin Mull**

"Push-ups, sit-ups, run in place. Each night I keep a grueling pace. With bleak results, I must divulge—I've lost the battle of the bulge."
—**Charles Ghinga**

# WHY ASK WHY?

*More questions without answers.*

"Ah! What is man? Wherefore does he why? Whence did he whence? Whither is he withering?"
—**Dan Leno**

"If truth is beauty, how come no one has their hair done in the library?"
—**Lily Tomlin**

"Is 'tired old cliché' one?"
—**Rod Schmidt**

"If you can't live without me, why aren't you dead already?"
—**Cynthia Heimel**

"Why is the alphabet in that order? Is it because of that song?"
—**Steven Wright**

"Why is the word 'abbreviation' so long?"
—**Jerry Seinfeld**

"You go to heaven. God sneezes. What do you say?"
—**Peter Houppermans**

"Why do we kill people who are killing people to show that killing people is wrong?"
—**Holly Near**

"Why is there so much month left at the end of the money?"
—**John Barrymore**

"If it doesn't matter who wins or loses, then why do they keep score?"
—**Vince Lombardi**

"If the banks are so friendly, how come they chain down the pens?"
—**Alan King**

"At Motel 6 in Amish Country, I wonder if they leave the light on for you?"
—**Jay London**

"Well, if I called the wrong number, why did you answer the phone?"
—**James Thurber**

"If a word in the dictionary were misspelled, how would we know?"
—**Steven Wright**

"When someone is impatient and says, 'I haven't got all day,' I always wonder: How can that be? How can you not have all day?"
—**George Carlin**

# THE HITCHHIKER'S GUIDE TO DOUGLAS ADAMS

*Combining a droll British sense of humor with science fiction, author Douglas Adams (1952–2001) garnered a huge cult following, thanks to witty—and bizarre—observations like these.*

"In the beginning, the Universe was created. This has made a lot of people very angry and has been widely regarded as a bad move."

"Nothing travels faster than the speed of light with the possible exception of bad news, which obeys its own special laws."

"It is no coincidence that in no known language does the phrase 'As pretty as an airport' appear."

"The major difference between a thing that might go wrong and a thing that cannot possibly go wrong is that when a thing that cannot possibly go wrong goes wrong it usually turns out to be impossible to get at or repair."

"If you try and take a cat apart to see how it works, the first thing you have in your hands is a non-working cat."

"I think fish is nice, but then I think that rain is wet, so who am I to judge?"

"I'm spending a year dead for tax reasons."

"If it looks like a duck, and quacks like a duck, we have at least to consider the possibility that we have a small aquatic bird of the family Anatidae on our hands."

"One always overcompensates for disabilities. I'm thinking of having my entire body surgically removed."

"The knack of flying is learning how to throw yourself at the ground and miss."

"You live and learn. At any rate, you live."

"I may not have gone where I intended to go, but I think I have ended up where I needed to be."

Douglas Adams chose the name of Pink Floyd's 1994 album, *The Division Bell.*

# HALL OF FAMERS

*Kenesaw Mountain Landis, the first commissioner of Major League Baseball, said, "Nearly every boy builds a shrine to some baseball hero, and before that shrine a candle always burns." On this page, we keep it burning.*

"Because there is always some kid who may be seeing me for the first or last time, I owe him my best."

—Joe DiMaggio

"Brooks Robinson never asked anyone to name a candy bar after him. In Baltimore, people name their children after him."

—Gordon Beard

"The team playing behind Sandy Koufax is the ghastliest scoring team in history. They pile up runs at the rate of one every nine innings. This is a little like making Rembrandt paint on the back of cigar boxes, giving Paderewski a piano with two octaves, Caruso singing with a high school chorus. With the Babe Ruth Yankees, Sandy Koufax would have been the first undefeated pitcher in history."

—Jim Murray, sportswriter

"I was thinking about making a comeback, until I pulled a muscle vacuuming."

—Johnny Bench

"If the human body recognized agony and frustration, people would never run marathons, have babies, or play baseball."

—Carlton Fisk

"Whether your name is Gehrig or Ripken, DiMaggio or Robinson, or that of some youngster who picks up his bat or puts on his glove, you are challenged by the game of baseball to do your very best day in and day out. That's all I've ever tried to do."

—Cal Ripken, Jr.

"I don't want them to forget Ruth, I just want them to remember me!"

—Hank Aaron, shortly before he broke Babe Ruth's lifetime home-run record

"A woman will be elected president before Wade Boggs is called out on strikes."

—George Brett

"Ain't no man can avoid being average, but there ain't no man got to be common."

—Leroy "Satchel" Paige

"Bob Gibson pitches as though he's double parked."
      —Vin Scully, broadcaster

"Fans don't boo nobodies."
      —Reggie Jackson

"Close don't count in baseball. Close only counts in horseshoes and hand grenades."
      —Frank Robinson

"You know why it's the most unique game in the world? Because it ameliorates the classic polarization between self-motivated individuals and collective ideology."
      —Ernie Banks

"I was born with the restless desire to do a thing as well as it could be done. That meant doing it a little better than the other fellow."
      —Ty Cobb

"I don't think these people at Wrigley Field ever saw but two players they liked—Billy Williams and Ernie Banks. Billy never said anything, and Ernie always said the right thing."
      —Ferguson Jenkins

"When they start the game, they don't yell, 'Work ball.' They say, 'Play ball.'"
      —Willie Stargell

"I drink beer, I swear, and I keep my hair short, so I guess you'd call me an all-American boy."

      —Tom Seaver

"There are two theories on hitting the knuckleball. Unfortunately, neither works." —Charlie Lau

# MEN AND WOMEN

*A few more thoughts on this whole gender thing.*

"The only thing worse than a man you can't control is a man you can."
—Jean Kerr

"Here's all you have to know about men and women: women are crazy, men are stupid. And the main reason women are crazy is that men are stupid."
—George Carlin

"If men can run the world, why can't they stop wearing neckties? How intelligent is it to start the day by tying a little noose around your neck?"
—Linda Ellerbee

"Male and female represent the two sides of the great radical dualism. But in fact they are perpetually passing into one another. Fluid hardens to solid, solid rushes to fluid. There is no wholly masculine man, no purely feminine woman."
—Margaret Fuller

"Dancing is a wonderful training for girls, it's the first way you learn to guess what a man is going to do before he does it."
—Christopher Morley

"Nature gave women too much power; the law gives them too little."
—William Henry

"Why are women so much more interesting to men then men are to women?"
—Virginia Woolf

"Inside every older lady is a younger lady, wondering what the hell happened."
—Cora Harvey Armstrong

"We've got a generation of women now who were born with semi-equality. They don't know how it was before, so they think, this isn't too bad. We're working. We have our attaché cases and our three-piece suits. I get very disgusted with the younger generation of women. We had a torch to pass, and they are just sitting there. They don't realize it can be taken away. Things are going to have to get worse before they join in fighting the battle."
—Erma Bombeck

"Men are only as loyal as their options."
—Bill Maher

"I'm just a person trapped inside a woman's body." —Elayne Boosler

# FREE ADVICE

*Uncle John's advice: "Read this page."*

"When buying a used car, punch the buttons on the radio. If all the stations are rock 'n' roll, there's a good chance the transmission is shot."
—**Larry Lujack**

"Be sure to wear a good cologne, a nice aftershave lotion, and a strong underarm deodorant. And it might be a good idea to wear some clothes, too."
—**George Burns**

"Have no fear of perfection, you'll never reach it."
—**Salvador Dali**

"If you're going to do something tonight that you'll be sorry for tomorrow, sleep late."
—**Henny Youngman**

"My advice to you is not to inquire why or whither but just enjoy your ice cream while it's on your plate."
—**Thornton Wilder,** *The Skin of Our Teeth*

"Laugh at yourself first, before anyone else can."
—**Elsa Maxwell**

"The best way to win an argument is to begin by being right."
—**Jill Ruckelshaus**

"If you know how to cheat, start now."
—**Earl Weaver**

"I know I'm not going to be the first parent that ever outsmarted a teenager, and I'm not trying. All I'm going to say is, everything they say is bad for you...pretty much is bad for you."
—**Jack Nicholson,** **to his teenage daughters**

"If it has tires or testicles, you're going to have trouble with it."
—**Linda Furney**

"Appear weak when you are strong, and strong when you are weak."
—**Sun Tzu**

"Often you just have to rely on your intuition."
—**Bill Gates**

"Be happy. It's one way of being wise."
—**Sidonie-Gabrielle Colette**

**"Many receive advice; only the wise profit from it." —Harper Lee**

# EASTERN WISDOM

*"Greetings, gentle reader. Sit back, release your worldly constraints, and let these quotations from some of history's most illuminated minds permeate your inner being. Om..."* —Uncle John

"The thought manifests as the word. The word manifests as the deed. The deed develops into habit. And the habit hardens into character. So watch the thought with care."
—**Buddha (560–480 B.C.)**

"Whenever you are confronted with an opponent, conquer him with love."
—**Mahatma Gandhi (1869–1948)**

"Everything has beauty, though not everyone sees it."
—**Confucius (551–479 B.C.)**

"Besides the noble art of getting things done, there is the noble art of leaving things undone. The wisdom of life consists in the elimination of nonessentials."
—**Lin Yutang (1895–1976)**

"Flow with whatever is happening and let your mind be free. Stay centered by accepting whatever you are doing. This is the ultimate."
—**Chuang Tzu (369–286 B.C.)**

"In dwelling, live close to the ground. In thinking, keep to the simple. In conflict, be fair and generous. In governing, don't try to control. In work, do what you enjoy. In family life, be completely present."
—**Lao Tzu (4th cent. B.C.)**

"Great is the man who does not lose his child mind."
—**Meng-Tse (372–289 B.C.)**

"The beauty of selfless love and service should not die away from the face of the earth. The world should know that a life of dedication is possible, that a life inspired by love and service to humanity is possible."
—**Ammachi (b. 1953)**

"Whether you go up the ladder or down it, your position is shaky. When you stand with your two feet on the ground, you will always keep your balance."
—**The *Tao Te Ching***

"Do your best, then don't worry, be happy."
—**Meher Baba (1894–1969)**

# MAMA ALWAYS SAID...

*Some more quotes of familial advice...some profound, some otherwise.*

"My mother taught me that when you stand in the truth and someone tells a lie about you, don't fight it."
—**Whitney Houston**

"My mother always said don't marry for money; divorce for money."
—**Wendy Liebman**

"Mom and Dad say I should make my life an example of the principles I believe in. But every time I do, they tell me to stop it."
—**Calvin, *Calvin and Hobbes***

"My father said to me that I had a good heart, but that he feared women would confuse and dominate my life."
—**Franz Liszt**

"There are only two families in the world, my old grandmother used to say, the Haves and the Have-nots."
—**Miguel de Cervantes**

"My father taught me all the tricks of the boys at an early age, which has made me very careful."
—**Kim Wilde**

"My mother said I must always be intolerant of ignorance but understanding of illiteracy. That some people, unable to go to school, were more educated and more intelligent than college professors."
—**Maya Angelou**

"Mother always said that honesty was the best policy, and money isn't everything. She was wrong about other things, too."
—**Gerald Barzan**

"My great-grandfather used to say to my great-grandmother, who in turn told my grandmother, who repeated it to my mother, who used to remind my sister, that to talk well and eloquently was a very great art, but that an equally great one was to know the right moment to stop."
—**Wolfgang Amadeus Mozart**

"I blame my mother for my poor sex life. All she told me was 'the man goes on top and the woman underneath.' For three years my husband and I slept in bunk beds."
—**Joan Rivers**

"If there are poor on the Moon, we shall go there too." —**Mother Teresa**

# TED TURNER

*Some see Turner as a visionary. Others write him off as a kook. But one thing is sure: He built the foundation for what is modern cable news coverage…and he's got something to say on almost every subject.*

"Maybe a little less 'pervert of the day.' I mean, there's a lot of perversion around, but is it really news?"

—*on how he would change* CNN

"I'd say the chances are about 50-50 that humanity will be extinct or nearly extinct within 50 years."

"The role of the government ought to be like the role of a referee in boxing, keeping the big guys from killing the little guys. But today the government has cast down its duty, and media competition is less like boxing and more like professional wrestling: The wrestler and the referee are both kicking the guy on the canvas."

"Sports is like a war without the killing."

"Having great wealth is one of the most disappointing things. It's overrated, I can tell you that. It's not as good as average sex."

"I've never run into a guy who could win at the top level in anything and didn't have the right attitude, didn't give it everything he had, at least while he was doing it."

"My son is now an 'entrepreneur.' That's what you're called when you don't have a job."

"I don't believe people should kill each other or hurt each other. It's stupid and uncivilized and expensive, all at a time when we need to use the money for education and healthcare and improving the human condition."

"The way I've interpreted religions, it seems to me that no matter how you see God, he wants us to be nice to each other. Virtually every religion that I've ever studied has 'Thou shalt not kill' as one of its tenets, yet killing goes on."

"I know what I'm having 'em put on my tombstone: 'I have nothing more to say.'"

---

Bill Gates could pay the salary of President George W. Bush for 132,000 years.

# ...AND GOD SAID, "LET THERE BE BEER"

*Who is St. Arnold? According to the Catholic Church, he's the patron saint of brewing beer. Here's some more proof that God loves beer.*

"From man's sweat and God's love, beer came into the world."
—Saint Arnoldus

"The good Lord has changed water into wine, so how can drinking beer be a sin?"
—Sign at a Belgian Monastery

"Of doctors and medicines we have in plenty more than enough. What you may, for the Love of God, send is some large quantity of beer."
—Dispatch from the Colony, New South Wales, 1854

"God made yeast, and loves fermentation just as dearly as he loves vegetation."
—Ralph Waldo Emerson

"This is grain, which any fool can eat, but for which the Lord intended a more divine means of consumption: BEER!"
—Friar Tuck, *Robin Hood, Prince of Thieves*

"Beer is proof that God loves us and wants us to be happy."
—Benjamin Franklin

"A good pub has much in common with a church, except that a pub is warmer, and there's more conversation."
—William Blake

"When we drink, we get drunk. When we get drunk, we fall asleep. When we fall asleep, we commit no sin. When we commit no sin, we go to heaven. So, let's all get drunk and go to heaven!"
—Brian O'Rourke

"If God had intended us to drink beer, He would have given us stomachs."
—David Daye

"I should like a great lake of ale, for the King of Kings. I should like the family of Heaven to be drinking it through time eternal."
—St. Brigid

"Religions change, but beer and wine remain." —Harvey Allen

# ENGLAND'S FAVORITE FRY

*Stephen Fry is an icon in England, having been a popular comedian, filmmaker, actor, and author since the 1980s. Here are some prime examples of why the Brits love him so much.*

"It is a cliché that most clichés are true, but then like most clichés, that cliché is untrue."

"I don't watch television, I think it destroys the art of talking about oneself."

"Many people would no more think of entering journalism than the sewage business—which at least does us all some good."

"I think animal testing is cruel. They get nervous and get all the answers wrong."

"I don't need you to remind me of my age. I have a bladder to do that for me."

"Smell is the most deeply embarrassing of all the five senses, the one which most clearly tells us precisely who and what we are."

"An original idea can't be too hard. The library must be full of them."

"The e-mail of the species is more deadly than the mail."

"Old professors never die; they just lose their faculties."

"Secret vices? I don't know. Rather too fond of chocolate. My wife tells me I overdo the heroin. Otherwise, not really."

"I was Princess Anne's assistant for a while, but I chucked that in because it was obvious they were never going to make me Princess no matter how well I did the job."

"If ignorance is bliss, why aren't there more happy people in the world?"

"You should try the fruit of every tree of every garden in the world. But 'try' is the word. Some fruits will be rotten, some will be poisonous, and some will be so seductive you eat nothing else and become malnutreated, if there is such a word."

# "SKIPPER, WHAT DO YOU THINK?"

*One of Major League Baseball's greatest managers, Earl Weaver,*
*never played in a big-league game in his life. Yet, as the skipper of the*
*Baltimore Orioles from 1968 to 1986, he won more than 1,000 games,*
*including four pennants and a World Series. Here he candidly describes*
*what it's like to tell a young kid at the end of spring training*
*that he doesn't have what it takes to play in the Bigs.*

You got a hundred more young kids than you have a place for on your club. Every one of them has had a going-away party. They have been given the shaving kit and the fifty dollars. They kissed everybody and said, "See you in the majors in two years!" You see these poor kids who shouldn't be there in the first place. You write on the report card "4-4-4 and out." That's the lowest rating in everything. Then you call 'em in and say, "It's the consensus among us that we're going to let you go back home." Some of them cry, some get mad, but none of them will leave until you answer them one question, "Skipper, what do you think?" And you gotta look every one of those kids in the eye and kick their dreams in the ass and say no. If you say it mean enough, maybe they do themselves a favor and don't waste years learning what you can see in a day. They don't have what it takes to make the majors, just like I never had it.

Earl Weaver still holds an American League record: most times ejected from a game (98).

# COMPLIMENTARY QUIZ

*See if you can guess which of these multiple choices
is getting lavished with all of this praise.*

**1.** "[He's] the most extraordinary combination of unbelievably powerful and passionate and he's so intricately subtle, it's like watching a glorious tapestry unveiled every time he's on the screen."

**—Kate Winslet is speaking about:**

**a:** Johnny Depp    **b:** Jude Law    **c:** Leonardo DiCaprio

**2.** "What more can I say about [him]? He is a brother, a friend, my godson's father. He is a unique and brave soul, someone that I would go to the ends of the earth for, and I know, full and well, he would do the same for me."

**—Johnny Depp is speaking about:**

**a:** Tim Burton    **b:** Keith Richards    **c:** Sean Penn

**3.** "[He] just keeps doing really good stuff. He's a really, really smart and good actor. I've written letters to him just so say, 'Hey, man, you're flaming great.'"

**—George Clooney is speaking about:**

**a:** Brad Pitt    **b:** Matt Damon    **c:** Johnny Depp

**4.** "I think [she] has a great deal of intelligence and capability. I have a lot of respect for her. She's taken her career and maximized it with intelligence and creativity."

**—Carole King is speaking about:**

**a:** Barbra Streisand    **b:** Madonna    **c:** Queen Latifah

**5.** "All modern American literature comes from one book. There was nothing before. There has been nothing as good since."

**—Ernest Hemingway is speaking about:**

**a:** *Moby Dick*, by Herman Melville

**b:** *Of Mice and Men*, by John Steinbeck

**c:** *Huckleberry Finn*, by Mark Twain

**6.** "I had two heroes, John Wayne and Roy Rogers. Then one day I saw [him] and I said, 'That's the way I want to look.' He represents a dream come true for every young man who wanted to be something, especially in the '60s. We saw in him everything we wanted to be."

—George Foreman is speaking about:

**a:** Muhammad Ali    **b:** Jim Brown    **c:** William Shatner

**7.** "[He] was arguably the best serve-and-volley man of all time, but then he was an exception to pretty much every predictive norm there was. At his peak (say 1980 to 1984), he was the greatest tennis player who ever lived—the most talented, the most beautiful, the most tormented: a genius."

—author David Foster Wallace wrote this in *Esquire* about:

**a:** Jimmy Connors    **b:** John McEnroe    **c:** Bjorn Borg

**8.** "There's not a hip-hop artist that didn't snatch of piece of [his music]. It's totally impossible."

—Wyclef Jean snatched a lot of music from:

**a:** James Brown    **b:** George Clinton    **c:** Bob Marley

**9.** "I do like [her]. I think she's cute. I think she's fun. And I like her records. You know, I'm not a pop snob whatsoever. I think she makes great pop records."

—Elton John is speaking about:

**a:** Britney Spears    **b:** Gwen Stefani    **c:** Jessica Simpson

**10.** Man, meeting [him] was like…black Jesus walking towards me. It was overwhelming to me to finally meet the guy I've looked up to my whole life."

—LeBron James, NBA star, is speaking about:

**a:** Shaquille O'Neal    **b:** Muhammad Ali    **c:** Michael Jordan

**11.** "It's a $3,000 Armani, but I'd throw it on the ground and step on it for [him]."

—Ben Affleck would ruin his jacket for:

**a:** Al Gore    **b:** Bill Clinton    **c:** Ted Kennedy

Answers: 1-b; 2-a; 3-c; 4-b; 5-c; 6-b; 7-b; 8-c; 9-a; 10-c; 11-a.

Michael Jordan always wore the shorts of his North Carolina uniform under his Bulls uniform.

# WORDS OF THE RINGS

*J.R.R. Tolkien (1892–1973) spoke to a generation of fantasy readers. Here's a sampling of Middle Earth wisdom from his books,* The Hobbit *and* The Lord of the Rings.

"It's a dangerous business, Frodo, going out your front door. You step into the Road, and if you don't keep your feet, there is no telling where you might be swept off to."
—**Bilbo Baggins**

"Many that live deserve death. And some die that deserve life. Can you give it to them? Be not too eager to deal out death in the name of justice, fearing for your own safety. Even the wise cannot see all ends."
—**Gandalf the Grey**

**Frodo:** I wish it need not have happened in my time.
**Gandalf:** So do all who live to see such times. But that is not for them to decide. All we have to decide is what to do with the time that is given us.

"Short cuts make long delays."
—**Hobbit proverb**

"If more of us valued food and cheer and song above hoarded gold, it would be a merrier world."
—**Thorin the Dwarf**

"He that breaks a thing to find out what it is has left the path of wisdom."
—**Gandalf**

"Nothing is evil in the beginning."
—**Elrond**

"When things are in danger: someone has to give them up so that others may keep them."
—**Frodo Baggins**

"The wise speak only of what they know."
—**Gandalf**

"Fair speech may hide a foul heart."
—**Samwise Gamgee**

"A traitor may betray himself and do good that he does not intend."
—**Gandalf**

"There is nothing like looking, if you want to find something."
—**Thorin the Dwarf**

"Not all those who wander are lost."
—**Boromir**

# FRIENDSHIP

*We at the Bathroom Readers' Institute are very proud to call you, our devoted readers, friends. Now, are you available next Thursday to help us move?*

"It is one of the blessings of old friends that you can afford to be stupid with them."
—**Ralph Waldo Emerson**

"Am I not destroying my enemies when I make friends of them?"
—**Abraham Lincoln**

"Friendship multiplies the good of life and divides the evil."
—**Baltasar Gracián**

"No person is your friend who demands your silence, or denies your right to grow."
—**Alice Walker**

"Don't believe your friends when they ask you to be honest with them. All they really want is to be maintained in the good opinion they have of themselves."
—**Albert Camus**

"Friendship is born at that moment when one person says to another: 'What! You, too? Thought I was the only one.'"
—**C. S. Lewis**

"Friendship marks a life even more deeply than love. Love risks degenerating into obsession; friendship is never anything but sharing."
—**Elie Wiesel**

"Friendship is a sheltering tree."
—**Samuel Coleridge**

"It's the friends you can call up at 4 a.m. that matter."
—**Marlene Dietrich**

"Men kick friendship around like a football, but it doesn't seem to crack. Women treat it like glass, and it goes to pieces."
—**Anne Morrow Lindbergh**

"When all is said and done, friendship is the only trustworthy fabric of the affections. Love is a delirious inhuman state of mind: when hot it substitutes indulgence for fair play; when cold it is cruel, but friendship is warmth in cold, firm ground in a bog."
—**Miles Franklin**

# CLASSIC COMEDIANS

*They were funny then; and they're still funny today.*

"My wife Mary and I have been married for 47 years, and not once have we had an argument serious enough to consider divorce; murder, yes, but divorce, never."
—Jack Benny

**George Burns:** Gracie, those are beautiful flowers. Where did they come from?
**Gracie Allen:** Don't you remember, George? You said that if I went to visit Clara Bagley in the hospital I should be sure to take her flowers. So when she wasn't looking, I did.

"Yes, darling, let me cover your face with kisses. On second thought, just let me cover your face."
—Groucho Marx

"I have enough money to last me the rest of my life, unless I buy something."
—Jackie Mason

"I don't get no respect. The time I got hurt, on the way to the hospital the ambulance stopped for gas."
—Rodney Dangerfield

"A guy bought a farm. He didn't know anything about farms, but he bought one anyway. He decides he's going to plant something. Anything. 'What are you going to plant?' his friend asks. 'Razor blades and cabbages.' His friend looks at him. 'Razor blades and cabbages? What could you possibly get out of that?' 'Coleslaw.'"
—Buddy Hackett

"Speaking of trade relations, almost everyone would like to."
—Henny Youngman

"A fellow told me he was going to hang-glider school. He said, 'I've been going for three months.' I said, 'How many successful jumps do you need to make before you graduate?' He said, 'All of them.'"
—Red Skelton

"I don't like country music, but I don't mean to denigrate those who do. And for the people who like country music, denigrate means 'put down.'"
—Bob Newhart

# HENRY ROLLINS

*He made his mark in the punk band Black Flag, then as a spoken-word artist.*
*These days, he hosts a movie-discussion show on IFC and entertains*
*troops with the USO. What will Henry Rollins think of next?*

"I've always seen it as the role of an artist to drag his inside out, give the audience all you've got. Writers, actors, singers, all good artists do the same. It isn't supposed to be easy."

"Life will not break your heart. It'll crush it."

"If you hate your parents, the man, or the establishment, don't show them up by getting wasted and wrapping your car around a tree. If you really want to rebel against your parents: outdream them, outlive them, and know more than they do."

"I get immediately bored with anyone complaining about how boring their life is, or how bad their town is. Leave and go somewhere else. Or don't."

"Honestly, I don't think music can do much to change anything. If it could, then it already would have happened."

"My optimism wears heavy boots and is loud."

"If you can fit it on a bumper sticker, it's not a reason to go to war."

"Don't do anything by half. If you love someone, love them. If you hate someone, hate them until it hurts."

"On occasion I am a pretty nice guy, but I hold my anger in high regard."

"Go without a coat when it's cold; find out what cold is. Go hungry; keep your existence lean. Wear away the fat, get down to the lean tissue and see what it's all about. The only time you define your character is when you go without."

"Half of life is messing up— the other half is dealing with it."

"As miserable as life may be, I hold it pretty precious."

# HOW TO SUCCEED

*Who knows the key to success? These folks do. Let these quotations inspire you to make your own dreams come true.*

"Talent is cheaper than table salt. What separates the talented individual from the successful one is a lot of hard work."
—**Stephen King**

"The rules are simple. Take your work, but never yourself, seriously. Pour in the love and whatever skill you have, and it will come out."
—**Chuck Jones**

"It seems to be a law of nature, inflexible and inexorable, that those who will not risk cannot win."
—**John Paul Jones**

"If you want to succeed, double your failure rate."
—**Thomas Watson, founder of IBM**

"Success is more permanent when you achieve it without destroying your principles."
—**Walter Cronkite**

"In order to succeed, you must fail…so that you know what not to do the next time."
—**Anthony D'Angelo**

"All you umpires, back to the bleachers. Referees, hit the showers. It's my game. I pitch, I hit, I catch. I run the bases. At sunset, I've won or lost. At sunrise, I'm out again, giving it the old try."
—**Ray Bradbury**

"The difference between a successful person and others is not a lack of strength, not a lack of knowledge, but rather in a lack of will."
—**Vince Lombardi**

"Yes, risk taking is inherently failure-prone. Otherwise, it would be called sure-thing-taking."
—**Jim McMahon**

"Some of the world's greatest feats were accomplished by people not smart enough to know they were impossible."
—**Doug Larson**

"Success is not the key to happiness. Happiness is the key to success. If you love what you are doing, you will be successful."
—**Albert Schweitzer**

**"It is never too late to be what you might have been."** —**George Eliot**

"It takes 20 years of hard work to become an overnight success."
—Diana Rankin

"If you hear a voice within you say 'you cannot paint,' then by all means paint, and that voice will be silenced."
—Vincent Van Gogh

"A successful person is one who can lay a firm foundation with the bricks that others throw at him or her."
—David Brinkley

"To follow, without halt, one aim: There's the secret of success."
—Anna Pavlova

"Of course there is no formula for success except perhaps an unconditional acceptance of life and what it brings."
—Arthur Rubinstein

"Success usually comes to those who are too busy to be looking for it."
—Henry David Thoreau

"All you need in this life is ignorance and confidence; then success is sure."
—Mark Twain

"Success isn't permanent, and failure isn't fatal."
—Mike Ditka

"Success isn't the result of spontaneous combustion. You must set yourself on fire."
—Reggie Leach

"Success is the ability to go from one failure to another with no loss of enthusiasm."
—Sir Winston Churchill

"Many of life's failures are people who did not realize how close they were to success when they gave up."
—Thomas Edison

"Eighty percent of success is showing up."
—Woody Allen

"Success is often the result of taking a misstep in the right direction."
—Al Bernstein

"Flaming enthusiasm, backed up by horse sense and persistence, is the quality that most frequently makes for success."
—Dale Carnegie

"In order to succeed, your desire for success should be greater than your fear of failure."
—Bill Cosby

"Failure is success, if we learn from it."
—Malcolm Forbes

"No pessimist ever sailed to an uncharted land." —Helen Keller

# SAY WHAT?

*Warning: Trying to read these quotations may give*
*you a headache (they sure did that to us).*

"We must be willing to pay a price for freedom, for no price that is ever asked for it is half the cost of doing without it."
—**H. L. Mencken**

"The Sequoia School District now has a minority population of 57%."
—*San Francisco Chronicle*

"I mean a child that doesn't have a parent to read to that child or that doesn't see that when the child is hurting to have a parent and help out or neither parent there enough to pick up the kid and dust him off and send him back into the game at school or whatever, that kid has a disadvantage."
—**George H. W. Bush**

"I see the world in very fluid, contradictory, emerging, interconnected terms, and with that kind of circuitry I just don't feel the need to say what is going to happen or will not happen."
—**Jerry Brown, former Governor of California**

"We are having to live with paying the price for what happened before."
—**Felix Sabates**

"The problem with beauty is that it's like being born rich and getting poorer."
—**Joan Collins**

"Action seems to follow feeling, but really action and feeling go together; and by regulating the action, which is under the more direct control of the will, we can indirectly regulate the feeling, which is not."
—**William James**

"I would not say that the future is necessarily less predictable than the past. I think the past was not predictable when it started."
—**Donald Rumsfeld**

"To say of what is that it is not, or of what is not that it is, is false, while to say of what is that it is, and of what is not that it is not, is true."
—**Aristotle**

# FOOD STUFFS

*Note to reader: Can't write witty intro…too hungry after gathering all these delicious food quotations…going to lunch now. —Uncle John*

"There is no love sincerer than the love of food."
—**George Bernard Shaw**

"Super-skinny women really irritate me. I hate when they say, 'Sometimes I just forget to eat.' Now, I've forgotten my anniversary and where I parked my car. But I've never forgotten to eat."
—**Sela Ward**

"When we lose, I eat. When we win, I eat. I also eat when we're rained out."
—**Tommy Lasorda**

"I doubt whether the world holds for anyone a more soul-stirring surprise than the first adventure with ice cream."
—**Heywood Broun**

"Candy Corn is the only candy in the history of America that's never been advertised. And there's a reason. All of the candy corn that was ever made was made in 1911."
—**Lewis Black**

"I prefer Hostess fruit pies to pop-up toaster tarts because they don't require as much cooking."
—**Carrie Snow**

"Bad dinners go hand in hand with total depravity, while a well-fed man is already half saved."
—**Helen Woodward**

"Why does man kill? He kills for food. And not only food: frequently there must be a beverage."
—**Woody Allen**

"One can say everything best over a meal."
—**George Eliot**

"Laurie got offended that I used the word 'puke.' But to me, that's what her dinner tasted like."
—**Jack Handey**

"When one has tasted watermelon, he knows what the angels eat."
—**Mark Twain**

In an average lifetime, a person will eat around 60,000 pounds of food.

# HARD-BOILED

*Whether you're a dame with gams that just won't quit or a mook with a smoldering cigar and something to prove, you've got a lot of moxie for checking out these film noir quotes, kid!*

"The streets were dark with something more than night."
—Professor Wanley (Edward G. Robinson), *The Woman in the Window*

"She liked me. I could feel that. The way you feel when the cards are falling right for you, with a nice little pile of blue and yellow chips in the middle of the table. Only what I didn't know then was that I wasn't playing her. She was playing me, with a deck of marked cards and the stakes weren't any blue and yellow chips. They were dynamite."
—Walter Neff (Fred Mac-Murray), *Double Indemnity*

"'Okay Marlowe,' I said to myself. 'You're a tough guy. You've been sapped twice, choked, beaten silly with a gun, shot in the arm until you're crazy as a couple of waltzing mice. Now let's see you do something really tough—like putting your pants on.'"
—Philip Marlowe (Dick Powell), *Murder, My Sweet*

"I know you like a book, you little tramp. You'd sell your own mother for a piece of fudge. You've got a great big dollar sign there where most women have a heart."
—Johnny Clay (Sterling Hayden), *The Killing*

Wilmer (Elisha Cook): Keep on riding me, and they're gonna be picking iron out of your liver.
Sam Spade (Humphrey Bogart): The cheaper the crook, the gaudier the patter, eh?
—*The Maltese Falcon*

"Experience has taught me never to trust a policeman. Just when you think one's alright, he turns legit."
—Doc Riedenschneider (Sam Jaffe), *Asphalt Jungle*

"My feelings? About ten years ago, I hid them somewhere and haven't been able to find them."
—Whit (Kirk Douglas), *Out of the Past*

"It happens to be against two laws:
God's and man's. I'm booking her
on the second."

—Lt. Diamond (Cornell Wilde),
*The Big Combo*

"What I like about you is you're
rock bottom. I wouldn't expect you
to understand this, but it's a great
comfort for a girl to know she could
not possibly sink any lower."

—Chiquita (Jane Greer),
*The Big Steal*

John Dillinger was the first criminal ever designated Public Enemy #1 by the FBI.

# LEONARDO DICAPRIO

*As you can tell from these quotations, Leonardo DiCaprio goes out of his way to remain a normal person in the midst of what has become "superstardom."*

"It's not getting your face recognized that's the payoff—it's having your film remembered."

"Don't think for a moment that I'm really like any of the characters I play. That's why it's called acting."

"I want to be a jerk like the rest of my friends, and have fun, and not care about the consequences, but I just can't now."

"People want you to be a crazy, out-of-control teen brat. They want you miserable, just like them. They don't want heroes; what they want is to see you fall."

"As soon as enough people give you enough compliments and you're wielding more power than you've ever had in your life, it's not that you become arrogant or rude to people, but you get a false sense of your own importance. You actually think you've altered the course of history."

"I hate this whole 'hunk' thing! I feel when I see myself in that, that I'm just part of this meat factory, like, 'Wow! Here's the hunk of the month! This month we're shoving Leonardo DiCaprio down your throat! Isn't he cute? Let's put him on the cover and we'll sell so many more magazines.' That's definitely not what I want to be, and I've tried to get away from that whole situation."

"It's easy to fall into the trap of believing all the hype that's written about you. Who knows? In a couple of years, you might find me in the loony bin."

"There are so many people out there who are suffering trillions of times more than I'll ever suffer, and would love to be me. I am a lucky little bastard."

"If you can do what you do best and be happy, you're further along in life than most people."

---

**Real newspaper headline: "One-Legged Man Competent To Stand Trial"**

# STRAIGHT TALK ABOUT...

*For some, the subject may be taboo. But that doesn't mean
it isn't a popular (and common) topic of conversation.*

"I was raised around heterosexuals, as all heterosexuals
are. That's where us gay
people come from—you
heterosexuals."
—Ellen DeGeneres

"I've always said that if anyone
ever thought I was straight
they must need glasses, but
when I finally came out and
said, 'Yes, I do sleep with
men and I'm gay,' yeah, I lost
record sales. There's no
question—big, big time."
—Boy George

"I've had enough of being a
gay icon! I've had enough of
all this hard work, because,
since I came out, I keep
getting all these parts, and
my career's taken off."
—Ian McKellen

"I think people should be
free to engage in any sexual
practices they choose; they
should draw the line at goats,
though."
—Elton John

"Why is it that, as a culture,
we are more comfortable
seeing two men holding guns
than holding hands?"
—Ernest Gaines

"The Bible contains six admonishments to homosexuals and
362 admonishments to
heterosexuals. That doesn't
mean that God doesn't love
heterosexuals. It's just that
they need more supervision."
—Lynn Lavner

"I do not believe we can
blame genetics for adultery,
homosexuality, dishonesty,
and other character flaws."
—Jerry Falwell

"I realize that homosexuality
is a serious problem for anyone who is—but then, of
course, heterosexuality is a
serious problem for anyone
who is, too. And being a man
is a serious problem and being
a woman is, too. Lots of things
are problems."
—Edward Gorey

Roman Emperor Nero married his male slave Scorus in a public ceremony.

# SPACED-OUT SPORTS

*There's a fine line between stupid and surreal. This page has crossed that line, but was then called for a 15-yard encroachment penalty and had to swim back to second base until the goalie scored three free throws.*

"We talked five times. I called him twice, and he called me twice."
—**Larry Bowa, California Angels coach**

"I'll fight Lloyd Honeyghan for nothing if the price is right."
—**Marlon Starling**

"The Yankees, as I told you later, are in a slump."
—**Dizzy Dean**

"Okay, everyone, now inhale... and then dehale."
—**Maury Wills, Los Angeles Dodgers captain**

"I don't think we learned a lesson. I think it was a learning experience for us."
—**Shaquille O'Neal**

"This is the earliest I've ever been late."
—**Yogi Berra**

"That picture was taken out of context."
—**Jeff Innis, MLB pitcher, on an unflattering photo**

"I felt like the track came to us, but then it went beyond us."
—**Dale Earnhardt Jr., on the California Speedway**

"Good pitching will always stop good hitting, and vice-versa."
—**Casey Stengel**

"Football coaches have a way to get it done with what they give you. You're going to get it done. If you don't get it done, you don't have to worry about getting it done because you're done."
—**Paul Pasqualoni, college football coach**

"It's a catch-21 situation."
—**Kevin Pietersen, cricket player, on his withdrawal from the A-squad**

"Sometimes even Superman gets a chink in his armor."
—**Steve Francis, NBA player, on being injured**

"I think we're capable of going exactly as far as we go."
—**Chris Ford, NBA coach**

"Randy Moss is like a beautiful woman who can't cook, doesn't want to clean, and doesn't want to take care of kids. You really don't want her, but she's so beautiful that you can't let her go. That's how Randy is."
—Deion Sanders, NFL player

"I didn't know big guys had groins. I'm finding out today that I actually have one."
—Norman Hand, NFL player, after straining his groin

"My mom was real happy. She was elated at everything, too."
—Steve Karsay, on being the #1 pick in the 1990 baseball draft

"I've had marriages that have lasted shorter than this."
—John Daly, on a rain delay at a golf tournament

"It really left a taste in my mouth."
—Vladimir Guerrero, Anaheim Angels, after being swept in the playoffs

"I don't want to shoot my mouth in my foot, but those are games we can win."
—Sherman Douglas, NBA player

"On our team we got a lot of young guys and they always want to poke at you and tickle you and stuff and I really hate that."
—Eddy Curry, NBA player

"My most memorable Christmas memory was having all of my uncles and aunties out of prison for one Christmas, and that includes me. We had a lot of run-ins with the law, and to have us all out at one time was great."
—Caron Butler, NBA player

"We had lost four in a row, so it was very important to win this game. If we lose to Miami, it's like losing three games."
—Hakeem Olajuwon, NBA player

"I've never seen anything like it. I'm not going to say it was a miracle, because that's crippled people getting up and walking, the blind seeing. But that's the closest thing to it I've ever seen."
—Larry Foote, on a Pittsburgh Steelers playoff win

"Everybody in the room gets to punch you in the face."
—Tom Rossley, NFL coach, on what happens if a player's cell phone rings during a team meeting

The first World Series unassisted triple play was made by Bill Wambsganns in 1920.

# LINUS PAULING

*What Einstein was to physics, Linus Pauling was to chemistry. Awarded the Nobel Prize in chemistry in 1954, Pauling also won the Nobel Peace Prize in 1962 for speaking out against above-ground nuclear testing.*

"I have something that I call my Golden Rule. It goes like this: 'Do unto others twenty-five percent better than you expect them to do unto you.' The twenty-five percent is for error."

"Science cannot be stopped. Man will gather knowledge no matter what the consequences —and we cannot predict what they will be."

"I know that great, interesting, and valuable discoveries can and will be made. But I know also that still more interesting discoveries will be made that I have not the imagination to describe."

"If you want to have good ideas, you must have many ideas. Most of them will be wrong, and what you have to learn is which ones to throw away."

"Never put your trust into anything but your own intellect."

"Your elder, no matter whether he has gray hair, no matter whether he is a Nobel laureate, may be wrong."

"Do not let medical authorities or politicians mislead you. Find out what the facts are, and make your own decisions about how to live a happy life and how to work for a better world."

"Satisfying one's curiosity is one of the greatest sources of happiness in life."

"It no longer makes sense to kill 20 million or 40 million people because of a dispute between two nations who are running things, or decisions made by the people who really are running things. Nobody wins."

"Science will go on. More interesting discoveries will be made that I have not the imagination to describe and I am awaiting them, full of curiosity and enthusiasm."

Only 13.5% of scientists are female.

# I APOLOGIZE

*With our sincerest regrets, we're very sorry to bring you this collection of some of the funniest and strangest apologies ever uttered.*

"We apologize for the error in last week's paper in which we stated that Mr. Arnold Dogbody was a defective in the police force. We meant, of course, that Mr. Dogbody is a detective in the police farce."
—*Ely Standard* **(U.K.)**

"My family and I are deeply sorry for all that Vice President Cheney and his family have had to go through this past week."
**—Harry Whittington, Washington lawyer, after Dick Cheney shot *him* in the face**

"In previous issues of this newspaper, we may have given the impression that the people of France were snail swallowing, garlic munching surrender-monkeys whose women never bother to shave their armpits. We now realise that the French football team can stop the Portuguese from getting to the World Cup Final. We apologise profusely to France. *Vive la France!*"
**—*Daily Star* (U.K.), after France beat the U.K.'s rival, Portugal, in the 2006 World Cup semifinals**

"I am so terribly sorry for urinating outside of a public place in your city. It was not a very intelligent thing to do."
**—a man charged with public urination in Fond du Lac, Wisconsin, where all offenders now have to write letters of public apology**

"I'm sorry I bet on baseball."
**—Pete Rose, written on 300 baseballs that he then priced at $1,000 each**

"Oh, goodness, I regret it, it was a mistake! I'm solely responsible for it, and I'm very, very sorry. It was a mistake, I was wrong, it's my fault, and I'm very, very sorry to hurt anyone."
**—Sen. George Allen (R–VA), after referring to an Indian-American constituent as a "macaca"**

"We ate everything but his boots."
**—part of an apology from the Navatusila tribe of Fiji, who killed and ate a British missionary in 1867, to the missionary's descendants**

# PRESIDENTIAL LAST WORDS

*No more campaign promises, stump speeches, or State of the Union addresses—just one final utterance.*

"I die hard, but am not afraid to go."
—George Washington, 1799

"This is the last of earth. I am content."
—John Quincy Adams, 1848

Mary Todd Lincoln: What will Miss Harris think of my hanging on to you so?
Abraham Lincoln: She won't think anything about it.
—while watching a play at the Ford Theater, 1865

"History will vindicate my memory."
—James Buchanan, 1868

"I love you, Sarah. For all eternity, I love you."
—James K. Polk, to his wife, 1849

"Oh, do not cry. Be good children and we will all meet in heaven."
—Andrew Jackson, 1845

"Is it the Fourth?"
—Thomas Jefferson, July 4, 1826

"The nourishment is palatable."
—Millard Fillmore, 1874

"Water."
—Ulysses S. Grant, 1885

"I always talk better lying down."
—James Madison, 1836

"Put out the light."
—Theodore Roosevelt, 1919

"I am ready."
—Woodrow Wilson, 1924

"I have a terrific headache."
—Franklin Delano Roosevelt, 1945

"That's obvious."
—John F. Kennedy, when told by Mrs. John Connally, "You can't say that Dallas doesn't love you," 1963

What do Presidents Harrison and Taylor have in common? They both died in the White House.

# THE POWER OF MUSIC

*How do we know Uncle John believes in the power of music? Because
we can always hear humming coming from the bathroom.*

"It's easy to play any musical instrument: all you have to do is touch the right key at the right time, and the instrument will play itself."
—J. S. Bach

"There are more love songs than anything else. If songs could make you do something, we'd all love one another."
—Frank Zappa

"Should any part of my music offend you, please do not close your ears to it. Just take what you can use and go on."
—Ani DiFranco

"Music is the mediator between the spiritual and the sensual life."
—Ludwig van Beethoven

"Some people think a song without singing is not a song. Tell that to Beethoven and he'll kick your ass."
—Eddie Van Halen

"Whenever society gets too stifling and the rules get too complex, there's some sort of musical explosion."
—Slash, Guns N' Roses

"Music is the poetry of the air."
—Jean Paul Richter

"Extraordinary how potent cheap music is."
—Noel Coward

"After silence, that which comes nearest to expressing the inexpressible is music."
—Aldous Huxley

"There are two kinds of music, the good and bad. I play the good kind."
—Louis Armstrong

"The whole problem can be stated quite simply by asking, 'Is there a meaning to music?' My answer would be, 'Yes.' And, 'Can you state in words what the meaning is?' My answer to that would be, 'No.'"
—Aaron Copland

"Music is your own experience, your thoughts, your wisdom. If you don't live it, it won't come out of your horn. They teach you that music has boundaries. But, man, there's no boundary line to art."
—Charlie Parker

Tchaikovsky suffered from a paralyzing fear that his head would fall off.

# THE GRIDIRON

*Alright, football quotes on 2. Hut 1…Hut 2…Hike!*

"Some people think football is a matter of life and death. I don't like that attitude. I can assure them it is much more serious than that."
—**Bill Shankly**

"He had no teeth, and he was slobbering all over himself. I'm thinking, 'You can have your money back, just get me out of here. Let me go be an accountant.' I can't tell you how badly I wanted out of there."
—**John Elway,** *Denver QB, describing Jack Lambert of the Steelers, who knocked him out of his first pro game*

"When I played pro football, I never set out to hurt anyone deliberately—unless it was, you know, important, like a league game or something."
—**Dick Butkus**

"Men are clinging to football on a level we aren't even aware of. For centuries, we ruled everything, and now, in the last ten minutes, there are all these incursions by women. It's our Alamo."
—**Tony Kornheiser**

"You have to play this game like somebody just hit your mother with a two-by-four."
—**Dan Birdwell**

"Kicking is very important in football. In fact, some of the more enthusiastic players even kick the ball, occasionally."
—**Alfred Hitchcock**

"Football is an honest game. It's true to life. It's a game about sharing. Football is a team game. So is life."
—**Joe Namath**

"I do not like football, which I think of as a game in which two tractors approach each other from opposite directions and collide. Besides, I have contempt for a game in which players have to wear so much equipment. Men play basketball in their underwear, which seems just right to me."
—**Anna Quindlen**

"Football is, after all, a wonderful way to get rid of your aggressions without going to jail for it."
—**Heywood Hale Broun**

# THOU ART A FLESH-MONGER!

*The Bard's best barbs.*

"Go, prick thy face, and over-red thy fear, Thou lily-liver'd boy."
—*Macbeth*

"Thou art like a toad; ugly and venomous."
—*As You Like It*

"He's a disease that must be cut away."
—*Coriolanus*

"Thou art a flesh-monger, a fool and a coward."
—*Measure for Measure*

"Thy tongue outvenoms all the worms of Nile."
—*Cymbeline*

"You scullion! You rampallian! You fustilarian! I'll tickle your catastrophe!"
—*Henry IV, Part 2*

"Peace, ye fat guts!"
—*Henry IV, Part 2*

"Methink'st thou art a general offence and every man should beat thee."
—*All's Well That Ends Well*

"Thou clay-brained guts, thou knotty-pated fool, thou whoreson obscene greasy tallow-catch!"
—*Henry IV, Part 1*

"You are as a candle, the better burnt out."
—*Henry IV, Part 2*

"I scorn you, scurvy companion. What, you poor, base, rascally, cheating, lack-linen mate! Away, you mouldy rogue!"
—*Henry IV, Part 2*

"Thou art unfit for any place but hell."
—*Richard III*

"Thine face is not worth sunburning."
—*Henry V*

"It is certain that when he makes water, his urine is congealed ice."
—*Measure for Measure*

"I do wish thou wert a dog, That I might love thee something."
—*Timon of Athens*

The city of Verona, Italy, receives about 1,000 letters addressed to "Juliet" every Valentine's Day.

"A knave, a rascal, an eater of broken meats; a base, proud, shallow, beggarly, three-suited, hundred-pound, filthy worsted-stocking knave; a lily-livered, action-taking, glass-gazing, super-serviceable, finical rogue; one-trunk-inheriting slave; one that art nothing but the composition of a knave, beggar, coward, pander, and the son and heir to a mongrel bitch: one whom I will beat into clamorous whining if thou deni'st the least syllable of thy addition."

—*King Lear*

# NO TALKING!

*Shhhhhh…*

"Four-fifths of all our troubles would disappear if we would only sit down and keep still."
—Calvin Coolidge

"The best cure for the body is a quiet mind."
—Napoleon Bonaparte

"Speech is human, silence is divine, yet also brutish and dead: therefore we must learn both arts."
—Thomas Carlyle

"It's so simple to be wise. Just think of something stupid to say, and then don't say it."
—Sam Levenson

"Cultivate quietness in your speech, in your thoughts, in your emotions. Speak habitually low. Wait for attention and then you low words will be charged with dynamite."
—Elbert Hubbard

"Silence is the true friend that never betrays."
—Confucius

"The inability to stay quiet is one of the conspicuous failings of mankind."
—Walter Bagehot

"He who establishes his argument by noise and command shows that his reason is weak."
—Michel de Montaigne

"Noise proves nothing. Often a hen who has merely laid an egg cackles as if she laid an asteroid."
—Mark Twain

"The most basic and powerful way to connect to another person is to listen. Just listen. Perhaps the most important thing we ever give each other is our attention."
—Rachel Naomi Remen

"Many attempts to communicate are nullified by saying too much."
—Robert Greenleaf

"You never saw a fish on the wall with its mouth shut."
—Sally Berger

**"If sometimes you can't hear me, (it's because I'm speaking in parentheses)." —Steven Wright**

# YOU'RE MY INSPIRATION

*Famous people divulge their most important influences.*

"My idol was Bugs Bunny, because I saw a cartoon of him playing ball—you know, the one where he plays every position himself with nobody else on the field but him? Now that I think of it, Bugs is still my idol. You have to love a ballplayer like that."
—**Nomar Garciaparra**

"My original inspiration was my mom: A few years after the death of my dad, she started dating one my teachers!"
—**Meg Cabot, author of** *The Princess Diaries*

"Whereas Billie Holiday is the perfect interpretive singer, and more of a jazz singer, I wanted to do what Frank Sinatra did, in revering and tipping my hat to the actual tune, the way it was written on the sheet music."
—**Carly Simon**

"Insomnia is my greatest inspiration."
—**Jon Stewart**

"I get inspired, in America, by a certain kind of sleaziness."
—**Helmut Newton**

"I grew up with *The Mary Tyler Moore Show* and both of Bob Newhart's shows. When you look back on those Norman Lear shows now, some of them are so hilariously preachy, you can't believe that they got away with it. But the shows were also character-driven. And really, really funny."
—**Tina Fey**

"See, I've always seen Jacques Cousteau as a hero, mate. He's a legend—like my dad, just a legend."
—**Steve Irwin**

"My heroine was Jessica Mitford. I named my daughter after her. I found her inspiring because she was a brave and idealistic person—the qualities I most admire."
—**J. K. Rowling (Mitford was a British woman of nobility who gave up family wealth to come to the U.S. and become a civil rights activist)**

"I am driven by a wonderful muse called alimony."
—**Dick Schaap**

# ED WOOD
# IF HE COULD

*Celebrated as one of the worst filmmakers of the 20th century, Ed Wood (1924–78) probably had more fun making his movies than most people did watching them. Here are some classic excerpts.*

"The world is a strange place to live in. All those cars. All going someplace. All carrying humans, which are carrying out their lives."
—**Narrator,** *Glen or Glenda?*

"Sometimes I find plastic surgery to be hard and very, very complicated."
—**Dr. Gregor,** *Jail Bait*

**Paula:** I've never seen you in this mood before.
**Jeff:** I guess that's because I've never been in this mood before.
—*Plan 9 from Outer Space*

**Inspector:** I'd like to hear the story to the fullest.
**Dr. Alton:** Only the infinity of the depths of a man's mind can really tell the story.
—*Glen or Glenda?*

"This afternoon we had a long telephone conversation earlier in the day."
—**Dr. Gregor,** *Jail Bait*

**Tanna:** Do we have to kill them? It seems such a waste.
**Eros:** Wouldn't it be better to kill a few now than permit them to destroy the entire universe?
**Tanna:** You're always right, Eros.
—*Plan 9 from Outer Space*

"This swamp is a monument to death. Snakes, alligators, quicksand…all bent on one thing: destruction."
—**Lt. Craig,** *Bride of the Monster*

**Silas:** I'm gonna get ahold of some of the boys and blast them right off the river, the dirty scum.
**Honey Bee:** But Pa, how am I ever gonna get a husband if you killin' off all my chances?
—*Shotgun Wedding*

**Lt. Harper:** It was a saucer.
**Patrolman:** A *flying* saucer?
—*Plan 9 from Outer Space*

"The cinema is not a slice of life, but a piece of cake." —Alfred Hitchcock

**Col. Edwards:** This is the most fantastic story I've ever heard.
**Jeff:** And every word of it's true, too.
**Col. Edwards:** That's the fantastic part of it.
—*Plan 9 from Outer Space*

"There's only two things worthwhile for a girl: men and money!"
—*Toni, Five Loose Women*

"We are all interested in the future, for that is where you and I are going to spend the rest of our lives. And remember, future events will affect you in the future."
—Criswell,
*Plan 9 from Outer Space*

**Preacher:** Young lady, are you a milkmaid or an angel in disguise?
**Lucianne:** What do *you* say?
**Preacher:** I see you are a milkmaid. You present such a charming picture of bucolic simplicity.
**Lucianne:** Huh?
—*Shotgun Wedding*

"Beware! Beware of the big green dragon that sits on your doorstep. He eats little boys, puppy dog tails, and big fat snails. Beware! Take care."
—Scientist, *Glen or Glenda?*

"These aren't kids. These are morons!"
—Detective,
*The Violent Years*

## DEATH OF A FILMMAKER

In 1978 Ed Wood was drunk, broke, and living in Hollywood. While watching a football game one day, he yelled upstairs to his wife: "Kathy, I'm dying! I'm dying!" He often said this, so she ignored him. Ninety minutes later, Kathy went to check on Ed. She found the 54-year-old filmmaker dead from a massive heart attack.

# DIS-SECTION

*Call us cynical, but there are few things more rewarding than hearing famous people say nasty things about other famous people.*

"It is not a criticism, rather a suggestion that he do some exercises and go on a diet. I'm doing this for the gentleman's health."
—**Fidel Castro, describing Florida Governor Jeb Bush as President Bush's "fat little brother"**

"In a very Christian way, as far as I'm concerned, he can go to hell."
—**Jimmy Carter, on the Rev. Jerry Falwell**

"Jon Stewart and Stephen Colbert make a living putting on video of old ladies slipping on ice and people laughing. They exist in a small little place where they count for nothing."
—**Geraldo Rivera**

"I just think she's a vile, hideous, horrible human being with no redeeming qualities."
—**Boy George, on Madonna**

"Andy Warhol is the only genius I've ever known with an I.Q. of 60."
—**Gore Vidal**

"Colin Powell is permitted to come into the house of the master, as long as he will serve the master according to the master's plans. And when Colin Powell dares suggest something other than what the master wants to hear, he will be turned back out to pasture. And you don't hear much from those who live in the pasture."
—**Harry Belafonte**

"The Backstreet Boys were so ten years ago. Whatever."
—**Paris Hilton**

"When Newt Gingrich was a graduate student at Tulane University, I baptized him by immersion into the membership of the St. Charles Avenue Baptist Church. Perhaps I didn't hold him under long enough."
—**Rev. G. Avery Lee**

"I welcome him like I welcome cold sores. He's from England, he's angry, and he's got Mad Power Disease."
—**Paula Abdul, on Simon Cowell**

Clark Gable was listed on his birth certificate as a girl.

# ON POLITICS

*"There ain't no ticks like poly-ticks. Bloodsuckers all." —Davy Crockett*

"A politician thinks of the next election; a statesman, of the next generation."
　　—John Kenneth Galbraith

"In politics, a lie unanswered becomes truth within 24 hours."
　　—Willie Brown

"I'll show you politics in America. Here it is, right here. 'I think the puppet on the right shares my beliefs.' 'I think the puppet on the left is more to my liking.' Hey, wait a minute, there's one guy holding out both puppets!"
　　—Bill Hicks

"It doesn't matter who votes. What matters is who counts the votes."
　　—Joseph Stalin

"Bad officials are elected by good citizens who do not vote."
　　—George Jean Nathan

"In order to become the master, the politician poses as the servant."
　　—Charles de Gaulle

"Politicians are the same all over. They promise to build a bridge even where there is no river."
　　—Nikita Krushchev

"Those who are too smart to engage in politics are punished by being governed by those who are dumber."
　　—Plato

"On some great and glorious day the plain folks of the land will reach in their heart's desire at last, and the White House will be adorned by a downright moron."
　　—H. L. Mencken

"Politics would be a hell of a good business if it weren't for the g*dd*mned people."
　　—Richard Nixon

"The only politics I am willing to devote myself to is serving those around us: serving the community and serving those who will come after us. Its deepest roots are moral because it is a responsibility expressed through action, to and for the whole."
　　—Václav Havel

# BILLY GRAHAM

*Perhaps the most famous televangelist ever, Graham has prayed
with 10 U.S. presidents and was number 7 on Gallup's
list of "admired people for the 20th century."*

"I don't understand it, and I can't prove it scientifically, but I believe it."

"Out of defeat can come the best in human nature."

"I believe there's a hell, but I think hell has been misunderstood. I think that hell is separation from God."

"I believe there are other ways of recognizing the existence of God, through nature for instance."

"There's a difference between an intellectual faith and a personal, heart faith."

"People confuse amassing money with security, but it is not so. What a pity to confuse real security with making money."

"Tears shed for self are tears of weakness, but tears shed for others are a sign of strength."

"'Fundamentalist' is a grand and wonderful word, but it got off track and into so many extreme positions."

"When wealth is lost, nothing is lost; when health is lost, something is lost; when character is lost, all is lost."

"Man has two great spiritual needs. One is for forgiveness. The other is for goodness."

"Hot heads and cold hearts never solved anything."

"The test of a preacher is that his congregation goes away saying, not, 'What a lovely sermon!' but, 'I will do something!'"

"You're born. You suffer. You die. Fortunately, there's a loophole."

"I've read the last page of the Bible. It's all going to turn out all right."

**In 1932, King George V became the first British monarch to broadcast a Christmas message.**

# LIKE, TOTALLY '80S!

*Ingredients for a 1980s teen movie: handsome boy, tomboy girl who gets a makeover, montages set to a Kenny Loggins song, a mean blond jock, Molly Ringwald, and lots of really earnest dialogue. Wolverines!*

**Allison:** When you grow up, your heart dies.
**Andrew:** Who cares?
**Allison:** I care.
—Ally Sheedy and Emilio Estevez, *The Breakfast Club*

"Suicide is never the answer, little trooper. And dying when you're not really sick is really sick, you know. Really!"
—Curtis Armstrong, *Better Off Dead*

"If somebody doesn't believe in me, I can't believe in them."
—Molly Ringwald, *Pretty in Pink*

"By night's end, I predict me and her will interface."
—Anthony Michael Hall, *Sixteen Candles*

"There are several quintessential moments in a man's life: losing his virginity, getting married, becoming a father, and having the right girl smile at you."
—Emilio Estevez, *St. Elmo's Fire*

"Life moves pretty fast. If you don't stop and look around once in awhile, you could miss it."
—Matthew Broderick, *Ferris Bueller's Day Off*

"If you want to be a party animal, you have to learn to live in the jungle."
—Kelly LeBrock, *Weird Science*

"I have this theory that good things always happen with bad things. I know you have to deal with them at the same time, but I just don't know why they have to happen at the same time. I just wish I could work out some schedule."
—Ione Skye, *Say Anything*

"I'm scared of everything. Most of all I'm scared of walking out of this room and never feeling the rest of my whole life the way I feel when I'm with you."
—Jennifer Grey, *Dirty Dancing*

"You're losing it. And when it's lost, all you are is a loser."
—**Mary Stuart Masterson,** *Some Kind of Wonderful*

**Brad:** Get a job, Spicoli.
**Spicoli:** What for?
**Brad:** You need money.
**Spicoli:** All I need are some tasty waves, a cool buzz, and I'm fine.
—**Judge Reinhold and Sean Penn,** *Fast Times at Ridgemont High*

"I'm young, I'm single, and I loves to mingle."
—**Gene Anthony Ray,** *Fame*

"My own brother a vampire! Oh, you wait 'til Mom finds out, buddy."
—**Corey Haim,** *The Lost Boys*

**Terry:** Listen, sex is not that big a deal.
**Buddy:** I'd like to form my own opinion.
—**Joyce Hyser and Billy Jayne,** *Just One of the Guys*

"Whenever I'm in a room with a guy, no matter who it is—a date, my dentist, anybody—I think, 'If we were the last two people on earth, would I puke if he kissed me?'"
—**Helen Hunt,** *Girls Just Want to Have Fun*

**Bill:** I agree that, in time, our band will be most triumphant. The truth is, Wyld Stallyns will never be a super band until we have Eddie Van Halen on guitar.
**Ted:** Yes, Bill. But I do not believe we will get Eddie Van Halen until we have a triumphant video.
**Bill:** Ted, it's pointless to have a triumphant video before we even have decent instruments.
**Ted:** Well, how can we have decent instruments when we don't really even know how to play?
**Bill:** That is why we *need* Eddie Van Halen!
**Ted:** And *that* is why we need a triumphant video.
—**Alex Winter and Keanu Reeves,** *Bill and Ted's Excellent Adventure*

"Why don't you just focus on girls and cars? Works for me."
—**Rob Lowe,** *The Outsiders*

"It's just that it's easier to say you don't care, than it is to try and fail."
—**Lea Thompson,** *SpaceCamp*

**Colonel:** All that hate's gonna burn you up, kid.
**Robert:** It keeps me warm.
—**Powers Boothe and C. Thomas Howell,** *Red Dawn*

Ha-ha: Atheism is a non-prophet organization.

# DEMS AND REPUBS

*-ocrats and -licans, that is.*

"Republicans have nothing but bad ideas, and Democrats have no ideas."
—**Lewis Black**

"The Democrats are the party that says government will make you smarter, taller, richer, and remove the crabgrass on your lawn. The Republicans are the party that says government doesn't work and then they get elected and prove it."
—**P. J. O'Rourke**

"Republicans study the financial pages of the newspaper. Democrats put them in the bottom of the bird cage."
—**Will Stanton**

"I hope the two wings of the Democratic Party may flap together."
—**William Jennings Bryan**

"The Republicans have a new healthcare proposal: Just say NO to illness!"
—**Mark Russell**

"You have to have been a Republican to know how good it is to be a Democrat."
—**Jacqueline Kennedy**

"My grandmother's brain was dead, but her heart was still beating. It was the first time we ever had a Democrat in the family."
—**Emo Phillips**

"A conservative is a man who wants the rules changed so that no one can make a pile the way he did."
—**Everett Dirksen**

"Liberal and conservative have lost their meaning in America. I represent the distracted center."
—**Jon Stewart**

"Liberals feel unworthy of their possessions. Conservatives feel they deserve everything they've stolen."
—**Mort Sahl**

"Republicans believe every day is the 4th of July. Democrats believe every day is April 15."
—**Ronald Reagan**

"If the Republicans will stop telling lies about the Democrats, we will stop telling the truth about them."
—**Adlai E. Stevenson**

---

"Life, liberty, and the pursuit of happiness" was penned by Englishman John Locke (17th century).

# UNCLE JOHN'S QUOTATIONARY

*Here's Part 7 of our quotation dictionary.*
*(Part 6 begins on page 246.)*

REALITY: the leading cause of stress among those in touch with it. (Lily Tomlin)

REASON: a slave to the emotions. (David Hume)

RELIGION: probably, after sex, the second oldest resource which human beings have available to them for blowing their minds. (Susan Sontag)

REPARTEE: something we think of twenty-four hours too late. (Mark Twain)

REVENGE: the weak pleasure of a little and narrow mind. (Decimus Junius Juvenal)

REVOLUTION: an abrupt change in the form of misgovernment. (Ambrose Bierce)

RIDICULE: the first and last argument of a fool. (Charles Simmons)

ROCK 'N' ROLL: music for the neck downwards. (Keith Richards)

ROMANCE: the glamour which turns the dust of everyday life into a golden haze. (Amanda Cross)

SATIRE: a sort of mirror, wherein beholders generally discover everybody's face but their own. (Jonathan Swift)

SCIENCE: a wonderful thing if one does not have to earn one's living at it. (Albert Einstein)

SECOND PLACE: the first loser. (Dale Earnhardt)

SECRECY: the beginning of tyranny. (Robert A. Heinlein)

SENSE OF HUMOR: common sense, dancing. (William James)

SEX: the most awful, filthy thing on Earth and you should save it for someone you love. (Butch Hancock)

SMOKING: always having to

say you're sorry. (Dr. Tom Ferguson)

**SOFTWARE:** where the people in your company's hardware section will tell you the problem is. (Dave Barry) *See "Hardware"—page 103*

**SOCIOLOGY:** journalism without news. (P. J. O'Rourke)

**SPORTS:** war without the killing. (Ted Turner)

**STATESMAN:** a dead politician. (James Freeman Clarke)

**STATUS QUO:** Latin for "the mess we're in." (Ronald Reagan)

**STYLE:** self-plagiarism. (Alfred Hitchcock)

**TACT:** the knack of making a point without making an enemy. (Carlos Castaneda)

**TAXPAYER:** someone who works for the federal government, but doesn't have to take a civil service examination. (Ronald Reagan)

**TAX REFORM:** taking the taxes off things that have been taxed in the past and putting taxes on things that haven't been taxed before. (Art Buchwald)

**TELEVISION:** that insidious beast, that Medusa which freezes a billion people to stone every night, that Siren which called and sang and promised so much and gave, after all, so little. (Ray Bradbury)

**TODAY:** yesterday's pupil. (Benjamin Franklin)

**TORONTO:** a kind of New York operated by the Swiss. (Peter Ustinov)

**TORTILLA:** a sleeping bag for ground beef. (Mitch Hedberg)

**TRADITION:** what you often resort to when you don't have the will, time or money to do it right. (Kurt Adler)

**TRUE FRIEND:** someone who thinks that you are a good egg even though he knows that you are slightly cracked. (Bernard Meltzer)

**TRUTH:** the cry of all, but the game of few. (George Berkeley)

*For more, see page 364.*

The band U2 was originally called Feedback.

# MORE WISDOM

*Read and be wiser.*

"Out beyond ideas of wrongdoing and right-doing, there is a field. I will meet you there."
—Rumi

"We are what we pretend to be. So we must be careful what we pretend to be."
—Kurt Vonnegut

"Man is a complex being: he makes deserts bloom—and lakes die."
—Gil Stern

"The true art of memory is the art of attention."
—Samuel Johnson

"The optimist proclaims that we live in the best of all possible worlds, and the pessimist fears this is true."
—James Branch Cabell

"Both optimists and pessimists contribute to our society. The optimist invents the airplane, and the pessimist the parachute."
—Gil Stern

"You never really learn much from hearing yourself talk."
—George Clooney

"Grief and tragedy and hatred are only for a time. Goodness and love have no end."
—George W. Bush

"If a problem has no solution, it may not be a problem, but a fact—not to be solved, but to be coped with."
—Shimon Peres

"If you can do something with your eyes closed, it's time to find something new."
—Kathie Lee Gifford

"True audacity is the trick of knowing how far you can go in going too far."
—Jean Cocteau

"A positive attitude may not solve all your problems, but it will annoy enough people to make it worth the effort."
—Herm Albright

"In three words I can sum up everything I've learned about life: it goes on." —Robert Frost

# SIMON SAYS:

*Read this page.*

"If I said to most of the people who auditioned, 'Good job, awesome, well done,' it would have made me actually look and feel ridiculous. It's quite obvious most of the people who turned up for this audition were hopeless."
—**Simon Cowell**

"Take care of your husband. And make him feel important. And if you can do that, you'll have a happy and wonderful marriage. Like two out of every ten couples."
—**Neil Simon**

"In Germany, when I finished playing, I was thinking, 'I hate "Homeward Bound."' Then I thought, Well, that's not a bad song at all for a 22-year-old kid."
—**Paul Simon**

"To be a liberal doesn't mean you're a wastrel."
—**Sen. Paul Simon**

"Are you looking at me bum? You cheeky monkey!"
—**Simon (Mike Myers),** *Saturday Night Live*

**A.J.:** Rick, she called you—quite accurately I might add—an overgrown adolescent with no romance in his soul.
**Rick:** What do I need a romantic soul for? The Power Wagon's got bench seats.
—*Simon & Simon*

"In Mexico we have a word for sushi: Bait."
—**Jose Simon**

"I remember being onstage once when I didn't have fear. I got so scared that I didn't have fear that it brought on an anxiety attack."
—**Carly Simon**

**Peasants:** Where is the traitor to the kingdom? Where is the spoiler of the commons?
**Simon of Sudbury:** Neither a traitor, nor despoiler am I, but thy archbishop.
—**June 1381, shortly before being beheaded by a mob**

"We want to be the band to dance to when the bomb drops."
—**Simon Le Bon,** **of Duran Duran**

---

In 1987 Paul Simon the singer and Paul Simon the senator co-hosted *Saturday Night Live.*

# CALVIN-ISMS

*From 1985 to 1995, Bill Watterson delighted millions of readers with his comic strip, Calvin and Hobbes. Calvin—a six-year-old boy whose best pal was a stuffed tiger named Hobbes—was both an example of what's best about modern society...and what's not so best.*

"I'm learning real skills that I can apply throughout the rest of my life...procrastinating and rationalizing."

"In my opinion, we don't devote nearly enough scientific research to finding a cure for jerks."

"I imagine bugs and girls have a dim perception that nature played a cruel trick on them, but they lack the intelligence to comprehend the magnitude of it."

"When birds burp, it must taste like bugs."

"To make a bad day worse, spend it wishing for the impossible."

"Life's disappointments are harder to take when you don't know any swear words."

"Happiness is being famous for your financial ability to indulge in every kind of excess."

"A little rudeness and disrespect can elevate a meaningless interaction to a battle of wills and add drama to an otherwise dull day."

"There's never enough time to do all the nothing you want."

"Nothing is permanent. Everything changes. That's the one thing we know for sure in this world. But I'm still going to gripe about it."

"I was put on this earth to accomplish a certain number of things. Right now I'm so far behind I will never die."

"I liked things better when I didn't understand them."

"That's the difference between me and the rest of the world! Happiness isn't good enough for me! I demand euphoria!"

"You know, Hobbes, some days even my lucky rocketship underpants don't help."

The comic strip *Peanuts* was originally called *Li'l Folks*.

# HUMBLE ACTORS?

*Are they really humble? Or are they just trying to formulate a humble image for PR's sake? You be the judge. (For some refreshingly un-humble actor quotes, check out Samuel L. Jackson on page 224.)*

"I telephoned my grandparents the other day, and my grandfather said to me, 'We saw your movie.' 'Which one?' I said, and he shouted, 'Betty, what was the name of that movie I didn't like?' I thought that was just classic."
—**Brad Pitt**

"I had a video made of my recent knee operation. The doctor said it was the best movie I ever starred in."
—**Shirley MacLaine**

"When I was on my way to the podium a gentleman stopped me and said I was as good a politician as I was an actor. What a cheap shot!"
—**Arnold Schwarzenegger**

"There are people who would rather choke than go see my movies. They write me letters all the time."
—**Alec Baldwin**

"Sometimes I wonder if I'm doing a Jimmy Stewart imitation of myself."
—**Jimmy Stewart**

"I'm not Jack Nicholson. I'm not Marlon Brando. But I do mumble."
—**Benicio del Toro**

"I'm always described as 'cocksure' or 'with a swagger,' and that bears no resemblance to who I feel like inside. I feel plagued by insecurity."
—**Ben Affleck**

"My eyes droop, the mouth is crooked, the teeth aren't straight, the voice sounds like a mafioso pallbearer."
—**Sylvester Stallone**

"I'm a meathead. I can't help it, man. You've got smart people and you've got dumb people."
—**Keanu Reeves**

"I'm better off not socializing. I make a better impression if I'm not around."
—**Christopher Walken**

"I'm in so many movies that are on TV at 2:00 a.m. that people think I'm dead."
—**Michael Caine**

"Modesty is the artifice of actors, similar to passion in call girls." —Jackie Gleason

# UNCLE ALBERT

*In the 20th century, Albert Einstein made his mark as a scientist. But as the years go by, it becomes more and more apparent that he was as much a philosopher as he was anything else...and a pretty wise one at that.*

"We should take care not to make the intellect our god; it has, of course, powerful muscles, but no personality."

"The intuitive mind is a sacred gift and the rational mind is a faithful servant. We have created a society that honors the servant and has forgotten the gift."

"The ideals which have lighted my way, and time after time have given me new courage to face life cheerfully, have been Kindness, Beauty, and Truth. The trite subjects of human efforts, possessions, outward success, and luxury have always seemed to me contemptible."

"When you look at yourself from a universal standpoint, something inside always reminds you that there are bigger and better things to worry about."

"If you are out to describe the truth, leave elegance to the tailor."

"The tragedy of life is what dies inside a man while he lives."

"Laws alone can not secure freedom of expression; in order that every man present his views without penalty there must be spirit of tolerance in the entire population."

"Anger dwells only in the bosom of fools."

"Great spirits have always encountered opposition from mediocre minds. The mediocre mind is incapable of understanding the man who refuses to bow blindly to conventional prejudices and chooses instead to express his opinions courageously and honestly."

"Reading, after a certain age, diverts the mind too much from its creative pursuits. Any man who reads too much and uses his own brain too little falls into lazy habits of thinking."

"I know not with what weapons World War III will be fought, but World War IV will be fought with sticks and stones."

"The important thing is not to stop questioning. Curiosity has its own reason for existing. One cannot help but be in awe when he contemplates the mysteries of eternity, of life, of the marvelous structure of reality. It is enough if one tries merely to comprehend a little of this mystery every day. Never lose a holy curiosity."

"Human beings can attain a worthy and harmonious life only if they are able to rid themselves, within the limits of human nature, of the striving for the wish fulfillment of material kinds. The goal is to raise the spiritual values of society."

"The devil has put a penalty on all things we enjoy in life. Either we suffer in health or we suffer in soul or we get fat."

"A human being is a part of the whole, called by us Universe, a part limited in time and space. He experiences himself, his thoughts and feelings as something separated from the rest—a kind of optical delusion of his consciousness. This delusion is a kind of prison, restricting us to our personal desires and to affection for a few persons nearest to us. Our task must be to free from this prison by widening our circle of compassion to embrace all living creatures and the whole nature in its beauty."

"Life is sacred, that is to say, it is the supreme value, to which all other values are subordinate."

"Whoever undertakes to set himself up as a judge of Truth and Knowledge is shipwrecked by the laughter of the gods."

—Albert Einstein

# HOMER RULES

*If you have to ask "Homer who?" then
you're not watching enough TV.*

"If these big stars didn't want people going through their garbage and saying they're gay, then they shouldn't have tried to express themselves creatively."

"When a woman says nothing's wrong, it means everything's wrong. When a woman says everything's wrong, it means everything's wrong. And when a woman says that something isn't funny, you'd better not laugh."

"Just because I don't care doesn't mean I'm not listening."

"With $10,000, we'd be millionaires!"

"Facts are meaningless. You could use facts to prove anything that's even remotely true."

"The three little sentences that will get you through life. Number 1: Cover for me. Number 2: Oh, good idea, boss! Number 3: It was like that when I got here."

"I'm normally not a praying man, but if you're up there, please save me, Superman!"

*(drunk)* "Look, the thing about my family is there's five of us. Marge, Bart, Girl Bart, the one who doesn't talk, and the fat guy. How I loathe him."

"Books are useless! I only ever read one book, *To Kill a Mockingbird*, and it gave me absolutely no insight on how to kill mockingbirds! Sure it taught me not to judge a man by the color of his skin…but what good does that do me?"

"That guy impressed me, and I am *not* easily impressed. Wow! A blue car!"

"When I look at the smiles on all the children's faces, I just know they're about to jab me with something."

"If you don't like your job, you don't strike. You go in every day and do it really half-assed. That's the American way."

**Fox Television forbids Dan Castellanata from doing Homer Simpson's voice in public.**

# THE STATE OF ROCK 'N' ROLL

*Is 21st-century rock music so different from what it was back in its golden years? Here's what some modern (and not-so-modern) artists say about it.*

"There are groups at the top of the charts that are hailed as the saviors of rock 'n' roll and all that, but they are amateurs. They don't know where the music comes from."
—**Bob Dylan**

"Videos destroyed the vitality of rock 'n' roll. Before that, music said, 'Listen to me.' Now it says, 'Look at me.'"
—**Billy Joel**

"Rock 'n' roll is absurd. In the past, U2 was trying to duck that. Now we're wrapping our arms around it and giving it a great big kiss."
—**Bono**

"The Smashing Pumpkins love rock 'n' roll, we absolutely love it, but we also think it's a flatulent, ego-serving kiddie playground."
—**Billy Corgan**

"There are two kinds of artists left: those who endorse Pepsi and those who simply won't."
—**Annie Lennox**

"A lot of pop music is about stealing pocket money from children."
—**Ian Anderson**

"Today, you can go into the studio and not even be a musician, just start beating on stuff and they can take parts out, move it around and make you sound like Slash. You don't have work at it like you did back in the day."
—**Mick Mars, guitarist, Mötley Crüe**

"Rock 'n' roll is dead. The attitude isn't dead, but the music is no longer vital."
—**David Byrne**

"You know what I hate about rock? I hate tie-dyed t-shirts."
—**Kurt Cobain**

"The biggest problem with American music right now is that kids don't listen. When people go to concerts, they say, 'I'm going to see,' not, 'I'm going to hear.'"
—**Branford Marsalis**

**"The worst crime is faking it." —Kurt Cobain**

# THE BLIND LEADING THE SIGHTED

*Here is some advice from people who can't see—but can help us to see better.*

"The best and most beautiful things in the world cannot be seen nor even touched, but just felt in the heart."
—**Helen Keller**

"Yet, taught by time, my heart has learned to glow for others' good, and melt at others' woe."
—**Homer**

"We all have inconveniences of one kind or another. How you deal with them ultimately determines how successful you are."
—**Craig MacFarlane,**
*blind motivational speaker*

"There are many spokes on the wheel of life. First, we're here to explore new possibilities."
—**Ray Charles**

Portland, Oregon, got its name in a coin toss...tails, and it would have been Boston, Oregon.

# COMEDIANS ON COMEDY

*More thoughts from some funny folks on
what it takes to make people laugh.*

"The Four Levels of Comedy:
Make your friends laugh,
Make strangers laugh, Get
paid to make strangers laugh,
and Make people talk like you
because it's so much fun."
—**Jerry Seinfeld**

"The saving grace of humor
is that if you fail, no one is
laughing at you."
—**A. Whitney Brown**

"Wit is the key to anybody's
heart. Show me the person
who doesn't like to laugh and
I'll show you a person with a
toe tag."
—**Julia Roberts**

"Humor is always based on a
modicum of truth. Ever heard
a joke about a father-in-law?"
—**Dick Clark**

"It's not surprising that some
comedians start thinking they
can save the world. But that's
one of most dangerous things
in show business: the journey
from comedian to humorist to
satirist to out of the business."
—**Jay Leno**

"Comedy has to be based on
truth. You take the truth and
you put a little curlicue at
the end."
—**Sid Caesar**

"Laughter gives us distance. It
allows us to step back from an
event, deal with it, and then
move on."
—**Bob Newhart**

"A man who feels, views
life as a tragedy. A man who
thinks, views life as a
comedy."
—**Taylor Caldwell**

"Your anger can be 49% and
your comedy 51%, and you're
okay. If the anger is 51%, the
comedy is gone."
—**Joan Rivers**

"Comedy is the last refuge of
the nonconformist mind."
—**Gilbert Seldes**

"At least one way of measuring
the freedom of any society is
the amount of comedy that is
permitted."
—**Eric Idle**

"He deserves Paradise who makes his companions laugh." —**The Koran**

# FELLINI

*Considered one of the greatest movie directors of all time, Federico Fellini (1920–93) was known for his use of dream sequences and flashbacks. Here are some of his thoughts on the process—and business—of filmmaking.*

"All art is autobiographical. The pearl is the oyster's autobiography."

"Talking about dreams is like talking about movies. Years can pass in a second, and you can hop from one place to another. It's a language made of image. In the cinema, every object and every light means something, as in a dream."

"A different language is a different vision of life."

"Hype is the awkward and desperate attempt to convince journalists that what you've made is worth the misery of having to review it."

"Style is what unites memory, ideology, sentiment, nostalgia, presentiment, to the way we express all that. It's not what we say but how we say it that matters."

"Nietzsche claimed that his genius was in his nostrils, and I think that is a very excellent place for it to be."

"God may not play dice, but he enjoys a good round of Trivial Pursuit every now and again."

"I don't believe in total freedom for the artist. Left on his own, free to do anything he likes, the artist ends up doing nothing at all. If there's one thing that's dangerous for an artist, it's precisely this question of total freedom, waiting for inspiration."

"Money is everywhere, but so is poetry. What we lack are the poets."

"Going to the cinema is like returning to the womb; you sit there, still and meditative in the darkness, waiting for life to appear on the screen."

"The visionary is the only true realist."

"There is no end. There is no beginning. There is only the passion of life."

"Don't tell me what I am doing. I don't want to know."

---

Fellini was nominated for an Oscar 12 times (for writing or directing). Number of wins: 0.

# DON'T

*Some more quotes of people telling you what not to do.*

"Don't criticize what you can't understand."
—Bob Dylan

"Don't go backwards; you have already been there."
—Ray Charles

"Don't think. Thinking is the enemy of creativity. It's self-conscious, and anything self-conscious is lousy. You can't try to do things. You simply must do things."
—Ray Bradbury

"Don't try to take on a new personality; it doesn't work."
—Richard Nixon

"Don't let yesterday use up too much of today."
—Will Rogers

"Don't confuse fame with success. Madonna is one; Helen Keller is the other."
—Erma Bombeck

"Don't listen to friends when the friend inside you says, 'Do this.'"
—Mahatma Gandhi

"Don't overestimate the decency of the human race."
—H. L. Mencken

"Don't limit a child to your own learning, for he was born in another time."
—Rabbinical saying

"Don't ever take a fence down until you know why it was put up."
—Robert Frost

"Don't flatter yourself that friendship authorizes you to say disagreeable things to your intimates. The nearer you come into relation with a person, the more necessary do tact and courtesy become."
—Oliver Wendell Holmes

"Don't fear the future; shape it."
—George W. Bush

"Don't part with your illusions. When they are gone, you may still exist, but you have ceased to live."
—Mark Twain

# PRIMETIME PROVERBS

*More deep thoughts from people who live in that box in the living room.*

## ON HONESTY:

**Larry:** I didn't lie. At most, I massaged the truth a little.

**Balki:** Massaged? You gave it a full body scrub and a mud bath.

—*Perfect Strangers*

## ON REALITY:

**Jerri:** Dreams *can* happen.

**Sara:** It's nice that you think that, dear.

—*Strangers With Candy*

## ON BIGOTRY:

"I hate racists. I hate everything about them—their music, their food, the way their men are so skinny and their wives are all so fat. But mostly, I hate the way they judge people based on tired stereotypes."

—*Byron, Andy Richter Controls the Universe*

## ON BEHAVIOR:

**Andy:** Do me a favor. You know how you normally behave?

**Ephram:** Distant and miserable?

**Andy:** Yeah. Do the opposite.

—*Everwood*

## ON GEOGRAPHY:

**Ali G:** What was it like being the head of the NYPD?

**Daryl Gates:** Not NY, LAPD.

**Ali G:** Well, you say tomato, I say potato.

—*Da Ali G Show*

## ON POLICE WORK:

**Andy:** Barney, you can't give Otis a sobriety test now; he's had all night to sleep it off. The time to give him a sobriety test was last night when you picked him up.

**Barney:** I couldn't give him the test last night!

**Andy:** Why?

**Barney:** He was too drunk.

—*The Andy Griffith Show*

## ON LOGIC:

**Shame:** You sissy, you couldn't drive nails in a snow bank.

**Batman:** Why would I want to?

—*Batman*

## ON EGOTISM:

"Maybe I sometimes say things that are selfish and self-centered, but that's who I am."

—*Hilary, The Fresh Prince of Bel-Air*

# WILLIAM JAMES

*Hailed as the father of American psychology, William James
(1842–1910) is equally known as a brilliant modern-day
philosopher. Here is some of his psycho-philosophy.*

"The deepest principle in human nature is the craving to be appreciated."

"We have grown literally afraid to be poor. We despise anyone who elects to be poor in order to simplify and save his inner life. If he does not join the general scramble and pant with the money-making street, we deem him spiritless and lacking in ambition."

"Everybody should do at least two things each day that he hates to do, just for practice."

"Acceptance of what has happened is the first step to overcoming the consequences of any misfortune."

"Compared to what we ought to be, we are half awake."

"If you believe that feeling bad or worrying long enough will change a past or future event, then you are residing on another planet with a different reality system."

"It is well for the world that in most of us, by the age of 30, the character has set like plaster, and will never soften again."

"All natural goods perish. Riches take wings; fame is a breath; love is a cheat; youth and health and pleasure vanish."

"Objective evidence and certitude are doubtless very fine ideals to play with, but where on this moonlit and dream-visited planet are they found?"

"Man can alter his life by altering his thinking."

"The best argument I know for an immortal life is the existence of a man who deserves one."

"Act as if what you do makes a difference. It does."

"Great emergencies and crises show us how much greater our vital resources are than we had supposed."

# SUPER EGOS

*Some folks who could use a heaping helping of humble pie.*

"I'm not conceited. Conceit is a fault, and I have no faults."
—**David Lee Roth**

"I have enormous personal ambition. I want to shift the entire planet. And I'm doing it. I am now a famous person."
—**Newt Gingrich**

"I admit I do have a very nice butt. Some say my career was built on it."
—**Jean-Claude Van Damme**

"When I sing, people shut up."
—**Barbra Streisand**

"The interesting thing is how one guy, through living out his own fantasies, is living out the fantasies of so many other people."
—**Hugh Hefner**

"I never lie. I believe everything I say, so it's not a lie."
—**Mark Wahlberg**

"I'm more than an actor. I'm an icon, an industry."
—**Corey Feldman**

"I won't apologize for the high ticket prices. We consider ourselves elite."
—**Glenn Frey, of the Eagles**

"Compared to contemporary painters, I am the most big genius of modern time...but modesty is not my specialty."
—**Salvador Dali**

"I'm not bragging, but my movies have grossed well over a billion dollars."
—**Steve Guttenberg**

"I have the stardom glow."
—**Jennifer Lopez**

"I'm working my way toward divinity."
—**Bette Midler**

"In every relationship, I've overwhelmed the girl. They just can't handle all the love."
—**Justin Timberlake**

"It's possible that the universe exists only for me. If so, it's sure going well for me, I must admit."
—**Bill Gates**

There are 132 countries whose gross domestic product is less than Bill Gates's net worth.

# JAPAN THROUGH WESTERN EYES

*Don't worry; the Japanese think Westerners are weird, too.*

### On Work:

"In Japan, employees occasionally work themselves to *death*. It's called *karoshi*. I don't want that to happen to anybody in my department. The trick is to take a break as soon as you see a bright light and hear dead relatives beckon."

—**Scott Adams**

### On Food:

"Japanese food is very pretty and undoubtedly a suitable cuisine in Japan, which is largely populated by people of below-average size. Hostesses hell-bent on serving such food to Occidentals would be well advised to supplement it with something more substantial and to keep in mind that almost everybody likes french fries."

—**Fran Lebowitz**

### On Manners:

"The Japanese have perfected good manners and made them indistinguishable from rudeness."

—**Paul Theroux**

### On Lawyers:

"There are more lawyers in just Washington, D.C. than in all of Japan. They've got about as many lawyers as we have sumo wrestlers."

—**Lee Iacocca**

### On Golf:

"The Japanese eat, sleep, and breathe golf; the only thing they don't do is actually play it, because to get on a course, you have to make a reservation roughly 137 years in advance, which means that by the time you actually get to the first tee you are deceased."

—**Dave Barry**

### On Language:

"The only English words I saw in Japan were Sony and Mitsubishi."

—**Bill Gullickson**

"In Japan, you have no idea what they're saying, and they can't help you, either. They're very polite, but you feel like a joke is being played on you the entire time you're there."

—**Bill Murray**

In Japan it is considered very bad manners to eat in the street.

# PRESIDENTIAL WISDOM

*Time to go easy on the commanders-in-chief of the United States and print
some of the wisest things they've ever said...or heard somewhere else
and then repeated...or were written for them by speechwriters.*

"Keep your eyes on the stars and feet on the ground."
—Theodore Roosevelt

"If we cannot end now our differences, at least we can help make the world safe for diversity."
—John F. Kennedy

"It is not strange to mistake change for progress."
—Millard Fillmore

"He serves his party best who serves the country best."
—Rutherford B. Hayes

"It is easier to do a job right than to explain why you didn't."
—Martin Van Buren

"I know in my heart that man is good, that what is right will eventually triumph."
—Ronald Reagan

"A man is known by the company he keeps, and also by the company from which he is kept out."
—Grover Cleveland

"If government is to serve any purpose, it is to do for others what they are unable to do for themselves."
—Lyndon Johnson

"The sad duty of politics is to establish justice in a sinful world."
—Jimmy Carter

"There never was a time when some way could not be found to prevent the drawing of the sword."
—Ulysses S. Grant

"A house divided against itself cannot stand."
—Abraham Lincoln

"I believe that God has planted in every heart the desire to live in freedom."
—George W. Bush

"The earth belongs to the living, not the dead."
—Thomas Jefferson

"Great is the guilt of an unnecessary war."
—John Adams

Q: Which president appeared on the most covers of *Time* magazine? A: Richard Nixon (55).

"It is common sense to take a method and try it. If it fails, admit it frankly and try another. But above all, try something."
—**Franklin D. Roosevelt**

"The advancement and diffusion of knowledge is the only guardian of true liberty."
—**James Madison**

"Government is not reason; it is not eloquence; it is force! Like fire, it is a dangerous servant and a fearful master."
—**George Washington**

"America's present need is not heroics but healing; not revolution but restoration."
—**Warren Harding**

"A man who has never lost himself in a cause bigger than himself has missed one of life's mountaintop experiences. Only in losing himself does he find himself."
—**Richard Nixon**

"I pity the man who wants a coat so cheap that the man who produces the cloth will starve in the process."
—**Benjamin Harrison**

"It ain't what they call you, it's what you answer to."
—**Bill Clinton**

"Truth is the glue that holds governments together. Compromise is the oil that makes governments go."
—**Gerald Ford**

"The problem to be solved is, not what form of government is perfect, but which of the forms is least imperfect."
—**James Madison**

"You can not stop the spread of an idea by passing a law against it."
—**Harry S. Truman**

"One man with courage is a majority."
—**Thomas Jefferson**

"Oh, that lovely title: 'ex-president.'"
—**Dwight D. Eisenhower**

First person to be born in the White House: James Madison Randolph, in 1806.

# JAY LENO

*Funny jokes from America's favorite gray-haired, big-chinned Everyman.*

"President Bush is extremely loyal to his staff. He never likes to fire his staff. Not out of loyalty; he hates having to learn new names."

"Today more al-Qaeda and Taliban prisoners were flown to Guantanamo Bay in Cuba. On the plane they are bound, they are sedated, they are chained to their chairs. Or, as Continental Airlines calls it, coach."

"I don't think President Bush fully understands this immigration thing. Like today, when they asked him about amnesty, he said it's horrible when anyone loses their memory."

"The United States has developed a new weapon that destroys people but it leaves buildings standing. It's called the stock market."

"Earlier this week the Senate voted 97 to 0 for tougher regulations. For example, when corporations buy a senator, they must now get a receipt."

"When they closed Denver's old Stapleton Airport, the gift shop had a big clearance sale, everything was 90 percent off. This was great: You could get a bottle of aspirin for twenty dollars."

"A congresswomen announced she will enter rehab after she fell down drunk in Congress after a big vote. Who says women can't hold the same jobs as men?"

"Pour kitty litter in your shoes, and it'll take away the odor. Unless, of course, you own a cat."

"A couple got married on a Continental Airlines flight last week. They had the service on the plane. That's kind of odd, don't you think? All your life you dream about walking down the aisle, the big moment comes, and you're stuck behind the beverage cart "

"I'm addicted to placebos. I'd give them up, but it wouldn't make any difference."

# BASEBALL GREATS

*Who are the greatest baseball players of all time?*
*Who better to ask than their fellow ballplayers?*

"Throwing a fastball to Henry Aaron is like trying to sneak the sun past a rooster."
—**Curt Simmons**

"Jimmy Foxx could hit me at midnight with the lights out."
—**Vernon "Lefty" Gomez**

"Cool Papa Bell was so fast he could turn out the light and jump in bed before the room got dark."
—**Satchel Paige**

"Rod Carew's the only guy I know who can go 4-for-3."
—**Alan Bannister**

"He hit 'em so high that everyone on the field thought he had a chance to get it. They'd all try to get under it to make the catch, and it looked like a union meeting."
—**Casey Stengel,** *on Babe Ruth*

"I can see how he won 25 games. What I don't understand is how he lost five."
—**Yogi Berra,** *after Sandy Koufax went 25–5*

"Lou Gehrig never learned that a ballplayer couldn't be good every day."
—**Hank Gowdy**

"The only thing Cy Young didn't win was the Cy Young Award."
—**Joe Torre**

"I'm beginning to see Brooks Robinson in my sleep. If I dropped this paper plate, he'd pick it up on hop and throw me out at first."
—**Sparky Anderson**

"Jackie Robinson was the greatest competitor I ever saw. He didn't win. He triumphed."
—**Ralph Branca**

"What's the best way to pitch to Stan Musial? That's easy. Walk him and then try to pick him off first base."
—**Joe Garagiola**

"Tom Seaver's so good that blind people come to the park just to hear him pitch."
—**Reggie Jackson**

---

Most seasons as a major-league umpire: Bill Klem, 37 years. He also officiated 18 World Series.

# HOW TO GET FIRED

*Are you a TV or radio personality, or perhaps in some other position
where you speak to a lot of people? Be very careful of what you say.
You could find yourself like these folks—out of a job. (Warning:
There are some very shocking statements in here.)*

**JOHN DEPETRO**
**Job:** Radio talk-show host on WRKO-AM, Boston
**Quote:** "I wish someone would tell that big fat lesbian to
shut up!"
**You're Fired!** He was referring to Grace Ross, the Green Rainbow
candidate for Massachusetts governor in 2006, who is openly gay.
DePetro was mad that Ross took up too much time talking during
a debate for an office she could never hope to be elected to.
DePetro's boss, Jason Wolfe, told reporters. "In the context of
what he said and the tone with which he said it, the comments
were completely inappropriate, derogatory, and will
not be tolerated."

For her part, Grace responded with bemusement: "Big? Fat?
I guess that's his way of saying he doesn't like somebody."

**DOUG TRACHT** (better known as "The Greaseman")
**Job:** Radio disc jockey and talk-show host at WARW in
Washington, D.C.
**Quote:** "No wonder people drag them behind trucks."
**You're Fired!** On February 24, 1999, the white disc jockey was
playing a song by black artist Lauryn Hill and stopped it halfway
through to make the comment. Tracht was referring to a current
news story about the James Byrd, Jr. trial in Texas. Byrd, an
African American, was killed by three white men, who
dragged him behind their truck. While the country was trying to
make sense of the crime, Tracht's line created a public outcry.
Even though he apologized profusely, Tracht was fired that day. A
rival morning host on WPGC named Donnie Simpson summed it
up the next day: "It's not just black folks who should be offended
by this—it's folks."

## TRENT LOTT

**Job:** Senate majority leader

**Quote:** "I want to say this about my state: When Strom Thurmond ran for president, we voted for him. We're proud of it. And if the rest of the country had followed our lead, we wouldn't have had all these problems over all these years, either."

**You're Fired!** Lott made the comments on December 5, 2002, at the 100th birthday party for fellow Mississippi senator Strom Thurmond. In 1948 Thurmond had run for president on the Dixiecrat ticket with a single issue: racial segregation. Lott's comments were interpreted to mean that if Thurmond had won the election, segregation would still be in place, and the United States would be in better shape. Lott tried to dismiss the comment, saying he was referring to Thurmond's national defense ideas, not his racial views. After calls from both Democrats and Republicans for his dismissal and a public admonition from President Bush, Lott resigned his post as Senate majority leader.

## MICHAEL HANSCOM

**Job:** An employee of Microsoft

**Quote:** "Even Microsoft wants G5s."

**You're Fired!** Hanscom posted this endorsement of Apple Computers, Microsoft's main competitor, on his own personal Web site in 2003. A few days later, he was called into his boss's office, where he was asked, "Is this page hosted on any Microsoft computer? Or is it on your own?"

"It's on mine," Hanscom replied. "Well, it's on a hosted site that I pay for, but no, it's not on anything of Microsoft's."

"Good," his boss replied. "That means that as it's your site on your own server, you have the right to say anything you want. Unfortunately, Microsoft has the right to decide that because of what you said, you're no longer welcome on the Microsoft campus."

## BILL MAHER

**Job:** Host of the ABC show *Politically Incorrect*

**Quote:** "We have been the cowards lobbing cruise missiles from 2,000 miles away. That's cowardly. Staying in the airplane when it hits the building, say what you want about it, it's not cowardly."

**You're Fired!** Maher made this comment just days after the terrorist attacks of September 11, 2001. At a time when the nation was mourning the victims, Maher's observation sparked outrage from viewers and sponsors alike. Many of the show's advertisers—including FedEx and Sears—pulled their ads, and several affiliates dropped the show. News commentators from around the U.S. called for Maher's dismissal (except for Rush Limbaugh, who pointed out that Maher was merely making a distinction between "physical and moral cowardice"). Interestingly, Maher wasn't even the one who brought the subject of cowardice up; it was his guest, conservative political commentator Dinesh D'Souza. Maher was just agreeing with and repeating what D'Souza said. But as the show's host, Maher took the brunt of the backlash. ABC declined to renew his contract for the following year, saying the show had lost too many viewers and was no longer profitable.

## MICHAEL SAVAGE
**Job:** Talk-show host
**Quote:** "Oh, you're one of the sodomites. You should only get AIDS and die, you pig. How's that? Why don't you see if you can sue me, you pig. You got nothing better than to put me down, you piece of garbage. You have got nothing to do today, go eat a sausage and choke on it!"
**You're Fired!** Although best known as a no-holds-barred radio host, Savage said this in 2003 on his television call-in show on cable news channel MSNBC. The unidentified caller was talking about wanting to smoke while on an airplane when Savage launched his tirade. He then cut the call and said, "These bums mean nothing to me." The show was barely over when Savage got the axe. Commented MSNBC spokesman Jeremy Gaines: "His comments were extremely inappropriate and the decision was an easy one."

"I just don't know what to think. I play in Colorado, they tell me they like me, and I get traded. I play in Calgary, and at the end of the season the GM tells me he likes me, and I get traded. I just hope my fiancee doesn't tell me she likes me."
—**Chris Drury, NHL player**

---

Roger Staubach holds the record for most career Super Bowl fumbles, with 5.

# DIVA WISDUMB

*Obviously, talent and intelligence don't always go together.*

"If I pop everyone who calls me a diva then I'm going to spend the rest of my life in prison."
—**Chaka Khan**

"Hair has always been important."
—**Diana Ross**

"I'm not a diva. I'm a tadpole trying to be a frog."
—**Toni Braxton**

"Half the time I don't even know what I'm nominated for."
—**Shania Twain**

"I don't know much about football. I know what a goal is, which is surely the main thing about football."
—**Victoria Beckham, former Spice Girl, now wife of soccer superstar David Beckham**

"I have sometimes been an emotional Chernobyl."
—**Liza Minnelli**

"I don't get anything for free. I pay for all my beauty treatments."
—**Jennifer Lopez**

"I'm not afraid to look ridiculous. It's a dirty job, but somebody's got to do it."
—**Cher**

"I've always been a thin girl. I'm not going to be fat, ever. Let's get that straight."
—**Whitney Houston**

"I don't mean to be a diva, but some days you wake up and you're Barbra Streisand."
—**Courtney Love**

"I am simple, complex, generous, selfish, unattractive, beautiful, lazy, and driven."
—**Barbra Streisand**

"Sorry, I don't eat buffalo."
—**Jessica Simpson, asked if she wanted Buffalo wings**

"Sometimes you have to sacrifice your performance for high heels."
—**Gwen Stefani**

"I give money to this company that manufactures hearing aids. More people should really hear me sing. I have a gift from God."
—**Christina Aguilera**

# EPITAPHS

*What do you want on your tombstone?*

Peace at last
—**Lenny Bruce**

The greatest honor history
can bestow is the title of
peacemaker.
—**Richard Nixon**

"The Entertainer": He did it all
—**Sammy Davis, Jr.**

Together Again
—**George Burns
and Gracie Allen**

There Goes the Neighborhood
—**Rodney Dangerfield**

And the Beat Goes On
—**Sonny Bono**

One Heart and One Soul
—**John Candy**

Thank you for the many
beautiful songs. They will live
long and longer.
—**Hank Williams**

I'll see you
in apple blossom time.
—**Tip O'Neill**

An American soldier and
defender of the Constitution
—**Jefferson Davis**

Sleep after toil, port after
stormy seas, ease after war,
death after life, does
greatly please.
—**Joseph Conrad**

Called back.
—**Emily Dickinson**

Steel true, blade straight
—**Sir Arthur Conan Doyle**

Don't try.
—**Charles Bukowski**

That nothing's so sacred
as honor and nothing's
so loyal as love.
—**Wyatt and Josephine Earp**

A friend to honesty and a foe
to crime.
—**Allan Pinkerton**

The passive master lent his
hand, to the vast soul which
o'er him planned.
—**Ralph Waldo Emerson**

**"Death is that after which nothing is of interest." —Rozinov**

# NELSON MANDELA

*After spending 27 years in a prison cell for protesting apartheid in South Africa, Mandela became that country's president.*

"A good head and a good heart are always a formidable combination. But when you add to that a literate tongue or pen, then you have something very special."

"There is nothing like returning to a place that remains unchanged to find the ways in which you yourself have altered."

"True reconciliation does not consist in merely forgetting the past."

"As we are liberated from our own fear, our presence automatically liberates others."

"Money won't create success; the freedom to make it will."

"And as we let our own light shine, we unconsciously give other people permission to do the same."

"There can be no keener revelation of a society's soul than the way in which it treats its children."

"There is no such thing as part freedom; it is all or nothing."

"After climbing a great hill, one only finds that there are many more hills to climb."

"If you talk to a man in a language he understands, that goes to his head. If you talk to him in his language, that goes to his heart."

"We must use time wisely and forever realize that the time is always ripe to do right."

"There is no passion to be found playing small, in settling for a life that is less than the one you are capable of living."

"If you want to make peace with your enemy, you have to work with your enemy."

"You can never have an impact on society if you have not changed yourself."

"It always seems impossible until it's done."

---

If you had eaten an apple a day until you were 30, you would have eaten 10,957 apples.

# NOVEMBER 6

*Quotes from some Scorpios who were
born on the 6th of November.*

"The invention of basketball
was not an accident. It was
developed to meet a need.
Those boys simply would not
play 'Drop the Handker-
chief.'"
—**James Naismith (b. 1861),
inventor of basketball**

"Except for a few guitar
chords, everything I've
learned in my life that is of
any value I've learned from
women."
—**Glenn Frey (b. 1948)**

"Don't think of him as a
Republican. Think of him
as the man I love, and if
that doesn't work, think of
him as the man who can
crush you."
—**Maria Shriver
(b. 1955), introducing
Arnold Schwarzenegger
to her uncle, Ted Kennedy**

"Being with an insanely jealous person is like being in the
room with a dead mammoth."
—**Mike Nichols (b. 1931),
director**

"My agent said, 'You aren't
good enough for movies.' I
said, 'You're fired.'"
—**Sally Field (b. 1946)**

"I kill flies, I eat meat, you
know, whatever."
—**Ethan Hawke (b. 1970)**

"There is one thing that
freezes a musician more than
the deadliest physical cold,
and that is the spiritual chill
of an unresponsive audience."
—**John Philip Sousa
(b. 1854)**

"I loved being a judge, and
sometimes I miss the power of
the gavel, but this is a lot
more fun."
—**Catherine Crier
(b. 1954), journalist**

"I can't believe that having
said what I said was interpreted as having been what I said
when I said it, because I said
it where I said it, when I said
it, and who I said it to."
—**Don King (b. 1932)**

**November 6, 1947: *Meet The Press* makes its television debut.**

# WE LOVE LUCY

*After struggling through Hollywood B-movies for 20 years, Lucille Ball (1911–1989) achieved superstardom in the TV sitcom I Love Lucy. Here are some observations on life and the biz from the "Queen of Comedy."*

"I was shy in my early days in Hollywood until I figured out that no one really gave a damn if I was shy or not, and I got over my shyness."

"I'm not funny. What I am is brave."

"Luck? I don't know anything about luck. I've never banked on it and I'm afraid of people who do."

"Knowing what you cannot do is more important than knowing what you can do."

"It wasn't love at first sight. It took a full five minutes."
—**on meeting Desi Arnaz**

"In life, all good things come hard, but wisdom is the hardest to come by."

"Women's lib? It doesn't interest me one bit. I've been so liberated it hurts."

"I would rather regret the things that I have done than the things that I have not."

"Not everything that is faced can be changed, but nothing can be changed until it is faced."

"How was *I Love Lucy* born? We decided that instead of divorce lawyers profiting from our mistakes, we'd profit from them."

"It's not what we set out to get, but how we go about the daily task of living."

"What could I do? I couldn't dance. I couldn't sing. I could talk."

"A man who correctly guesses a woman's age may be smart, but he's not very bright."

"I suppose I've grown old gracefully—'gracefully' meaning I've stemmed the tide, but there's a leak in the dike."

"Love yourself first, and everything else falls into line. You really have to love yourself to get anything done in this world."

---

To dye for: Everyone's favorite redhead, Lucille Ball, actually had brown hair.

# ON RELIGION AND GOD

*Instead of separating out the faithful, agnostics, and atheists, we thought we'd make this like the real world and just throw them all in there together—with the hope that that they may have a civil discussion about the nature of God.*

"A friendly study of the world's religions is a sacred duty."
—**Mahatma Gandhi**

"Religion today is not transforming people; rather it is being transformed by the people. It is not raising the moral level of society; it is descending to society's own level, and congratulating itself that it has scored a victory because society is smilingly accepting its surrender."
—**A. W. Tozer**

"Being religious means asking passionately the question of the meaning of our existence and being willing to receive answers, even if the answers hurt."
—**Paul Tillich**

"Faith is believing what you know ain't so."
—**Mark Twain**

"God is our refuge and our strength, a very present help in trouble."
—**Psalms 16:1**

"To surrender to ignorance and call it God has always been premature, and it remains premature today."
—**Isaac Asimov**

"Christianity, if false, is of no importance, and if true, of infinite importance. The only thing it cannot be is moderately important."
—**C. S. Lewis**

"The last true Christian died on the cross."
—**Friedrich Nietzsche**

"To have a positive religion is not necessary. To be in harmony with yourself and the universe is what counts, and this is possible without positive and specific formulation in words."
—**Goethe**

"Religion altars the mind."
—**Tony Follari**

"A church steeple with a lightning rod on top shows a lack of confidence."
—**Doug McLeod**

---

Q: Did you hear about the dyslexic atheist?   A: He didn't believe in Dog.

"Going to church does not make you a Christian any more than going to the garage makes you a car."
—Laurence J. Peter

"When I told the people of Northern Ireland that I was an atheist, a woman in the audience stood up and said, 'Yes, but is it the God of the Catholics or the God of the Protestants in whom you don't believe?'"
—Quentin Crisp

"A little philosophy inclineth man's mind to atheism, but depth in philosophy bringeth men's minds about to religion."
—Francis Bacon

"In the absence of any other proof, the thumb alone would convince me of God's existence."
—Isaac Newton

"I think people who don't believe in God are crazy. How can you say there is no God when you hear the birds singing these beautiful songs you didn't make?"
—Little Richard

"It is the final proof of God's omnipotence that He need not exist in order to save us."
—Peter De Vries

"If I were doing something that the Bible condemns, I have two choices. I can straighten up my act, or I can somehow distort the meaning of the Bible."
—Jerry Falwell

"All national institutions of churches, whether Jewish, Christian or Turkish, appear to me no other than human inventions, set up to terrify and enslave mankind, and monopolize power and profit."
—Thomas Paine

"Scientific views end in awe and mystery, lost at the edge in uncertainty, but they appear to be so deep and so impressive that the theory that it is all arranged as a stage for God to watch man's struggle for good and evil seems inadequate."
—Richard P. Feynman

"And the day will come, when the mystical generation of Jesus, by the Supreme Being as His Father, in the womb of a virgin, will be classed with the fable of the generation of Minerva, in the brain of Jupiter."
—Thomas Jefferson

"If there is no God, who pops up the next Kleenex?"
—Art Hoppe

The youngest Pope was 11 years old.

# MORE DIRECTORS

*That last "Directors on Directors" page seemed kind of flat.
Let's try it one more time with feeling. And...action!*

"I am not a director of action; I'm a director of gestures and silences."
—**Sergio Leone**

"I can't, in words, say what I say in film."
—**David Lynch**

"When you understand what makes a great Western painting, you'll be a great Western director."
—**John Ford**

"I associate my motion picture career more with being scared, or being under the gun, than with anything pleasant."
—**Francis Ford Coppola**

"Directing while acting is one less person to argue with."
—**Roman Polanski**

"The hell with the trains, the helicopters, the Mafia, the FBI, the car crashes, the pursuits, the stakeouts, the barricades...all of those things that we pump into movies because we're afraid to make movies about people."
—**Barry Levinson**

"The directing of a picture involves coming out of your individual loneliness and taking a controlling part in putting together a small world."
—**John Huston**

"Cinema is a matter of what is in the frame and what is out."
—**Martin Scorsese**

"I love doing big movies. It's awesome! You have all these toys. Like they always say, directors have the biggest train sets! Don't tell anyone, but I'd do this for free."
—**Michael Bay**

"Getting the audience to cry for the Terminator at the end of *T2*, for me that was the whole purpose of making that film. If you can get the audience to feel emotion for a character that in the previous film you despised utterly and were terrified by, then that's a cinematic arc."
—**James Cameron**

"After all, it's only moving shadows on a silver screen."
—**Richard Fleischer**

"Good luck has its storms." —George Lucas

# EULOGIES

*How would you like to be honored at your funeral?*

"In her own lifetime she created a myth of what a poor girl from a deprived background could attain. For the entire world she became a symbol of the eternal feminine."
—Lee Strasberg, on Marilyn Monroe

"As millions of race fans mourn the loss of the man they knew as 'The Intimidator,' the sport and the race that he truly loved has taken from me one of my best friends. I feel fortunate that I had the opportunity to race with, tangle with, sometimes outrun, and most usually finish behind the greatest driving talent NASCAR racing has ever seen."
—Dale Jarrett, on Dale Earnhardt, Sr.

"He was a Dostoevsky, a Melville, and a Tolstoy all rolled up in one. He was an uncompromising giant unafraid to tackle controversial issues and explore the human condition through his unique vision."
—Edward Champion, on Stanley Kubrick

"He had a natural reserve to him, but when he admired people, he went all out to tell them about it. And because there was no deception in him, his praise meant more than just about anything else. If Chet was a fan of yours, you never needed another one. He was not a saint. He liked synthesizers more than he maybe ought to have. He sometimes kicked the golf ball to improve his lie."
—Garrison Keillor, on guitarist Chet Atkins

"We will never forget them, nor the last time we saw them, this morning, as they prepared for their journey and waved good-bye and 'slipped the surly bonds of earth' to 'touch the face of God.'"
—Ronald Reagan, on the Challenger astronauts

"Here lies the body of my good horse, 'The General.' For 20 years he bore me around the circuit of my practice, and in all that time he never made a blunder. Would that his master could say the same!"
—President John Tyler

St. John was the only one of the 12 apostles to die a natural death.

# COURAGE!

*"What makes the elephant charge his tusk in the misty mist, or the dusky dusk? What makes the muskrat guard his musk? Courage!"*
—The Cowardly Lion, The Wizard of Oz (1939)

"Our deepest fear is not that we are inadequate. Our deepest fear is that we are powerful beyond measure. It is our light, not our darkness, that most frightens us."
—**Nelson Mandela**

"Life shrinks or expands according to one's courage."
—**Anaïs Nin**

"Courage without conscience is a wild beast."
—**Robert G. Ingersoll**

"People react to fear, not love—they don't teach that in Sunday School, but it's true."
—**Richard Nixon**

"Become so wrapped up in something that you forget to be afraid."
—**Lady Bird Johnson**

"You gain strength, courage, and confidence by every experience in which you really stop to look fear in the face."
—**Eleanor Roosevelt**

"It is curious—curious that physical courage should be so common in the world, and moral courage so rare."
—**Mark Twain**

"Courage is going from failure to failure without losing enthusiasm."
—**Winston Churchill**

"Courage is not the absence of fear, but rather the judgment that something else is more important than fear."
—**Ambrose Redmoon**

"A timid person is frightened before a danger, a coward during the time, and a courageous person afterwards."
—**Jean Paul Richter**

"When a brave man takes a stand, the spines of others are often stiffened."
—**Billy Graham**

"Fear was absolutely necessary. Without it, I would have been scared to death."
—**Floyd Patterson, boxing champion**

"Courage is the power to overcome danger, misfortune, fear, injustice, while continuing to affirm inwardly that life with all its sorrows is good; that everything is meaningful even if in a sense beyond our understanding; and that there is always tomorrow."

—Dorothy Thompson

# HENRY FORD

*Timeless wisdom from America's greatest industrialist.*

"A business absolutely devoted to service will have only one worry about profits. They will be embarrassingly large."

"A market is never saturated with a good product, but it is very quickly saturated with a bad one."

"Money doesn't change men, it merely unmasks them. If a man is naturally selfish or arrogant or greedy, the money brings that out, that's all."

"The man who will use his skill and constructive imagination to see how much he can give for a dollar, instead of how little he can give for a dollar, is bound to succeed."

"Thinking is the hardest work there is. Which is the probable reason why so few engage in it."

"My best friend is the one who brings out the best in me."

"It has been my observation that most people get ahead during the time that others waste."

"Before everything else, getting ready is the secret of success."

"Failure is simply the opportunity to begin again, this time more intelligently."

"No two men are just alike. Every new life is a new thing under the sun; there has never been anything just like it before, never will be again. A young man ought to get that idea about himself; he should look for the single spark of individuality that makes him different from other folks, and develop that for all he is worth. Society and schools may try to iron it out of him; their tendency is to put it all in the same mold, but I say don't let that spark be lost; it is your only real claim to importance."

"Don't find fault, find a remedy."

"One of the greatest discoveries a man makes, one of his great surprises, is to find he can do what he was afraid he couldn't do."

If you are an average driver, you will lock yourself out of your car nine times in your life.

# IT'S A GREAT COUNTRY

*Say these people…*

"The creation of the United States of America is the greatest of all human adventures."
—**Paul Johnson**

"America is more than just a country, it's an idea—an idea that's contagious."
—**Bono**

"America is the greatest, freest and most decent society in existence. It is an oasis of goodness in a desert of cynicism and barbarism. This country, once an experiment unique in the world, is now the last best hope for the world."
—**Dinesh D'Souza**

"America has never been united by blood or birth or soil. We are bound by ideals that move us beyond our backgrounds, lift us above our interests, and teach us what it means to be citizens."
—**George W. Bush**

"I love America more than any other country in this world; and, exactly for this reason, I insist on the right to criticize her perpetually."
—**James Baldwin**

"America is the greatest country in the world. What I've accomplished could not have been done anywhere else."
—**boxing promoter Don King**

"The good things about America are football, kindness, and jazz bands."
—**George Santayana**

"America is a vast conspiracy to make you happy."
—**John Updike**

"We must always remember that America is a great nation today not because of what government did for people but because of what people did for themselves and for one another."
—**Richard M. Nixon**

"Ours is the only country deliberately founded on a good idea."
—**John Gunther**

"You'll be sorry that you messed with the U.S. of A. 'Cause we'll put a boot in your a**. It's the American way"
—**Toby Keith, "Courtesy of the Red, White & Blue"**

# IT'S A FREE COUNTRY

*Say these people…*

"Too many of us look upon Americans as dollar chasers. This is a cruel libel, even if it is reiterated thoughtlessly by the Americans themselves."
—**Albert Einstein**

"In America you can say anything you want, as long as it doesn't have any effect."
—**Paul Goodman**

"America is a melting pot; the people at the bottom get burned while all the scum floats to the top."
—**Charlie King**

"The Americans have invented so wide a range of pithy and hackneyed phrases that they can carry on a conversation without giving a moment's reflection to what they are saying and so leave their minds free to consider the more important matters of big business and fornication."
—**W. Somerset Maugham**

"The IQ and life expectancy of the average American recently passed each other going in opposite directions."
—**George Carlin**

"Americans keep telling us how successful their system is—then they remind us not to stray too far from our hotel at night."
—**European official during the G-8 economic summit in Denver, 1997**

"Americans are getting stronger. Twenty years ago, it took two people to carry ten dollars worth of groceries. Today, a five-year-old can do it."
—**Henny Youngman**

"In America, through pressure of conformity, there is freedom of choice, but nothing to choose from."
—**Peter Ustinov**

"Americans can eat garbage, provided you sprinkle it liberally with ketchup, mustard, chili sauce, Tabasco sauce, cayenne pepper, or any other condiment which destroys the original flavor of the dish."
—**Henry Miller**

"America's one of the finest countries anyone ever stole."
—**Bobcat Goldthwaite**

"With public sentiment, nothing can fail. Without it, nothing can succeed." —Abraham Lincoln

# LOVE, COURTNEY

*Courtney Love, lead singer of the rock band Hole, has had troubles with the law, drugs, and her friends, and endured the death of her husband, Kurt Cobain of Nirvana. And she's also tested with a genius-level IQ.*

## ON MUSIC:

"If I write a song about being a teenage prostitute, that doesn't mean that I was a teenage prostitute."

"Drugs have nothing to do with the creation of music. They are dumb and self-indulgent, kind of like sucking your thumb."

"I tell lies, but not in my lyrics."

"One thing I haven't conquered is the usage of the word 'love.' I can't say it out loud in a song."

## ON LIFE:

"I wish I ruled the world. I think it'd be a better place."

"Being offended is part of being in the real world."

"I want every girl in the world to pick up a guitar and start screaming."

"Only dumb people are happy."

"I'm not a woman. I'm a force of nature."

## ON HER IMAGE:

"I don't like small talk, and I behave in an extremely normal, wholesome manner for the most part in my daily life."

"I used to do drugs, but don't tell anyone or it will ruin my image."

"My number-one thing to work on is not being reactive—but appropriateness doesn't come easily to me sometimes."

## ON FAME:

"Being a rock star is like being a cult leader. You really have to be in your own religion."

"Since my persona is so demonized and so huge and so not what I'm about, I can practically do anything I want behind that persona, artistically. That's kind of a gift."

"In rock stardom, there's an absolute economic upside to self-destruction."

"I'm real bored of fame. I like power better."

---

Lovely name origin: Courtney Harrison's mother called her little girl "Courtney Love."

# VOICES FROM HISTORY

*Some quotes from the past that may send a chill down your spine.*

"They were well built, with good bodies and handsome features....They do not bear arms, and do not know them, for I showed them a sword, they took it by the edge and cut themselves out of ignorance. They would make fine servants....With fifty men we could subjugate them all and make them do whatever we want."
—**Christopher Columbus, on natives he encountered in what is now the Bahamas**

"I thought I was benefiting the Indians as well as the government, by taking them all over the United States, and giving them a correct idea of the customs, life, etc., of the pale faces, so that when they returned to their people they could make known all they had seen."
—**"Buffalo" Bill Cody, writing about his Wild West Show of 1878**

"For a short time we lived quietly. But this could not last. White men had found gold in the mountains around the land of winding water."
—**Chief Joseph, 1879**

"The great masses of the people will more easily fall victims to a big lie than to a small one."
—**Adolf Hitler**

"Our government has kept us in a perpetual state of fear—kept us in a continuous stampede of patriotic fervor—with the cry of grave national emergency. Always there has been some terrible evil at home or some monstrous foreign power that was going to gobble us up if we did not blindly rally behind it by furnishing the exorbitant funds demanded. Yet, in retrospect, these disasters seem never to have happened, seem never to have been quite real."
—**General Douglas MacArthur, 1957**

"It suddenly struck me that that tiny pea, pretty and blue, was the Earth. I put up my thumb and shut one eye, and my thumb blotted out the planet Earth. I didn't feel like a giant. I felt very, very small."
—**Neil Armstrong**

"We cannot do everything at once, but we can do something at once." —Calvin Coolidge

# NEVER SAY NEVER

*"Never stop reading in the bathroom." —Uncle John*

"Never face facts; if you do, you'll never get up in the morning."
—Marlo Thomas

"Never under any circumstances take a sleeping pill and a laxative on the same night."
—Dave Barry

"Never trust the advice of a man in trouble."
—Aesop

"Never ruin an apology with an excuse."
—Kimberly Johnson

"Never put a sock in a toaster."
—Eddie Izzard

"Never, never listen to anybody who tries to discourage you."
—Mariah Carey

"Never help a child with a task at which he feels he can succeed."
—Maria Montessori

"Never love anything that can't love you back."
—Joan Crawford

"Never mistake knowledge for wisdom. One helps you make a living, the other helps you make a life."
—Sandra Carey

"Never insult anyone by accident."
—Robert A. Heinlein

"Never run in the rain with your socks on."
—Billie Joe Armstrong, of Green Day

"Never believe anything in politics until it has been officially denied."
—Otto von Bismarck

"If you want to be something, be conceited about it. Never say you're no good; that will never get you anywhere."
—Mike McLaren

"Never apologize for showing feeling. When you do so, you apologize for the truth."
—Benjamin Disraeli

"Never play a thing the same way twice."
—Louis Armstrong

# MORE AMERICAN INDIAN PROVERBS

*Timeless wisdom from ancient peoples.*

The one who tells the stories, rules the world.
—Hopi

There are no secrets. There is no mystery. There is only common sense.
—Onondaga

Don't let yesterday use up too much of today.
—Cherokee

Every animal knows more than you do.
—Nez Perce

If you see no reason for giving thanks, the fault lies in yourself.
—Minquass

Force, no matter how concealed, begets resistance.
—Lakota

The frog does not drink up the pond in which he lives.
—Sioux

Each bird loves to hear himself sing.
—Arapaho

It is better to have less thunder in the mouth and more lightning in the hand.
—Apache

When you were born, you cried and the world rejoiced. Live your life so that when you die, the world cries and you rejoice.
—Cherokee

The man who gives his opinion freely should be ready to fight fiercely.
—Iowa

When the fox walks lame, the old rabbit jumps.
—Oklahoma

There is nothing as eloquent as a rattlesnake's tail.
—Navajo

Misfortunes do not flourish on one path; they grow everywhere.
—Pawnee

We will be known forever by the tracks we leave.
—Dakota

The name Pocahontas means "playful one."

# GOOD VS. EVIL

*Round 2...*

"No man chooses evil because it is evil; he only mistakes it for happiness, for the good he seeks."
—**Mary Wollstonecraft**

"To do an evil act is base. To do a good one without incurring danger is common enough. But it is part of a good man to do great and noble deeds though he risks everything in doing them."
—**Plutarch**

"Whatever is done for love always occurs beyond good and evil."
—**Friedrich Nietzsche**

"Non-cooperation with evil is as much a duty as is cooperation with good."
—**Mahatma Gandhi**

"If a man sets his heart on benevolence, he will be free from evil."
—**Confucius**

"Evil can be transmuted into good. What is evil at one time becomes good at another time to somebody else."
—**Sivananda**

"The only good is knowledge, and the only evil is ignorance."
—**Diogenes Laërtius**

"At the bottom of the heart of every human being, from infancy until the tomb, there is something that goes on expecting, in the teeth of all experience of crimes committed, suffered, and witnessed, that good and not evil will be done."
—**Simone Weil**

"Every minute you are thinking of evil, you might have been thinking of good instead. Refuse to pander to a morbid interest in your own misdeeds. Pick yourself up, shake yourself, and go on again."
—**Evelyn Underhill**

"When good people cease their vigilance and struggle, then evil men prevail."
—**Pearl S. Buck**

"Goodness alone is never enough. Goodness without wisdom invariably accomplishes evil."
—**Robert Heinlein**

---

**"If there is any good in philosophy, it is that it never inspects pedigrees." —Seneca**

# NOBEL'S PRIZES

*Alfred Nobel was an engineer who invented dynamite and encouraged the development of science through the Nobel Prize—and world peace, through the Nobel Peace Prize. Still, he remained cynical about the human condition.*

"A heart can no more be forced to love than a stomach can be forced to digest food by persuasion."

"Hope is nature's veil for hiding truth's nakedness."

"If I have a thousand ideas and only one turns out to be good, I am satisfied."

"Second to agriculture, humbug is the biggest industry of our age."

"For my part, I wish all guns with their belongings and everything could be sent to hell, which is the proper place for their exhibition and use."

"Lying is the greatest of all sins."

"Contentment is the only real wealth."

"We build upon the sand, and the older we become, the more unstable this foundation becomes."

"The truthful man is usually defeated by the liar."

"The savants will write excellent volumes. There will be laureates. But wars will continue just the same until the forces of the circumstances render them impossible."

"Justice is to be found only in the imagination."

"I intend to leave after my death a large fund for the promotion of the peace idea, but I am skeptical as to its results."

"It is not sufficient to be worthy of respect in order to be respected."

"Worry is the stomach's worst poison."

"My dynamite will sooner lead to peace than a thousand world conventions. As soon as men will find that in one instant whole armies can be utterly destroyed, they surely will abide by golden peace."

Q: Who invented the hula-hoop? A: Spud Melvin.

# CREATIVITY

*Can you just turn it on like a faucet? Why not?*

"Confidence in nonsense is a requirement for the creative process."
—**M. C. Escher**

"Creativity requires the courage to let go of certainties."
—**Erich Fromm**

"The idea is there, locked inside. All you have to do is remove the excess stone."
—**Michelangelo**

"Emptiness is a symptom that you are not living creatively. You either have no goal that is important enough to you, or you are not using your talents and efforts in a striving toward an important goal."
—**Dr. Maxwell Maltz**

"The creative person is both more primitive and more cultivated, more destructive, a lot madder, and a lot saner than the average person."
—**Frank Barron**

"One must accept that one has uncreative moments. The more honestly one can accept that, the quicker these moments will pass."
—**Etty Hillesum**

"Creativity is discontent translated into arts."
—**Eric Hoffer**

"The secret to creativity is knowing how to hide your sources."
—**Albert Einstein**

"One of the advantages of being disorderly is that one is constantly making exciting discoveries."
—**A. A. Milne**

"The function of the creative artist consists in making laws, not in following laws already made."
—**Ferruccio Busoni**

"Nothing encourages creativity like the chance to fall flat on one's face."
—**James D. Finley**

"The truly creative people I know all live lousy lives, never have time to see you, don't take care of themselves properly, have weird tastes in women, and behave badly. They don't wash and they eat disgusting stuff, they are mentally unstable and are absolutely brilliant."
—**Toke Nygaard**

"Creativity is allowing yourself to make mistakes. Art is knowing which ones to keep." —Scott Adams

"Creativity often consists of merely turning up what is already there. Did you know that right and left shoes were thought up only a little more than a century ago?"

—Bernice Fitz-Gibbon

"An activity is creative when the doer cares about doing it right...or doing it better." —John Updike

# ALFRED HITCHCOCK

*The master of the macabre was also a master of sardonic wit.*

"I have a perfect cure for a sore throat: cut it."

"Disney has the best casting. If he doesn't like an actor he just tears him up."

"If I made *Cinderella*, the audience would immediately be looking for a body in the coach."

"There is no terror in a bang, only in the anticipation of it."

"When an actor comes to me and wants to discuss his character, I say, 'It's in the script.' If he says, 'But what's my motivation?,' I say, 'Your salary.'"

"I am scared easily. Here is a list of my adrenaline production. 1: small children; 2: policemen; 3: high places; 4: that my next movie will not be as good as the last one."

"Some of our most exquisite murders have been domestic, performed with tenderness in simple, homey places like the kitchen table."

"Always make the audience suffer as much as possible."

"Even my failures make money and become classics a year after I make them."

"There is a dreadful story that I hate actors. I can't imagine how such a rumor began. Of course it may possibly be because I was once quoted as saying that actors are cattle. My actor friends know I would never be capable of such a thoughtless, rude, and unfeeling remark, that I would never call them cattle. What I probably said was that actors should be treated like cattle."

"If it's a good movie, the sound could go off and the audience would still have a perfectly clear idea of what was going on."

"Blondes make the best victims. They're like virgin snow that shows up the bloody footprints."

"I enjoy playing the audience like a piano."

"B.M.," which appears on a ring in Hitchcock's *Shadow of a Doubt*, stands for "Bowel Movement."

# LITTLE WEBBYS

*The annual Webby Awards (the "Oscars of the Internet") honor the best sites on the World Wide Web. Because they give out roughly 125 awards over the course of the evening, award winners must adhere to a simple rule: "No acceptance speech can be more than five words long."*

**SITE:** *JDate.com*, a dating service for "Jewish singles looking for kosher love."
**AWARD:** Social/Networking Site
**SPEECH:** "Jewish American Princesses—Sssmokin'!"

**SITE:** *RememberSegregation.org*, dedicated to civil rights
**AWARD:** Best Home/Welcome Page
**SPEECH:** "Two crackers, fighting racism, yo!"

**SITE:** *huffingtonpost.com*, Arianna Huffington's blog site
**AWARD:** Blog—Political
**SPEECH:** "Dahlings, make blogs, not war."

**WINNER:** Al Gore
**AWARD:** Lifetime Achievement
**SPEECH:** "Please don't recount this vote."

**SITE:** *nationalgeographic.com/genographic*, National Geographic's DNA study that tracks the history of human migration
**AWARD:** Magazine online edition
**SPEECH:** "More than just bare breasts."

**SITE:** *TripAdvisor.com*
**AWARD:** Community
**SPEECH:** "Because some hotels really suck."

**SITE:** *myspace.com*
**AWARD:** Breakout of the Year
**SPEECH:** "Fun for the whole family."

---

Monaco's national orchestra is larger than its army.

**SITE:** *Bebo.com*
**AWARD:** Social/Networking
**SPEECH:** "In your face, myspace."

**SITE:** New Zealand International Arts Festival
**AWARD:** Events
**SPEECH:** "New Zealanders, a day ahead."

**SITE:** *NPGMusicclub.com*, music artist Prince's site from which he releases his albums
**AWARD:** Celebrity/Fan
**SPEECH:** "Prince says: Eliminate the middleman."

**SITE:** *BabyCenter.com*
**AWARD:** Family/Parenting
**SPEECH:** "You push, we deliver."

**SITE:** *ESPN.com*
**AWARD:** Sports
**SPEECH:** "Sports? Pornography? Sports…pornography…SPORTS!"

**SITE:** *WashingtonPost.com*
**AWARD:** Newspaper online edition
**SPEECH:** "We're deeper than Deep Throat."

**SITE:** *Monster.com*
**AWARD:** Employment
**SPEECH:** "Note to self: update resume."

**And finally,** *had Uncle John won an award for our gloriously beautiful Web site, www.bathroomreader.com, he would have said:*
"Go with the Flow. Tanks."
*Maybe next year…*

# OH, CANADA!

*We at the BRI love our neighbors to the North!*
*(Although not everyone on this page does.)*

"If some countries have too much history, we have too much geography."
—Mackenzie King

"Very little is known of the Canadian country, since it is rarely visited by anyone but the Queen and illiterate sport fishermen."
—P. J. O'Rourke

"Canada and Mexico, as the saying goes, have one common problem between them."
—J. C. Ogelsby

"The beaver, which has come to represent Canada as the eagle does the United States and the lion Britain, is a flat-tailed, slow-witted, toothy rodent known to bite off its own testicles or to stand under its own falling trees."
—June Callwood

"The great themes of Canadian history are as follows: keeping the Americans out, keeping the French in, and trying to get the Natives to somehow disappear."
—Will Ferguson

"In Canada, there are nine months of winter and three months of road repair."
—Peter Hanson

"The beginning of Canadian cultural nationalism was not, 'Am I really that oppressed?' but, 'Am I really that boring?'"
—Margaret Atwood

"Canada is an interesting place. The rest of the world thinks so, even if Canadians don't."
—Terence M. Green

"Canada is like an old cow. The West feeds it. Ontario and Quebec milk it. And you can well imagine what it's doing in the Maritimes!"
—Tommy Douglas

"Americans are so benevolently ignorant about Canada, while Canadians are malevolently well informed about the United States."
—J. Bartlet Brebner

"Canada has never been a melting pot; more like a tossed salad."
—Arnold Edinborough

# 'TOON TALK

*Just because they're two-dimensional and fictional doesn't mean cartoons can't be sort of smart.*

"It doesn't matter what you look like on the outside, whether you're white, black, or Sasquatch, even. As long as you follow your dream… except for Sasquatch. If you're Sasquatch, the rules are different."
—Meatwad, *Aqua Teen Hunger Force*

"Let me guess, you picked out yet another colorful box with a crank that I'm expected to turn and turn until OOPS!, big shock, a jack pops out and you laugh and the kids laugh and the dog laughs and I die a little inside."
—Stewie, *Family Guy*

**Darryl:** How 'bout my cousin Earl and his wife? They're nice and they like to travel.
**Wanda:** Avoiding a subpoena is not liking to travel.
—*Baby Blues*

"If you love something, and you set it free, and it doesn't come back, you're a dumbass."
—Butt-Head, *Beavis and Butt-Head*

"Bears are crazy. They'll bite your head if you're wearing a steak on it."
—Space Ghost, *Space Ghost Coast to Coast*

"If you're in a bus station and they sell postcards for Bizzaro World, you have to assume you're in Bizzaro World."
—Captain Hero, *Drawn Together*

"I do my best work when I'm being worshiped as a god."
—Johnny, *Johnny Bravo*

"You never forget how to fight. It's like beating up a bicycle."
—Stan, *American Dad*

"There's a time and place for everything and it's called 'college.'"
—Chef, *South Park*

"I'll tell you a little story called 'The Ugly Barnacle': Once there was a very ugly barnacle. He was so ugly that everybody died. The End."
—Patrick, *SpongeBob SquarePants*

Walt Disney first started drawing cartoons in exchange for free haircuts.

# LEONARD COHEN

*A successful poet and novelist in Canada, Cohen came to the United States in his late 30s to try his hand at music. He joined the folk music boom of the 1960s and has since become an influential singer/songwriter who never forgot his poetic roots.*

"What is most original in a man's nature is often that which is most desperate."

"I see a song as the ashes of existence."

"There is a crack in everything; that's how the light gets in."

"The term 'clinical depression' finds its way into too many conversations these days. One has a sense that a catastrophe has occurred in the psychic landscape."

"New systems are forced on the world by men who simply cannot bear the pain of living with what is. Creators care nothing for their systems except that they be unique."

"The last refuge of the insomniac is a sense of superiority to the sleeping world."

"Children show scars like medals. Lovers use them as secrets to reveal. A scar is what happens when the word is made flesh."

"Prayer is translation. A man translates himself into a child asking for all there is in a language he has barely mastered."

"Zen Buddhism is the very contrary of dropping out. Most people can't wait to get home to their house or apartment and shut that door and turn on the TV. To me, that's dropping out."

"I've always felt that the most important thing in this vale of tears was relationships. This was the real politics and that all these institutions were the desperate and dismal alternatives to a failed embrace."

"If your life is burning well, poetry is just the ash."

---

**Mötley Crüe drummer Tommy Lee has a Starbucks in his home.**

# RANDOM QUOTES

*A few more thoughts that were too good to leave out.*

"They say such nice things about people at funerals that it makes me sad to realize that I'm going to miss mine by just a few days."
—**Garrison Keillor**

"What's the use of a fine house if you haven't got a tolerable planet to put it on?"
—**Henry David Thoreau**

"Sometimes to realize you were well, someone must come along and hurt you."
—**Perry Farrell**

"Unless a man undertakes more than he possibly can do, he will never do all that he can."
—**Henry Drummond**

"If you wish success in life, make perseverance your bosom friend, experience your wise counselor, caution your elder brother, and hope your guardian genius."
—**Joseph Addison**

"My goal is to goad people into saying something that ruins their life."
—**Don Imus**

"This is unparalyzed in the state's history."
—**Gib Lewis, Texas Speaker of the House**

"Now, the only thing that remains unresolved is the resolution of the problem."
—**Thomas Wells, Ontario legislature minister**

"The person who makes a success of living is the one who sees his goal steadily and aims for it unswervingly."
—**Cecil B. DeMille**

"Live so that you wouldn't be ashamed to sell the family parrot to the town gossip."
—**Will Rogers**

"I am amazed at radio DJs today. I am firmly convinced that AM on my radio stands for Absolute Moron. I will not begin to tell you what FM stands for."
—**Jasper Carrott**

"There is no need to do any housework at all. After the first four years the dirt doesn't get any worse."
—**Quentin Crisp**

**"Take time to repair the roof when the sun is shining." —John F. Kennedy**

# SEX SEX SEX SEX SEX SEX

*More quotes on the birds and the bees.*

"A student undergoing a word-association test was asked why a snowstorm put him in mind of sex. He replied frankly: 'Because everything does.'"
—Honor Tracy

"When authorities warn you of the sinfulness of sex, there is an important lesson to be learned. Do not have sex with the authorities."
—Matt Groening

"To hear many religious people talk, one would think God created the torso, head, legs, and arms, but the devil slapped on the genitals."
—Don Schrader

"Sex is nature, and I believe in going along with nature."
—Marilyn Monroe

"I don't think anyone should be educated sexually. There's far too many people on the planet. If we could hush it up for a few years, that would help."
—John Cleese

"Anybody who believes that the way to a man's heart is through his stomach flunked geography."
—Robert Byrne

"Sex at age 90 is like trying to shoot pool with a rope."
—George Burns

"Seems to me the basic conflict between men and women, sexually, is that men are like firemen. To men, sex is an emergency, and no matter what we're doing we can be ready in two minutes. Women, on the other hand, are like fire. They're very exciting, but the conditions have to be exactly right for it to occur."
—Jerry Seinfeld

"God is in my head, but the devil is in my pants."
—Jonathan Winters

"We might as well make up our minds that chastity is no more a virtue than malnutrition."
—Edmund Waller

Men did not start wearing wedding rings until the early 1900s.

# THE CONAN ZONE

*What's tall, has a giant orange head, and is extremely funny? No, not the Great Pumpkin.* Late Night *host Conan O'Brien.*

"Now that Martha Stewart is out of jail, she's going back to writing for her magazine. This month's column explains how to hot-glue seashells to your electronic ankle bracelet."

"California Governor Arnold Schwarzenegger said America needs to work together to conserve oil. Then Arnold lit a cigar and drove over the crowd in his Hummer."

"The Chinese government launched China's first 24-hour news channel. And since the channel will only report stories that are favorable to the ruling party, they've decided to call it Fox News."

"Former Vice President Al Gore gave a passionate 10-minute speech where he criticized President Bush for, quote, 'repeatedly breaking the law.' Those who heard the speech called it 'the worst elevator ride ever.'"

"Today, the Senate voted to build a 370-mile fence along the Mexican border. Experts say a 370-mile fence is the perfect way to protect a border that is 1,900 miles long."

"A group of scientists warned that because of global warming, sea levels will rise so much that parts of New Jersey will be under water. The bad news? Parts of New Jersey *won't* be under water."

"The other day in New York, a department store unveiled the most expensive perfume in the world, which sells for over $215,000. Perfume experts say it smells like a combination of money and jackass."

"A man just set a new record for solving the Rubik's Cube by completing the puzzle in 11.13 seconds. For his next challenge he's going to see if he can escape from the 1980s."

"The *New York Daily News* reports that Leonard Nimoy, *Star Trek*'s Mr. Spock, will star in a pain-reliever ad during the Super Bowl. *Star Trek* fans were excited by this news and asked, 'What's the Super Bowl?'"

Conan O'Brien has written for *The Simpsons* and *Saturday Night Live*.

# P. J. O'ROURKE

*In the 1970s, he was an idealistic hippie. In the '80s and '90s,
his writing could best be described as conservative.
What is he now? You decide.*

"Politicians are interested in people. Not that this is always a virtue. Fleas are interested in dogs."

"When buying and selling are controlled by legislation, the first things to be bought and sold are legislators."

"Always read stuff that will make you look good if you die in the middle of it."

"A little government and a little luck are necessary in life, but only a fool trusts either of them."

"A hat should be taken off when you greet a lady and left off for the rest of your life. Nothing looks more stupid than a hat."

"Anything that makes your mother cry is fun."

"Politics should be limited in scope to war, protection of property, and the occasional precautionary beheading of a member of the ruling class."

"I can understand why mankind hasn't given up war. During a war you get to drive tanks through buildings and shoot foreigners—two things that are usually frowned on during peacetime."

"The mystery of government is not how Washington works, but how to make it stop."

"Then there's 'No Child Left Behind.' What if the child deserves to be left behind?"

"How much can you really say against a drug [marijuana] that makes teenage boys drive slow?"

"[George W.] Bush said that if illegal immigrants want citizenship, they'd have to do three things: pay taxes, hold meaningful jobs, and learn English. Bush doesn't meet those qualifications."

"Liberals have invented whole college majors—psychology, sociology, women's studies—to prove that nothing is anybody's fault."

Queen Victoria's wedding cake was more than nine feet in circumference.

"And by the way, I've about had it with this 'greatest generation' malarkey. You people have one stock market crash in 1929, and it takes you a dozen years to go get a job. Then you wait until Germany and Japan have conquered half the world before it occurs to you to get involved in World War II. After that you get surprised by a million Red Chinese in Korea. Where do you put a million Red Chinese so they'll be a surprise? You spend the entire 1950s watching Lawrence Welk and designing tail fins. You come up with the idea for Vietnam. Thanks. And you elect Richard Nixon. The hell with you."

—P. J. O'Rourke

Oscar's a grouch? Only seven comedies have ever won the Academy Award for Best Picture.

# CHIASMUS

*What's a chiasmus? It's a statement where the second half reverses the first half, resulting in an elegant play on words. Here are some favorites.*

"Many a man owes his success to his first wife and his second wife to his success."
—**Jim Backus**

"No woman has ever so comforted the distressed, or so distressed the comfortable."
—**Clare Boothe Luce, on Eleanor Roosevelt**

"You have to know how to accept rejection and reject acceptance."
—**Ray Bradbury**

"A comedian does funny things. A good comedian does things funny."
—**Buster Keaton**

"I do not get ideas; ideas get me."
—**Robertson Davies**

"I despise the pleasure of pleasing people that I despise."
—**Lady Mary Wortley Montagu**

"Half of our mistakes in life arise from feeling where we ought to think and thinking where we ought to feel."
—**John Churton Collins**

"If your religion does not change you, then you should change your religion."
—**Elbert Hubbard**

"A scout troop consists of 12 little kids dressed like schmucks following a big schmuck dressed like a kid."
—**Jack Benny**

"Don't sweat the petty things, and don't pet the sweaty things."
—**Jacquelyn Small**

"It is not enough to preach about family values. We must value families."
—**Hillary Rodham Clinton**

"Those who mind don't matter, and those who matter don't mind."
—**Bernard Baruch**

"A friend is one who loves you, but one who loves you isn't necessarily your friend."
—**Seneca the Younger**

"To fall in love is awfully simple, but to fall out of love is simply awful."
—**Bess Myerson**

If an Amish man has a beard, he's married.

# MORE LOVIN'

*Because there's no such thing as too much love.*

"Tell me whom you love, and I will tell you who you are."
—**Arsène Houssaye**

"In the arithmetic of love, one plus one equals everything, and two minus one equals nothing."
—**Mignon McLaughlin**

"Love cures people—both the ones who give it and the ones who receive it."
—**Karl Menninger**

"The absolute yearning of one human body for another particular one and its indifference to substitutes is one of life's major mysteries."
—**Iris Murdoch**

"Love at first sight is easy to understand; it's when two people have been looking at each other for a lifetime that it becomes a miracle."
—**Amy Bloom**

"We put a lot of emphasis on relationships, to the point where it's often our whole life, and if your relationship isn't going right, your life is wack."
—**Erykah Badu**

"Love is like an hourglass, with the heart filling up as the brain empties."
—**Jules Renard**

"The best part of a good man stays forever, for love is immortal and makes all things immortal."
—**William Saroyan**

"All we need is to imagine our ability to love developing until it embraces the totality of men and the earth."
—**Pierre Teilhard de Chardin**

"Love doesn't just lay there. It has to be made, like bread; re-made all the time, made new."
—**Ursula Le Guin**

"Love is a hidden fire, A pleasant sore, A delicious poison, A delectable pain, An agreeable torment, A sweet and throbbing wound, A gentle death."
—**Fernando de Pujas**

"We are all mortal until the first kiss and the second glass of wine."
—**Eduardo Galeano**

# HUMBUG!

*Christmas sure has changed over the years. It seems to be getting more and more commercial. But can the Christmas spirit rise above all of that?*

"If I could work my will, every idiot who goes about with 'Merry Christmas' upon his lips should be boiled with his own pudding, and buried with a stake of holly through his heart."
—**Ebenezer Scrooge, in Charles Dickens's** *A Christmas Carol*

"Christmas begins about the first of December with an office party and ends when you finally realize what you spent, around April 15th of the next year."
—**P. J. O'Rourke**

"Nothing says 'Holidays' like a cheese log."
—**Ellen DeGeneres**

"Next to a circus there ain't nothing that packs up and tears out faster than the Christmas spirit."
—**Kin Hubbard**

"There's nothing sadder in this world than to awake Christmas morning and not be a child."
—**Erma Bombeck**

"Christmas is when everybody wants his past forgotten and his present remembered."
—**Phyllis Diller**

"The Holiday Season, that very special time of year when we join with our loved ones in sharing centuries-old traditions, such as trying to find a parking space at the mall."
—**Dave Barry**

"Christmas is a time when you get homesick, even when you're home."
—**Carol Nelson**

"From a commercial point of view, if Christmas didn't exist, we would have to invent it."
—**Katharine Whitehorn**

"My idea of Christmas is simple: loving others. Come to think of it, why do we have to wait for Christmas to do that?"
—**Bob Hope**

"A lovely thing about Christmas is that it's compulsory, like a thunderstorm, and we all go through it together."
—**Garrison Keillor**

**Q:** Why does Scrooge love Rudolph the Red-Nosed Reindeer? **A:** Because every buck is dear to him.

# UNCLE JOHN'S QUOTATIONARY

*Here's Part 8 of our quotation dictionary.*
*(Part 7 begins on page 303.)*

**ULTIMATUM:** in diplomacy, a last demand before resorting to concessions. (Ambrose Bierce)

**UMPIRE:** a necessary evil to the luxury of baseball, like the odor that follows an automobile. (Christy Mathewson)

**UNDERWEAR:** an emotional thing. (Elle MacPherson)

**UNEMPLOYMENT:** capitalism's way of getting you to plant a garden. (Orson Scott Card)

**UNHAPPINESS:** the difference between our talents and our expectations. (Edward de Bono)

**UNITED STATES:** a nation of laws, badly written and randomly enforced. (Frank Zappa)

**UNIVERSE:** the periodical manifestation of this unknown Absolute Essence. (H. P. Blavatsky)

**UNIX:** a command-line-driven OS that only nerds could love. (*PC Magazine*)

**VACATION:** what you take when you can no longer take what you've been taking. (Earl Wilson)

**VARIETY:** the condition of harmony. (Thomas Carlyle)

**VASECTOMY:** never having to say you're sorry. (Larry Adler)

**VEGAS:** Everyman's cut-rate Babylon. (Alistair Cooke)

**VEGETARIAN:** a person who eats only side dishes. (Gerald Lieberman)

**VICE:** a function to keep virtue within reasonable bounds. (Samuel Butler)

**VIOLENCE:** the last refuge of the incompetent. (Isaac Asimov)

**VIRTUE:** an insufficient

---

Fashion designer Christian Dior died of choking on a fish bone.

temptation. (George Bernard Shaw)

**VISIONARY:** the only true realist. (Federico Fellini)

**VOTE:** the instrument and symbol of a freeman's power to make a fool of himself and a wreck of his country. (Ambrose Bierce)

**VULGARITY:** the garlic in the salad of life. (Cyril Connolly)

**WAFFLES:** pancakes with syrup traps. (Mitch Hedberg)

**WASHINGTON, D.C.:** where an insignificant individual may trespass on a nation's time. (Ralph Waldo Emerson)

**WINE:** the Mozart of the mouth. (Gérard Depardieu)

**WINNER:** someone who recognizes his God-given talents, works his tail off to develop them into skills, and uses these skills to accomplish his goals. (Larry Bird)

**WISDOM:** learning what to overlook. (William James)

**WIT:** a weapon; a masculine way of inflicting superiority. (Frank Muir)

**WORDS:** the assaults of thoughts on the unthinking. (John Maynard Keynes)

**WORK:** the scythe of time. (Napoleon Bonaparte)

**WRITER:** a frustrated actor who recites his lines in the hidden auditorium of his skull. (Rod Serling)

**X-FACTOR:** anything that is unexpected. (Dante Hall)

**XEROX MACHINE:** one of the biggest threats to national security ever devised. (Adm. Thomas Moorer)

**YALE:** going to classes, staggering on in the best fashion possible. (John Merriman)

**YANKEE:** one who, if he once gets his teeth set on a thing, all creation can't make him let go. (Ralph Waldo Emerson)

**YAWN:** a silent shout. (G. K. Chesterton)

**YOUNG LOVE:** a flame; very pretty, often very hot and

fierce, but still only light and flickering. (Henry Ward Beecher)

**Z**EALOTRY: the enemy of idealism. (Neil Kinnock)

**ZEN BUDDHISM:** a discipline where belief isn't necessary. (David Sylvian)

**ZEST:** the secret of all beauty. (Christian Dior)

**ZOO:** a form of idle and witless amusement, compared to which a visit to a penitentiary or even a state legislature in session, is informing, stimulating, and ennobling. (H. L. Mencken)

## RANDOM QUOTES

"By labor we can find food and water, but all of our labor will not find for us another hour."
—Kenneth Patton

"There is one kind of robber whom the law does not strike at, and who steals what is most precious to men: time."
—Napoloeon Bonaparte

"Except for the occasional heart attack, I've never felt better."
—Dick Cheney

"Beware the lollipop of mediocrity. Lick it once, and you'll suck forever."
—Brian Wilson

"Bugs Bunny is who we'd most like to be; Daffy Duck is probably who we are."
—Chuck Jones

"For marriage to be a success, every woman and every man should have her and his own bathroom. The end."
—Catherine Zeta-Jones

# ON STUPIDITY

*The great paradox of our time may be that we tend
to think that everyone else is stupid.*

"Genius may have its limitations, but stupidity is not thus handicapped."
—**Elbert Hubbard**

"A fool's paradise is a wise man's hell!"
—**Thomas Fuller**

"The dumber people think you are, the more surprised they're going to be when you kill them."
—**William Clayton**

"What Jefferson should have said was 'Life, liberty, and the pursuit of intelligence,' for the latter has never been a recognizable goal of our nation."
—**John Irving**

"Strange as it seems, no amount of learning can cure stupidity, and higher education positively fortifies it."
—**Stephen Vizinczey**

"To be ignorant of one's ignorance is the malady of the ignorant."
—**Amos Bronson Alcott**

"Nothing in the world is more dangerous than sincere ignorance and conscientious stupidity."
—**Martin Luther King, Jr.**

"Talk sense to a fool, and he calls you foolish."
—**Euripides**

"A great many people mistake opinions for thoughts."
—**Herbert V. Prochnow**

"Two things are infinite: the universe and human stupidity; and I'm not sure about the universe."
—**Albert Einstein**

"The dumbest people I know are those who know it all."
—**Malcolm Forbes**

"Just think of how stupid the average person is, and then realize half of them are even stupider."
—**George Carlin**

"Stupidity is better kept a secret than displayed."
—**Heraclitus of Ephesus**

---

"Solutions are not the answer." —**Richard Nixon**

# ROWLING'S MUSINGS

*Snippets of wisdom from the author of the*
*Harry Potter books, J. K. Rowling.*

"It takes a great deal of courage to stand up to your enemies, but even more to stand up to your friends."

"If you want to know what a man's like, take a good look at how he treats his inferiors, not his equals."

"It's a strange thing, but when you are dreading something, and would give anything to slow down time, it has a disobliging habit of speeding up."

"Humans have a knack of choosing precisely those things that are worst for them."

"Indifference and neglect often do much more damage than outright dislike."

"Differences of habit and language are nothing at all if our aims are identical and our hearts are open."

"Youth cannot know how age thinks and feels. But old men are guilty if they forget what it was to be young."

"It does not do to dwell on dreams and forget to live."

"Have you any idea how much tyrants fear the people they oppress?"

"It is our choices that show what we truly are, far more than our abilities."

"Fear of a name increases fear of the thing itself."

"Numbing the pain for a while will make it worse when you finally feel it."

"Destiny is a name often given in retrospect to choices that had dramatic consequences."

"The consequences of our actions are always so complicated that predicting the future is a very difficult business indeed."

"It is the unknown we fear when we look upon death and darkness, nothing more."

"What's coming will come, and we'll meet it when it does."

# POLITICIANSPEAK

*More select quotes from our vaunted public figures.*

"Our intent will not be to create gridlock. Oh, except maybe from time to time."
—**Bob Dole, on working with the Clinton administration**

"Life is indeed precious, and I believe the death penalty helps to affirm this fact."
—**Ed Koch, former New York City mayor**

"If crime went down 100%, it would still be 50 times higher than it should be."
—**John Bowman, Washington, D.C., councilman**

"My party is demonstrating that they are for states' rights unless they don't like what states are doing."
—**Rep. Christopher Shays (R–CT)**

"Racial discrimination does not always violate public policy."
—**Trent Lott**

"We need to stiffify these penalties."
—**Louisiana state rep. John Travis (D)**

"Considering the dire circumstances that we have in New Orleans, virtually a city that has been destroyed, things are going relatively well."
—**Michael Brown, FEMA director**

"The last time I checked, the Constitution said, 'Of the people, by the people, and for the people.' That's what the Declaration of Independence says."
—**Bill Clinton**

"The Congress didn't vote themselves a pay raise. We simply did not deny ourselves that normal increase in our cost of living that every other worker in America not only expects but insists upon."
—**Rep. Dick Armey, after raising congressional salaries to $155,000 a year**

"One of my role models, Xena the Warrior Princess, comes from here."
—**Sec. of State Madeleine Albright, in New Zealand**

"I will not tolerate intolerance!"
—**Bob Dole**

---

**"He who slings mud generally loses ground." —Adlai Stevenson**

# LEGAL BRIEFS

*Does anybody like lawyers?*
*These people say...nope.*

"If all the lawyers were hanged tomorrow,
and their bones sold to a mah-jongg factory,
we'd be freer and safer, and our taxes would
be reduced by almost half."
—**H. L. Mencken**

米

"The most innocent and irreproachable life
cannot guard a lawyer against the hatred
of his fellow citizens."
—**John Quincy Adams**

米

"The greatest scourge an angry Heaven ever
inflicted upon an ungrateful and sinning
people was an ignorant or corrupt judiciary."
—**John Marshall**

米

"I get paid for seeing that my clients have
every break the law allows. I have knowingly
defended a number of guilty men. But the
guilty never escape unscathed. My fees are
sufficient punishment for anyone."
—**F. Lee Bailey**

米

"I think we may class the lawyer in the
natural history of monsters."
—**John Keats**

# FAMOUS LAST WORDS

*They said a lot before, and nothing after.*

"I am about to—or I am going to—die. Either expression is correct."
—**Dominique Bouhours, French grammarian, 1702**

"I'm bored with it all."
—**Winston Churchill, 1965**

"Is it not meningitis?"
—**Louisa May Alcott, 1888**

"Leave the shower curtain on the inside of the tub."
—**Conrad Hilton, 1979**

"Die? I should say not, dear fellow. No Barrymore would allow such a conventional thing to happen to him."
—**John Barrymore, 1942**

"That was the best ice-cream soda I ever tasted."
—**Lou Costello, 1959**

"This is absurd, this is absurd."
—**Sigmund Freud, 1939**

"Does nobody understand?"
—**James Joyce, 1941**

"Lord help my poor soul."
—**Edgar Allan Poe, 1849**

"Write…write…pencil … paper."
—**Heinrich Heine, 1856**

"Don't turn down the light. I'm afraid to go home in the dark."
—**O. Henry, 1910**

"Why not? Why not? Why not? Why not? Yeah."
—**Timothy Leary, 1996**

"How were the receipts today at Madison Square Garden?"
—**P. T. Barnum, 1891**

"I've had 18 straight whiskies. I think that's the record."
—**Dylan Thomas, 1853**

"Please don't leave me. Please don't leave me."
—**Chris Farley, 1997**

"Is everyone else alright?"
—**Robert F. Kennedy, 1968**

"Leave me alone. I'm fine."
—**Barry White, 2003**

"Love one another."
—**George Harrison, 2001**

"Last words are for people who haven't said anything in life." —**Karl Marx**

# HOPE FOR THE FUTURE

*Our final collection of quotations puts every other collection
of quotations in the proper perspective: No matter
how bad things get, there is always hope.*

"As for the future, your task is not to foresee it, but to enable it."
—**Antoine de Saint-Exupéry**

"Some day, after we have mastered the winds, the waves, the tides, and gravity, we shall harness the energies of love. Then, for the second time in the history of the world, man will have discovered fire."
—**Pierre Teilhard De Chardin**

"Human salvation lies in the hands of the creatively maladjusted."
—**Martin Luther King, Jr.**

"To solve the human equation, we need to add love, subtract hate, multiply good, and divide between truth and error."
—**Janet Coleman**

"Everything you need for better future and success has already been written. And guess what? All you have to do is go to the library."
—**Henri-Frédéric Amiel**

"What you are is what you have been, and what you will be is what you do now."
—**Buddha**

"There is no greater legacy that we can leave our children and grandchildren than a peaceful and safer world."
—**Ted Turner**

"I like the dreams of the future better than the history of the past."
—**Thomas Jefferson**

"In times of change, learners inherit the Earth, while the learned find themselves beautifully equipped to deal with a world that no longer exists."
—**Eric Hoffer**

"I am not afraid of tomorrow, for I have seen yesterday and I love today."
—**William Allen White**

"Nobody gets to live life backward. Look ahead—that is where your future lies."
—**Ann Landers**

"The vast possibilities of our great future will become realities only if we make ourselves responsible for that future."
—**Gifford Pinchot**

"Your hopes, dreams, and aspirations are legitimate. They are trying to take you airborne, above the clouds, above the storms, if you only let them."
—**William James**

"There is no medicine like hope, no incentive so great, and no tonic so powerful as expectation of something better tomorrow."
—**Orison Swett Marden**

"Not only is another world possible, she is on her way. On a quiet day, I can hear her breathing."
—**Arundhati Roy**

"Once social change begins, it cannot be reversed. You cannot uneducate the person who has learned to read. You cannot humiliate the person who feels pride. You cannot oppress the people who are not afraid anymore. We have seen the future, and the future is ours."
—**César Chávez**

"I believe that imagination is stronger than knowledge—myth is more potent than history—dreams are more powerful than facts—hope always triumphs over experience—laughter is the cure for grief—love is stronger than death."
—**Robert Fulghum**

"The future is always beginning now."
—**Mark Strand**

"The best is yet to be."

—**Robert Browning**

...perhaps, the end of the beginning." —Winston Churchill

# INDEX BY NAME

# INDEX BY SUBJECT

204, 209, 236, 275, 289, 294, 303, 306, 312, 331, 342, 344, 355
names, 50, 55, 96
narcissist, 246
nationality, 84, 131
nature, 21, 173, 217, 220-221, 225, 231, 244, 246, 299
necessity, 85, 246
neurosis, 246
New York, 26, 50, 60, 69, 84, 107, 167, 246
night, 246
Nixon, Richard, 91, 360
no, 57, 157, 255
noise, 31, 246, 293
normal, 246
nostalgia, 247
nothing, 15, 35, 130, 307
novels, first lines of, 18
nudity, 22, 55, 128
ocean, 247, 255
Ono, Yoko, 78, 98, 174
opinion, 58, 85, 231, 237, 309, 345, 367
opportunity, 122, 222
optimism, optimist, 247, 275, 305
originality, 247
pain, 122, 356, 368
parents/parenting, 12, 42, 158, 247, 254, 263, 275, 278
party, 53, 119, 135, 168, 300
past, the, 14, 19, 98, 130, 278, 316, 330
patience, 163, 255
patriotism, 73, 144, 247
peace, 172, 177, 211, 238-239, 330, 347
people, 36-37, 148
perception, 34, 41, 58, 217, 250
perfection, 263
perseverance, 19, 41, 60, 122
pets, 138
philosophy, 85, 130, 203, 247, 334

photography, 34, 114, 154, 225, 248
plastic surgery, 30, 34, 184, 295
poetry/poets, 42, 149, 248, 355
politician, 89, 105, 233, 298, 304, 359
politics, 24, 26, 55, 57, 140, 161, 177, 197, 233, 241, 244, 248, 298, 302, 321, 331, 344, 359-360, 369
poverty, 14, 42, 49, 69, 173, 195, 318
power, 115, 172, 202, 206, 227, 239, 248, 254
prediction, prophecy, 145, 199, 248, 278, 368
prejudice, 254, 317, 369
presidency, 65, 103, 106, 140, 233, 241, 322
privacy, 11, 237
problems, 54, 122, 157, 313
procrastination, 205, 242, 307
progress, 65, 81
promises, 41, 121
proverbs, 15, 40-41, 139, 219, 249, 272, 345
punk rock, 160
puns, 44-45
queen, 248
questions, 21, 136, 185, 248
queue, 248
quizzes, 18, 270-271
quotations, 103, 226-227, 248
Ratherisms, 26
Reagan, Ronald, 78, 91, 173, 197
reality, 54, 57, 80, 236, 303
reason, 303
relationships, 12, 136, 138, 171, 355, 362
relaxation/rest, 15

religion, 124, 144, 211, 226, 246, 250, 266, 299, 303, 333-334, 355, 361, 366
repartee, 303
Republicans, 12
respect, 12, 195, 237, 274, 347
retirement, 120
revenge, 303
revolution, 73, 124, 190
reward, 102, 132, 148
rhymes, 168-169
right and wrong, 53, 305
rock 'n' roll, 303, 312
romance, 303
sailing/ships, 15, 39, 139, 156, 199
sanity, 58, 59, 80, 164, 169, 222
satire, 303
science, 37, 43, 131, 247, 286, 303, 307
searching, 136, 272
seasons, 34, 106
secrets, 41, 112, 151, 303
security, 14, 299
self, knowledge of, 14, 31, 56, 81, 121, 136, 138, 190, 332
self-esteem, 93, 106
Senate/senators, 91, 113, 323
sex, 61, 75, 90, 92, 129, 136, 237, 247, 248, 265, 303, 357
silence, 55, 82, 190, 196, 273, 293
simplicity, 112, 117
slavery, 81
sleep, 76, 77, 121, 164, 242, 246, 263, 355
smoking, 12, 13, 136, 198, 303
speech, speaking, 64, 73, 81, 91, 140, 144, 163, 177, 265, 272, 293, 305, 331
sports, 13, 32, 37, 54, 64, 103, 111, 123, 143, 178, 202, 222,

"If you don't find it in the Index, look very carefully through the entire catalogue."—*Consumer's Guide*, Sears, Roebuck and Co.

# UNCLE JOHN'S BATHROOM READER CLASSIC SERIES

Find these and other great titles from the *Uncle John's Bathroom Reader* Classic Series online at **www.bathroomreader.com.** Or contact us at:

Bathroom Readers' Institute
P.O. Box 1117
Ashland, OR 97520
(888) 488-4642

# THE LAST PAGE

**F**ELLOW BATHROOM READERS:
The fight for good bathroom reading should never be taken loosely—we must do our duty and sit firmly for what we believe in, even while the rest of the world is taking pot shots at us.

We'll be brief. Now that we've proven we're not simply a flush-in-the-pan, we invite you to take the plunge: Sit Down and Be Counted! Become a member of the Bathroom Readers' Institute. Log on to *www.bathroomreader.com*, or send a self-addressed, stamped, business-sized envelope to: BRI, PO Box 1117, Ashland, Oregon 97520. You'll receive your free membership card, get discounts when ordering directly through the BRI, and earn a permanent spot on the BRI honor roll!

---

If you like reading our books...
VISIT THE BRI'S WEB SITE!
*www.bathroomreader.com*

- Visit "The Throne Room"—a great place to read!
- Receive our irregular newsletters via e-mail
- Order additional *Bathroom Readers*
- Become a BRI member

*Go with the Flow...*

---

Well, we're out of space, and when you've gotta go, you've gotta go. Tanks for all your support. Hope to hear from you soon. Meanwhile, remember...

*Keep on flushin'!*